Jayhawker

Jayhawker

On History, Home, and Basketball

Andrew Malan Milward

University Press of Kansas

Published by the University Press of Kansas (Lawrence, Kansas 66045),
which was organized by the Kansas Board of Regents and is operated and
funded by Emporia State University, Fort Hays State University,
Kansas State University, Pittsburg State University, the University of Kansas,
and Wichita State University.

Library of Congress Cataloging-in-Publication Data
Names: Milward, Andrew Malan, author.
Title: Jayhawker : on history, home, and basketball / Andrew Malan Milward.
Description: Lawrence, Kansas : University Press of Kansas, [2019] |
Includes bibliographical references.
Identifiers: LCCN 2019019339
ISBN 9780700628674 (pbk. : alk. paper)
ISBN 9780700628681 (ebook)
Subjects: LCSH: University of Kansas—Basketball—History. | Kansas Jayhawks
(Basketball team)—Anecdotes.
Classification: LCC GV885.43.U52 M55 2019 | DDC 796.323/630978165—dc23
LC record available at https://lccn.loc.gov/2019019339.

British Library Cataloguing-in-Publication Data is available.

Printed in the United States of America

10 9 8 7 6 5 4 3 2 1

The paper used in this publication is recycled and contains 30 percent
postconsumer waste. It is acid free and meets the minimum requirements
of the American National Standard for Permanence of Paper for
Printed Library Materials Z39.48-1992.

For Todd Michael Heitshusen,
aka "the Clinic," my brother in obsession

Athletes are searchers for meaning. Behind the easygoing facades and the put-down humor, we are all a little restless with our lot. The games we play are sometimes beautiful. But there is more to life, and also less, as I think this book will demonstrate.

—Cleo Birdwell, *Amazons: An Intimate Memoir by the First Woman Ever to Play in the National Hockey League*

Contents

Jayhawker

LOSS

It was nine years ago now, a Saturday afternoon in mid-March of 2010. So long ago in one sense, and yet to remember my way back into it feels effortless and untroubled by all that has happened in my life and in the world between then and now. I was sitting at my desk in the upper floor of a house I shared with a roommate in a neighborhood of San Francisco called Bernal Heights. I had been writing all morning, which at the time would have meant making progress on a collection of short fiction I'd been working on for several years about the political history of the state I grew up in, Kansas. It would be more accurate to say, however, that I wasn't writing; I was *trying* to write, or at least convince myself that I was. Mostly I watched the cursor blink back at me, daring me to do something, anything, until I would inevitably flinch and steal a look at the clock in the upper right-hand corner of my computer screen, waiting for it to hit the designated hour when I could drop the pretense of doing anything remotely productive and just go watch basketball. And when that time finally came, I saved the current draft of the story I had long been trying to finish, X'ed out of Word, lowered the screen of my laptop, and began the five-minute walk to the bar where I watched games because I didn't have a television.

Just south of the Mission District, Bernal Heights sits atop a large hill overlooking the entire city, a truly magnificent view in a city with perhaps the highest per capita magnificent views in the country. Bernal was once the boonies, home to immigrants and the working poor of early last century, then later became known as "Red Hill" when it was occupied by movement socialists and communitarians, followed shortly—or perhaps joined simultaneously—by an influx of lesbians, making it the female answer to the Castro for a time, or so I'd been told. In the years before I

1

arrived it had become the destination for young professionals renovating homes and starting families. And while the cycle of gentrification is familiar, the various people who made up the neighborhood's history seemed to coexist with remarkable comity, or so it seemed to someone who did not fit neatly into any of these groups, who shared none of Bernal's history. The silver-haired hippies and lesbians were still there; so too were the working-class Hispanic families and now the young, white, heteronormative couples and their children, not to mention their dogs, who kind of ran the place. I belonged to a gym around the corner that allowed members to bring their dogs while they worked out. I still recall the wisps of shed fur floating dreamily past my head as I did crunches. The bar I was headed to this day, Stray Bar, welcomed its patrons' dogs inside to sniff your butt, to enjoy a cool dish of water, to occasionally knock over your beer with an errant tail wag, or to go suddenly apeshit for some reason lost on us humans. But everyone took it in stride, laughed it off. I did not have a dog, did not speak Spanish. I was not gay, nor did I have a family. A midwestern transplant with a car, I came for the parking and for the proximity to the Mission, where my girlfriend, H, lived.

But whatever.

None of that mattered as I hustled down Cortland Street, blowing right past the languid weekend gait of hand-holding couples, dodging street joggers, stroller pushers, and leash holders. I passed Skip's Tavern and Wild Side West, better bars than where I was headed, because Stray Bar had the good TVs and two-dollar PBR draws all day long, which in the bar scene in San Francisco was sort of like spotting a Yeti. Stray Bar was a lesbian sports bar but welcomed all. Because I didn't have a TV, I often wound up there on nights or weekends, staking out a spot at the rail to watch something while a postgame softball team bender swallowed up the women around me. And come March, when the best, most dramatic sporting event of all, the NCAA tournament, took over my life for three weeks, they should have just placed a beer helmet on my head and Velcroed me to the wall like an astronaut. I would have been content to stay there for the duration.

When I arrived, the bar had just opened and only Karina, the bartender, and her boyfriend Ryan were there. I set up shop on the left side of the bar before a large flat screen, making sure Karina programmed it to show the Midwest Regional games, then told her what regions to tune the other sets to. "I like to watch all the games," I said sheepishly when I saw I had annoyed her.

It is true that I liked to see all the games and would have been there, or somewhere with televisions, any day of the tournament, but I was especially invested and present that day because the University of Kansas Jayhawks, my team and my burden, were set to play their second-round game. And it was there, at Stray Bar, that I would watch Kansas, the top seed, the odds-on favorite to win the tournament, the team that had been ranked number one nearly the entire season, lose to the Northern Iowa Panthers, a nine seed, a team that looked as if it had fielded its squad five minutes before tipoff by going into a local bar in Cedar Falls and offering free drink tokens to anyone willing to suit up and take a beating from the Jayhawks on national television. This was where I watched Northern Iowa come out unintimidated by heavily favored KU, staking an early lead, causing frequent updates in other regions by CBS announcers (I could see and hear them on the TVs behind me and off to the side) to keep an eye on these upstart Panthers. This was where people in the bar would start to congregate around me, moving from moderate interest ("They're plucky, all right, but wait till Kansas wakes up") to serious investment in the improbable journey of the underdog, cheering loudly after every Panther jump shot and defensive stop, while I watched it unfold with a stoic calm that was an absolute ruse, a burying of the emotional pyrotechnics going on inside me that might most aptly be described as Episcopalian. I doubt anyone even knew I was pulling for Kansas, and frankly I preferred it that way. I didn't want to be that guy—lord knows, we've all seen him—who takes over the bar with his performance of team loyalty, high-fiving randos and spraying bystanders with his skunk-stink at every twist and turn. Instead, I watched, elbows on the bar, chin resting atop laced fingers that tented my pint of Pabst, aping the pose of impartial observer instead of what it actually was: the posture of the prayerful. Only occasionally did I close my eyes at a turnover, swallow a sigh on a slow defensive closeout, whisper into my fingers, "Get over the hump," as we cut the lead to five, to four, to three, but could never make the necessary defensive stop or drain the jumper to finally take the lead. At every step, Northern Iowa answered.

That afternoon in Stray Bar I listened to announcers contrast the "slow and smart" play of the overmatched Panthers with the "talent and athleticism" of the Jayhawks, racially coded language for styles of play attributed to white and black players. Normally, were they playing just about anyone other than Kansas, I would have jumped on the Northern Iowa bandwagon, but such was my lot to be in Goliath's corner that day. And for this crime I was made to bear witness to what would become an iconic moment in tournament history, something thereafter to be replayed at the beginning of every CBS tourney broadcast until the end of time.

Knowing it was their last opportunity to save the game, the Jayhawks made a furious comeback around the five-minute mark, and eventually cut the lead to one with forty-three seconds left. The Oklahoma City crowd, almost entirely Kansas fans, went nuts. You could see doubt come over the Panthers for the first time, sense the morning headlines already being written along press row—JAYHAWKS SURVIVE SCARE FROM PANTHERS—as they attempted to inbound the ball. The Kansas defense was swarming and NIU struggled to get it in. When they finally did, they nearly turned it over in the backcourt before outletting a pass to the only open Panther player, Ali Farokhmanesh.

Ah, Farokhmanesh, least likely owner of the boots that would stomp my heart into mush. All six feet, 190 pounds of him. He looked like a well-meaning goofball, someone given a spot on the squad to boost morale and team GPA. Not exactly the stuff of basketball legend. And yet all of this was just the unassuming guise of a cold-blooded assassin. When Farokhmanesh caught the ball on the wing, just outside the three-point line, there were thirty-eight seconds remaining on the game clock, which meant he could just hold it and KU would have to foul him and take their chances with him at the line, hoping to have a few seconds left to get up a shot to win or tie. But Farokhmanesh had no intention of running the clock down or waiting for the foul, as every armchair coach in country was cautioning him to do.

After receiving the pass, Farokhmanesh immediately squared to the basket. Three KU players ran toward him and one NIU teammate was deep in the opposite corner. The smart play would be to misdirect the KU players by passing to this teammate in the corner, trying to take as much time off the clock before Kansas could foul. But he didn't. After a millisecond, in which his brain considered these options and probably a few others, he went right into his shooting motion. There was still a chance that it was just a jump pass to that open teammate; no one thought anybody in his right mind would actually shoot a three in this situation, which accounts for why KU's star senior, Sherron Collins, was a little slow to close out on him, desperately trying to get a hand in his face only when Farokhmanesh's intention was clear. He let the ball go with 36.7 seconds and it dropped though the net at 35 flat; across the country in those 1.7 seconds millions of people were yelling, "What the hell are you doing!?" and "NO!" at their television sets, followed by "YES!" and "What a play!" Taking the shot had not been a lapse in judgment; Farokhmanesh knew exactly what he was doing. He knew that if Kansas got the ball back they would win or send it to overtime, where their momentum would carry them to victory.

It was all or nothing for Northern Iowa and there had been no doubt in his stroke. It is inspiring when you think about it, that moment of decisiveness and belief in himself, but that's something I can only see and appreciate now, so many years later, rewatching the game for the first time, running those final moments in slow motion, pausing the frame briefly at the moment the ball releases from his hands. Sometimes it still feels like there's a chance it might not go in.

The final seconds of the game dragged out a few more minutes, the futile timeouts and desperate fouling, but the celebration had already begun in the bar. I focused on the TV with the same stone-faced solemnity, cocooned in misery, until the buzzer sounded and the Panther bench stormed the court as my Jayhawks ambled dazed, hands on their heads, trying, like everyone, to process what had just happened. "On the first day of spring, number one has fallen," cried Kevin Harlan, the announcer, as the final score brought resolution to the drama, if not the trauma for Kansans like me.

#9 Northern Iowa 69
#1 Kansas 67

I remember sitting at the bar until the revelers moved on, turning their attention to other games in other regions. My cell phone lay next to my beer, but there were no signs of activity. My family had learned never to call me after a KU loss, especially one of this magnitude. A few minutes later Ryan bopped over and tried to get me to play foosball in the back room. He knew I was a Kansas fan, but he didn't understand. "Tough loss," he said, as if it could be shaken off so easily. "Come on, let's play." I declined and when he persisted I told him, "I'm not in the mood for foosball," in a tone that suggested, *Keep this up and I'll eat your face.* I sat and stewed awhile longer before finally getting off my stool and going outside to call my oldest friend, Todd. We grew up together in Lawrence, and by 2010 he lived with his wife and daughter in Kansas City. He is the only one I can speak to after losses, because he's the only one who can truly commiserate. Like me, he played basketball in college, so not only is he knowledgeable about the sport, he knows it intimately and experientially. But more importantly, Todd and I are the same age, so we have an equal amount of shared KU basketball consciousness and history to draw upon, thirty-plus years of victories and defeats, that help contextualize the particular agony of this loss.

I was outside Stray Bar, pacing before the doorway, and finally lost my cool, unleashing a deluge of random observations from the game on poor

Todd until I could only muster caustic self-criticism: "We pissed down our leg."

We.

Because, like most ardent fans, for us the team feels like an extension of ourselves, so we speak of it collectively, royally. Us. We.

Todd and I talked about the loss, unpacking the frustration and embarrassment of defeat at the hands of a team we were supposed to beat easily, while leaving unsaid the frustration and embarrassment that the loss had such power to wound us. We spoke until there was little more to say and it was time to go.

"I'm gonna mow the lawn," said Todd.

"I'm gonna set myself on fire and jump off the Bay Bridge," I answered, and then we said we loved one another and hung up.

The rest of the night is a blur to me now. I had plans to meet up with my friends Laura and Jenny, something I had agreed to in advance of knowing the game schedule of the tournament. I probably should have canceled but didn't. I met them a little while later down the street in a beer garden, content to let my toxic mood jaundice a nice night of sipping drinks on a bench under the starlight. Laura and Jenny had a friend visiting from out of town and told me how earlier that night they'd taken their friend to dinner in the Lower Haight and heard an eruption at bar area of the restaurant. "Everyone was screaming and high-fiving," said Laura. "Then I saw the TV and the score. I thought of you. I'm sorry."

I'm sorry for your loss, I thought, and saw myself in the receiving line at a wake for the 2009–2010 Kansas basketball team.

In a city where people were painstakingly diligent in asserting their beliefs, orientations, and affiliations, I self-identified as a Kansan. Always have, even though I wasn't born there, even though I've now lived most of my life elsewhere. If people know anything at all about me, there's a strong likelihood it's my connection to the state. It seems likely that something along the lines of "You know Andrew, that Kansas guy," has been uttered in conversations about me to which I have not been privy.

"I'm devastated," I said to Laura and Jenny and their friend whose name I can't remember, whose face I can't even picture. It was what I continued to say over the next week to anyone who told me they were sorry, to anyone who asked how I was doing. "I'm devastated," I said, and they smiled because they thought my grave admission was a humorous affectation since sports are so obviously inconsequential. It's just a game, after all. I might as well have told them I was writing an epic poem about *The Real Housewives of Orange County.* My pain was real, I wanted to tell them, and yet that pain also shamed me. I confided this to H when we spoke over the phone later that night. She was out of town on spring break with her family. We had been together over three years, so she was all too familiar with my KU basketball obsession, had suffered my black moods many times because of it, but even she would later tell me of that night on the phone after the Northern Iowa loss: "I'd never heard you like that. You'd have thought someone died. It was the sound of true despair."

Despair sounds dire, but later I came across a passage in William Styron's "memoir of madness," *Darkness Visible*, that seemed to capture perfectly what that afflicted time felt like: "It may be more accurate to say that despair, owing to some evil trick played upon the sick brain by the inhabiting psyche, comes to resemble the diabolical discomfort of being imprisoned in a fiercely overheated room. And because no breeze stirs this cauldron, because there is no escape from this smothering confinement, it is entirely natural that the victim begins to think ceaselessly of oblivion." The oblivion Styron is referring to is suicide, and while I have weathered my own battles with depression, I was not seeking oblivion; I was seeking a living escape and hopefully, later, an understanding of the intensity of my response to Kansas's loss.

I thought I might sleep it off, but the next morning I woke to find that the darkness had not left. I looked at the Sunday *Times* online. Headlines about Iraq and Afghanistan, more on the horrific aftermath from the earthquake in Haiti. Budgets being slashed, plans for national healthcare being gutted. Some of these were issues to which I had given a considerable amount of thought and political energy, but I cared little about them that morning. I drank coffee and sat in a chair trying to read, but my mind would not settle, not turning over the game so much as trying to discover a pathway out from under the mood and finding it impossible. A peculiar breed of soul sickness had overcome me. It was despair, as H had said and Styron had elucidated so aptly, and it was perplexing because at that point I was living my life in the most mindful way I ever had, trying to give my attention to things I believed were important. My rational mind knew that my hometown basketball team losing was not really a big deal and yet there I was existentially paralytic. I was also embarrassed that I felt as bad as I did, but that only seemed to compound the problem. I had felt plenty bad after other Kansas losses, sure, but how had this particular basketball game—something I could recognize as meaningless on the continuum of consequential events like wars, earthquakes, and public policy decisions that affect people's wellbeing in serious ways—been able to hold such sway over me? How had I come to care so much about something that ultimately meant so little? Was it inconsequential if I felt like this? If so, why couldn't I escape the sadness and futility I felt draping me like a burial shroud? What was the deal with me and basketball?

Suddenly I began scribbling in my notebook, writing about basketball and Kansas. When I look back at those notes now I see that not only were they written in such fury as to be barely legible but they read like the diary of a conspiracy theorist. *Resolution: no basketball for a year . . . Does competition ruin everything? Could I watch a basketball game in which no one won? . . . My own sexism: Why do I not watch women's basketball? . . . Impossible choice: Kansas wins title or I have health insurance?* I can see the notes now for what they were, the work of a troubled mind frantically trying to gain perspective on itself, but for that period of time—it was at least three hours—I wasn't fully conscious of what I was writing. I was just doing it, compelled to a state of automatic writing from which I might later find clues to my unconscious mind, my id's irrational love of and identification with basketball and Kansas.

It was only a call from my friend Cathy that broke the spell I was under. I suspect H must have sent up the Bat-Signal to alert some friends as to my distress, because soon Cathy was on her way to my apartment, even when I tried to convince her that I wanted to be alone. She picked me up and drove me over Golden Gate to the Marin Headlands, where we got out and looked at the ocean and clouds and felt like the small beings we were. Like a mother who knows that if she can't cure her son's broken heart at least she can make sure he goes to bed well fed, Cathy took me to In-N-Out Burger and we commiserated, animal-style.

Afterward, she dropped me off back in Bernal. I thought about work and dreaded going in the next day. Technically the Great Recession had ended, but we were still very much suffering its effects. I had moved to the Bay Area that previous summer upon receiving a writing fellowship that provided me with a modest stiped in exchange for minimal duties. While I was fortunate to have received the honor and grateful for the support, the fellowship money didn't come close to covering San Francisco's notorious cost of living. I had taken on two part-time jobs and still could not afford health or car insurance, still was accreting poverty-trapping credit card debt, to say nothing of the colossus of student loan debt that had been erected over the course of my years of higher education. And yet, as I was often reminded, I was lucky to have any kind of employment in those dark economic times. At my main job I taught creative writing at a day program for adults with developmental disabilities. My other job was seasonal; I was the JV tennis coach at a private high school in the city. While I enjoyed watching tennis, I had never been on a team and had little idea of how to coach the sport or how to conduct a tennis practice, but I had managed to fake my way through an interview with the school's athletic director thanks in large part to a close rereading of the tennis academy sections of *Infinite Jest*. I would receive a healthy ribbing from both groups of students in the coming week, and I dreaded their gloating: "What happened to Kansas? Your team choked!"

I sat at my desk, pondering what to do with myself. I sure as hell wasn't going to watch any more basketball. I was finished with that nonsense. I thought about working on my fiction or prepping for the teaching I had that week but couldn't muster the resolve. I looked at the clock, thought a moment, and then I was making my way back down to Cortland Street. The afternoon games were about to start, games that would decide who was moving on to the Sweet Sixteen the following weekend. I might have felt dead, but the tournament still carried on, stepping over my corpse in the inexorable march of the madness. I hated basketball, I told myself as I walked toward Skip's Tavern. (It would take me a little while before I could go back to Stray Bar, haunted as it was by the ghost of Farokhmanesh and his nuts of steel.) I didn't want to care about it anymore, to invest emotionally in a game that didn't really matter, that could pain me in this way and shame me for feeling so. Yet there I was, pulling up a stool to watch Michigan State play Maryland, looking on as the Spartans won by two and advanced to what was supposed to have been a much-anticipated rematch with Kansas from their close game in the tournament the previous year.

Elbows on the bar, I drank beer and watched basketball and felt nothing. Still under the compulsion to understand the game's hold on me, I began making more notes on what soon became a stack of napkins. I still have a few of them. One note, squeezed along the edge because I was running out of space, reads: *It's right that defeat is called a loss*. Which makes me think of something else Styron wrote: "Loss in all of its manifestations is the touchstone of depression." Though I would not realize it for a long time, I was in the germinal stages of writing a book I had no intention of setting out to write, one it has taken me all this time since then to complete because I kept trying to find reasons and excuses not to write it. To devote the time and energy it takes to compose an entire book about my relationship to basketball felt—at times, anyway—just as wrongheaded and frivolous as the time and energy I spend thinking and caring about the game itself. More so, even. And yet I came around to it, unable to let the book stay just an idea existing only in the form of disparate notes scattered across years of notebooks devoted largely to other writing projects. I did so because

I came to see that our obsessions, whatever they may be, are interesting and worthy of exploration since they are rarely only about the object of obsession. They encompass so much more, whether we realize or want to acknowledge it, and this was certainly the case for me.

The impact of the Northern Iowa loss marked a turning point in my love of the game. It did not make me stop caring about basketball. Even when I tried to swear it off, I always came back, as I continued to each new season. What it did was make me more aware of my fandom, more inquisitive about its roots and origins, more willing to look at it with a colder eye. In the year that followed, which much of this book details, I found myself beginning that process of understanding. But I didn't know that then, that day at Skip's Tavern scribbling on napkins. That would only come much later. On that day I simply watched the entire slate of games before heading home in the early evening to do something I swore I wouldn't: scroll past the front-page headlines of important world affairs in favor of the sports pages, so that I could read the online postmortems of the previous day's loss in the *Lawrence Journal-World* and *Kansas City Star*.

Portrait of the Ball Player as a Young Artist

For much of my early life, my identity—my sense of who I was and how I fit into the world around me—was intimately bound up in, and perhaps largely determined by, my ability to accurately throw a synthetic leather ball through an orange iron hoop. Naturally, it was confusing for everyone in my life, myself included, when I decided I didn't want to play basketball anymore. But to understand the end, I must talk about the beginning, and to do so would find me in Lawrence shooting baskets in the driveway by day and, like so many young boys and girls across Kansas, rushing inside to watch the Jayhawks play by night. Everything else—school, chores, dinner, homework—was something to be endured before we could get back to doing one or the other. Which is to say, I did what a lot of young children across the country do, only more so in a town like Lawrence and a state like Kansas.

We played in school gymnasiums and rec centers. We played in churches after services and at the Salvation Army, where homeless people sat beside our families, clapping. We played in driveways on hoops with bent or missing rims, on goals that were either planted in concrete or freestanding and had to be weighed down with sandbags, as was mine, and thus subject to rocking steadily in the wind. We shot on small plastic Nerf hoops attached to bedroom doors and in basements on three-foot goals meant for younger siblings. We traveled to other towns to play in their gyms and parks. We played in town leagues, school leagues, church leagues, travel leagues, and of course the best and toughest league there was: streetball pickup at the playground, where the rims were unforgiving, the game spontaneous and subject to the elements, and where we players—absent coaches and referees—controlled the game. It belonged only to us. Such, such were the joys.

11

This isn't wholly accurate. I did other things too, played other sports. My father had been an excellent tennis player as a young man and he instilled in my brother Brint and me a healthy love of the sport. So I dabbled in tennis as well, which in Lawrence was to be something of a novelty, like saying you loved ice hockey or cricket. But in Kansas, a state named after its original inhabitants, the Kansa Indians, "the people of the wind," tennis was only the name we gave to the spectacle that more closely resembled some strange fusion of jai alai and wiffle ball. Still, basketball was where my heart was. I remember my mother confronting me one day—I must have been about ten—and telling me that I had to choose between basketball and tennis and commit fully to try to be the best that I could. This stays with me not because it was a difficult decision but because of how out of character this authoritarian ultimatum was coming from a woman who had been a folk singer in the sixties, who had spent two years in Liberia as a Peace Corps volunteer, who had given my brother and me subscriptions to *Playboy* in middle school to open a dialogue about sex while sating our curiosity about the inscrutable female body. When I ask her about it now, she smiles drolly, like maybe she half remembers or maybe it had happened during some aberrant psychic "episode." She was a graduate student then at KU, working to earn her PhD in accounting, and a year or two later, when she successfully defended her dissertation and went on the job market, we left Kansas for Connecticut.

At the time, moving to the East Coast was devastating. It was not a particularly good time to go. I was twelve, right on the verge of those angst-ridden teenage years, and the thought of leaving my friends and home was terrifying and sad. I withdrew. In Lawrence I had been social and popular. In Avon, the small suburb of Hartford where we settled, I barely spoke. I was shy, oversensitive, and anxious. I missed my home. I mostly wanted to be left alone and then resented my peers when they obliged. This ambivalence, the competing desires to be both seen and unseen, characterized much of my teenage years as I weathered my depression unmedicated, and basketball helped me navigate it all. It became a crutch, a social lubricant, something that allowed me to exist in the company of others when the hard feelings inside me screamed otherwise. It helped that I was good at the sport and received validation for my ability. I spent my first several months in Avon an invisible boy, but tryouts for the school team were held that November and whether I wanted them to or not—and half the time I was crippled with a burning desire for one or the other—my peers took notice of the quiet kid from Kansas who could play ball.

Though I was someone who found it embarrassing and ill-mannered to utter aloud, I did know I was good. It was hard not to see that I was better than everyone else at my school. I stood out and people noticed, particularly the varsity coach, Jim Taft, who taught phys ed at the middle school and got to see me play every day in gym class. Sometime during my eighth-grade year he invited me to the high school to practice with the varsity, and when I asked him whether I had a shot at making junior varsity the following year as a freshman he told me to forget JV: he needed a point guard to lead the varsity team. So I went from playing power forward in eighth grade to starting at the point against players three or four years older as a freshman. This is not as impressive as it might sound. It was a small public high school of six hundred students. Still, it wasn't something that happened often.

The best part was that, for the first time in our lives, I got the chance to play on the same team as my brother. Brint is two and a half years older than me, and that year he was a senior. He was a grinder, what is often called a "glue guy," which is what people say about an essential player who doesn't need to have offensive plays run for him. A glue guy rebounds and defends, scores occasionally and opportunistically but mostly sets up his teammates—the type of player every good team requires but most people don't want to be because it is hard, selfless work that doesn't usually garner headlines. Because he was willing to do it, however, Brint had worked himself up from JV to a bench player on varsity and by his senior year he was starting. I'm sure that there were difficulties and perhaps indignities that came with seeing his kid brother gifted what he had worked so hard to earn, but he never said so. My mother used to joke that she was responsible for 40 percent of the starting lineup.

We were not a very good team that year, but we played well enough to make it to the state tournament. In our final game we were matched up against the number-one team in the state, Trinity Catholic, which boasted two excellent players who would win back-to-back Connecticut player of the year honors: Rashamel Jones, who went on to play at UConn, and Earl Johnson, who would play for Rutgers and Iona. It wasn't much of a game. At halftime the Trinity Catholic cheerleaders passed out post-card-sized pictures of Rashamel to our family members in case they wanted to get autographs after the game. Playing point guard was still new to me, and it didn't help that I was matched up against Earl, the best in the state, who in two years would be the Big East freshman of the year. He ate my lunch, plain and simple, took the ball from me at will. I remember one particular moment early in the second half when I was bringing the ball up court and I was so anxious that Earl would rip another steal from my shaky handle that I tried to pass to Brint on the wing before I had even crossed half court. The pass was telegraphed and Rashamel barely had to move to steal it. Suddenly he and and Earl were on a two-on-one break, and I was the only defender back. I was backpedaling and when it became clear that Rashamel had no intention of passing the ball there came a moment when I had a decision to make: I could stand tall and try to take a charge from the six-five, 215-pound freight train heading my way, or I could give up the breakaway dunk. I summoned all my bravery to establish position, but at the last second my will to live kicked in and I did an NBA-style *Toro!* defense. In my memory of the play, it happens so slowly, and I'm watching Rashamel's size-fifteens inch through the air before me at eye level like great barges navigating the ocean. He is so high I don't even see him throw it down; I just hear the gymnasium erupt.

And so it went. The next few years as I got better, so did the team. My sophomore year we lost a close game in the Final Four of the state tournament to the eventual champions. My junior year I was named all-state, but we lost in the quarters to a great Saint Thomas Aquinas squad. Lamar Odom was on their team, but he didn't play in the game. I can't remember if it was an academic issue or an injury, but their team was so stacked they didn't even need him to take care of us. He sat on the bench in khakis and a blue sweater, clapping for his teammates, and later in the handshake line he told me I played a good game even though I hadn't, which was a kindness. To this day, I think of him as the greatest player I ever shook hands against.

By my final year in high school, I knew we would have a great team, at the core of which were four of us who would play in college the following year, a significant feat for a small public school that didn't recruit players away from their hometowns the way the private schools did: Jeff ("Chief") was our tallest player but also had a great outside shot, and it seemed his points were the most spectacular: either dunks or deep threes; Ryan ("Nutso") had been playing ball for only four years but had developed—at light speed—a deadly crossover that in combination with his long arms and height allowed him to get to the hole on anyone; and though at only six three he was shorter than Chief, Matt ("Biff") was our center, an absolute beast on the glass, and far and away the best rebounder I ever played with.

My game had improved over the years. Perhaps my greatest strength stemmed from the fact that while I shot with my right hand I wrote with my left, meaning I was essentially ambidextrous. So if a defender tried to force me left, thinking it was my weak hand, I could just as easily blow by. I had always been a better athlete than skill player, my game predicated on being able to improvise, break people down off the dribble, and get to the hole. But sometime in my junior year—probably about the time Coach Taft made me get contacts—I had become a good shooter, and by senior year I was an excellent marksman. Now I had an inside-outside game that was pick-your-poison for opposing players: if a defender played off me to protect against the drive, I would hit a jumper in his eye; if he played me tight, I would penetrate into the lane. But being surrounded by good players meant I had the luxury of not needing to carry the team. Even if I was having an off night, someone else would pick up the slack. Not without reason, Coach Taft boasted publicly that he had the four best players in our league on his team.

He had high expectations for us, and as a measuring stick he scheduled the defending state champs, Marianapolis Prep, in the opening game of the season. I didn't have a great game, but we pulled out a tough victory. From that point on, we never looked back. We breezed through the rest of the nonconference and conference season undefeated, becoming the only Class S team (the division of the smallest schools) to be ranked in the top ten of the state alongside the big Class L and LL schools. Somewhere along the line I scored my thousandth point, at the time the third person in school history to do so, and became the school's all-time assist leader. Then, just as we had moved into the all-important postseason, I got injured.

It happened in the first round of the conference tournament against East Granby, the last-place team in our league. I dunked occasionally in practice and summer league games but never had in a school game. The guys busted my balls about it, so knowing the game against East Granby was likely to be a blowout I told them I would if I got the chance. Late in the game, when we were winning handily, I got out on a breakaway and decided it was the time. I jumped off of two feet from the right block at the bottom of the lane, rising in the air to throw it down with my left hand. I had enough height, but I was too excited and tried to dunk it too hard, and the ball ricocheted off the back of the rim and shot out past the three-point line. For a long time I imagined that the dunk attempt was when the injury happened, but the truth is I don't know. It's just the story I have told myself because the truth is much less certain and dramatic. At some point in the game, without realizing it, I tore the meniscus in my left knee. There was no fall-to-the-ground clutching at the injured limb that we see so often, no being carried off the court by teammates. I finished the game and went to bed that night feeling fine, perhaps sore but no more so than usual at that point in the season. It wasn't until the next day that I felt the pain and saw the swelling.

After the MRI, I sat with my mother and Coach Taft across the desk from the doctor, who told me that I didn't have to have the surgery immediately, that I could try to play and have it done after the season—my knee wouldn't worsen; the damage was done. There was no doubt that I would play, but as good as our team was, I worried our chances for the title had taken a hit.

My game changed after the injury; it had to. Because my left knee was essentially dead, I was several steps slower and had little explosion, which negated my ability to beat defenders off the dribble. I became a spot-up shooter, but even that was affected by the fact that I wasn't getting as much lift on my jump shot, even with my right knee compensating for my left. I wore a brace and the second the game was out of reach for our opponents, Coach pulled me and I would spend the rest of the game icing my knee on the bench. I was frustrated. Though it was a meaningless vanity, it nonetheless bothered me that my scoring dipped from over twenty a game to twelve or so, that reporters wanted to talk to my teammates after the game instead of to me. There was discomfort in the knee, some pain, but what bothered me most was not being able to do what I had done just weeks before, to know what I was capable of and to not be able to deliver it. I felt a burning desire to tell anyone who would listen that I was injured, that that was why my performance had dipped, but while my teammates knew the truth, we downplayed the severity of my injury publicly, not wanting to appear vulnerable. And still we won, closing out a perfect conference season with an easy win in the conference tournament title game on our home court. Afterward, Chief, Nutso, Biff, and I raised the trophy as the crowd clapped, then stood with our team as a banner was unfurled in the gymnasium honoring our 24–0 season. But we weren't done yet, we told reporters covering the game. We weren't satisfied with a perfect regular season. We wanted to win state.

As we began our postseason run, one of the intriguing storylines was that there were only two undefeated teams in the state and both were in Class S: us and Gilbert, a school in Winsted. When the bracket was released, we were set up on opposite sides with the expectation that we would meet in the final. All of us on the team were talking about it; we wanted to prove we were the best and only undefeated team in the state. We steamrolled through the first two rounds of the tournament and found ourselves in the Final Four, matched up against Tolland, a team from our conference that we'd already faced in the regular season and beaten on their home court. They were good and had played us tougher than most teams, but we were already thinking about a matchup with Gilbert in the title game. Overconfident, entitled, and looking ahead: the tragic flaws of many a great team.

My father, who rarely got to see me play and who had been getting the game-by-game updates of the season, flew in for the game from Tucson, Arizona, where he is a professor at the University of Arizona. I felt no pressure. I was excited. I wanted him to see how good I knew we were. And by "we," of course, I meant me. I felt good in warmups—my shots were falling—but that quickly changed once the ball was tipped.

Tolland played a one-three-one matchup zone that could give you fits if you didn't move the ball, attack the seams of the zone, and hit outside shots with some regularity. They were not a gifted offensive team the way we were, which meant that to have a chance they had to slow the game down, which is exactly what they did. If you're an athletic team used to flying up and down the court, it is incredibly frustrating to play against a team that intentionally holds the ball so you can't have it—doubly so because in high school basketball, at that point, anyway, there wasn't even a shot clock to compel the stalling team into doing *something* on offense. We had managed to handle it well in our first game against Tolland, but in the state semifinals we came out sluggish, turning the ball over and missing shots. This, coupled with the fact that they were hitting their shots, gave them confidence and shook ours. Though we had led most of the first half, Tolland closed on a rare offensive burst, heading into halftime on the momentum of a ten-zero run.

We were down twenty-six to nineteen at the half and Coach Taft lit into us in the locker room. "What the hell is wrong with you guys? Show some fight! This is the semifinals of state. I shouldn't have to yell at you to get you fired up for the game!" He was right, and yet I couldn't shake the lethargy that had overtaken me once the game began. The entire first half I had felt out of step, slow, as if the game were happening to me, and I'd made only a single basket on a breakaway layup. There in the locker room I felt tired and confused as to why I couldn't summon the urgency I knew I should feel. Even the shame of playing this poorly in front of my father wasn't motivating me to give maximal effort. I hoped my teammates would bail me out, get me through whatever this funk was, and maybe I would be myself again in the championship game.

However, things only worsened in the second half. My shot, so accurate pregame, so accurate all season, had gone completely off the rails. Coach Taft told me to keep shooting, as one says to slumping marksmen, and I did, but to little avail. Statistically and existentially, it was the worst game of my life. For my career I had excellent shooting percentages: 50 percent field-goal percentage, over 40 percent from three-point range and 80 percent from the free throw line. But on that night I shot two for twenty from the field, didn't make a single three-pointer, and missed half of my foul shots. I scored seven points, the only time all season I did not score double digits. I had never shot so often or so poorly, a deadly combination, and it was as if I were the contagion, my poor play infecting my teammates. Of our "big four" only Chief played well, as did a couple of our bench players, who kept us close. We even took the lead, 39–38, for the first time since the second quarter with 3:48 remaining in the fourth on a layup by Nutso. I remember thinking, *Finally, we're back in control.* It was going to be one of the ugly games every good team has to survive in a tournament if they are to win the championship. But Tolland answered with a basket of their own. We had several chances to tie or take the lead over the final minutes—including me missing the front end of a one-and-one with 1:44 remaining—but we never took advantage of the opportunities. Tolland won 49–45, our perfect season was gone, 26–1, and the state championship left to be hoisted the following week by Gilbert.

The whole game I felt like I was moving underwater and, strangely, the longer the game went on the less troubled I felt by my poor play and our impending loss. It wasn't that I choked; to say so would be to suggest that I cared more than I did about the game, whereas I was struggling to feel anything at all. When I think back on it now, I suspect perhaps this was the beginning of my burnout, something I would not become conscious of for another year or so. Perhaps the numbness, the odd feeling I had the entire game, was in some sense a relief that the season would soon be over. Perhaps I'm grasping at straws, trying to understand why I felt so little about something I thought meant everything.

When the team bus arrived back at school after the long, silent drive to Avon, I found my girlfriend waiting for me. We were a wonderful cliché: captain of the basketball team and captain of the cheerleading squad. We drove around awhile, not saying much, until I parked down the street from her house. I feigned a despondence I didn't quite feel. I told her I didn't want to go to school the next day, so ashamed was I of my performance. What I really wanted to do in that moment was to fool around, but her kisses were more conciliatory than amorous. She was being a good partner, consoling me, and when she realized my intentions, she pulled away. There were tears in her eyes and confusion on her face. She seemed to be trying to reconcile her sadness with the peculiar timing of my romantic overtures. I saw how awful I was in that moment and felt ashamed, less because I didn't feel the disappointment of the loss as she did than that I'd pretended I had only to try and get up her skirt. The slow burn of shame overtook me as she kissed me and got out of the car.

It is a strange thing, but I have no recollection of seeing my father after the loss. He surely stayed the night in Connecticut, probably stayed a couple of nights, and he would have taken me out for a nice dinner and likely would have come to visit me at my mother's house, engaging in pleasant conversation with her under the icy, silent stare of my stepfather. I'm sure these things happened, but I don't remember them. The only memory I have of his trip is seeing his outline in the stands of the gymnasium, looking on as I played the worst game of my life. But it wasn't just him. I don't remember interacting with my mother after the game either, or even talking about the loss with my friends and teammates. Other than that awful moment in the car with my girlfriend, I seem to have disappeared so much of the postloss fallout from memory. It's as though my brain has blocked it out to protect me, as our minds will sometimes do when we have undergone traumatic events.

Soon thereafter I had arthroscopic surgery on my knee. I had assumed I'd be laid up awhile, but my doctor told me I could get back to playing and working out in a week or so, which is what I did. That fall I was set to attend Western Connecticut State University, and I wanted to make sure I was coming in at full strength, ready to play. WestConn, as we called it, had been recruiting Chief and Nutso all season, but not me. It was a Division III school, which meant they couldn't offer athletic scholarships, and they assumed, I later learned, that I was going to play D-II or perhaps even D-I, both of which offered athletic scholarships. I had moderate interest from a number of schools, but the two I was deciding between were Northern Arizona University and Transylvania University. NAU was a good mid-major D-I school, which was then coached by Ben Howland, who would soon leave to become the University of Pittsburgh's coach, then take UCLA to three straight Final Fours, and is currently returning Mississippi State to respectability. Transy, as it is known, is in Lexington, Kentucky, where I was born and where much of my father's family lives. It was a National Association of Intercollegiate Athletics (NAIA) school, then led by legendary coach Don Lane.

With my father in Tucson and a host of uncles and cousins in Lexington, I had selected these schools because they were close to family and the idea of going to a place where I knew nobody was anxiety-producing. I struggled with the decision and I dealt with it mostly by not thinking about it. As the time neared, I had no idea what to do, partly out of indolence, partly out of indecision, but mostly out of fear. Biff was heading off to play at the University of Scranton, and Chief and Nutso were set to attend WestConn. I was envious; it seemed less scary to go with a friend. After one game late in the season, I told Chief to tell the WestConn scouts who had been attending all of our games that I was interested. It all happened quickly after that. Some last-minute paperwork and I was off to college to play ball with my buddies. It was safe, easy. College but not really. More like summer camp. Of course, I never owned up to anyone that I had made the decision out of fear. I self-aggrandized. I said the coaches came after me hard, implied the three of us were a package deal, exaggerated the coaches' delight over Western's recruiting coup. I couldn't say no.

WestConn is near the New York–Connecticut border in Danbury, the midway point in the two-hour drive between Hartford and Manhattan. Our team was made up entirely of players from the two states, though most of us were from Connecticut. Players were split evenly between black and white and came mostly from working-class towns like Bristol and New Britain or urban cities like Hartford and Bridgeport. The three of us from Avon—a suburban, affluent, and near-entirely white town—were something of anomalies. And like many who are anxious about their own privilege, I found the change refreshing. Still, there were times when the advantages the three of us had been given were so glaring as to be shameful, and more than material things—each of us had a car, a little more walking-around money, didn't have to carry a work-study job—the discrepancy was evident in education. Though I'd not realized it at the time, we had gone to one of the best public high schools in the state, a school—thanks to the strong tax base it drew upon—with excellent resources and well-qualified and well-compensated teachers. I remember one day in our dorm room when Chief showed me a paper one of our teammates from East Hartford had written. "Just read it," Chief said. This teammate was soft-spoken, kind, and smart, but his paper was nonsensical. Literally, the sentences lacked any semblance of coherence. The professor had given it a B+.

In high school I had been a just slightly above-average student. B− was my targeted sweet spot: just enough to avoid a C, that scarlet letter of plain averageness that might draw parental ire, but to do any better would require intelligence and effort I either did not have or was not willing to give. In college, however, I was making As. I finished with a 3.8 my first semester and would hold a 4.0 throughout the rest of my college career. In part, this was because I was encountering a different level of standards.

However, most of it was because classes in college were way more interesting than the ones I had in high school. At Avon High, with the exception of one or two English classes, school was utter drudgery, while at West-Conn the classes were interesting and the discussions lively. My sense of my own intelligence was recalibrating. The skills I had learned, almost despite myself, by enduring high school curricula synergized with the interest and effort I developed after encountering the expansive course offerings at the university level, and for the first time in my life I enjoyed being a student.

Adjusting to the demands of school proved far easier than meeting the demands of playing college basketball. People sometimes turn their noses up at D-III athletics as less serious or talented than D-I, and while that may generally be the case, it's true only insofar as saying someone with 20 million dollars in the bank is poorer than someone with 30 million saved. The commitment required is staggering. First, there are the time commitments that break a player's days into incremental blocks determined by the coaching staff: practice, team meetings, study halls, individual skill-development workouts, weightlifting, games, travel, team dinners, film sessions—your life does not belong to you anymore. If it was this way at Western Connecticut State, I remember thinking, what must it be like at an elite D-I program like Kansas?

Then, of course, there was the adjustment that came with competing at a higher level of play. So obvious it hardly need be said, but the players in college were bigger, stronger, faster, and more skilled. The game just moved quicker and there was a period of time I had to wait as my brain mutated, learning to process time and to respond not in seconds but in fractions of milliseconds. It didn't help that my knee had never properly healed. Throughout the summer before entering college I had noticed it was retaining fluid and the doctor told me that would go away, but by the fall, as we prepared to start the season, it worsened and swelled back to the size it had been after the initial injury. Eventually I'd have it drained and the problem would be resolved, but a recovery that was supposed to take a few weeks had stretched into months, delaying my readiness throughout the preseason, and I was finally healed only as the season commenced.

Our first practice was early on a Saturday morning in October. In addition to playing pickup every afternoon, we had been having informal workouts with the coaching staff since we arrived on campus in August, but this was the official start of the season. We were at a local high school because the arena that housed our home court was occupied. Nervous, I had gotten up early, drunk a power shake, and eaten a protein bar, trying to get myself physically and mentally prepared. When we arrived at practice, our head coach, Bob Campbell, who was one of winningest all-time coaches in D-III history, had us run single file around the perimeter of the court to warm up, and when it seemed we were ready, he had us continue to run for what memory suggests was the entirety of practice. I could feel it building long before it came—all that crap I had eaten to prepare for practice was being rejected by my body. As I rounded the baseline to the sideline, eyes locked on the jersey of the teammate in front of me, I suddenly flew out of line, ran out the door and down a hallway, vomited in a large silver garbage can next to a window displaying student artwork, turned around, sprinting, and slipped right back into line almost without breaking stride.

Even as my knee healed, I found my role reduced to what it had been the previous spring when I'd limped through the state tournament, merely a shooter. The inside-outside game I had worked to my advantage in high school was not going to work in college until I got stronger and quicker and could create my own shot. Until then, I would have to rely on my teammates setting screens for me to get open looks, and it's a good thing that at least I still had my shot, otherwise I wouldn't have seen the floor.

I began the season coming off the bench, relieving another freshman named Kevin who had won the starting spot at shooting guard. Coach Taft drove down from Avon for the first game to see how his three former players were doing. We all played well. I came into the game and knocked down several shots, hitting double figures, an auspicious beginning. This would be my role throughout the early part of the season. However, soon after returning from a tournament in Miami, with Kevin mired in a prolonged shooting slump, I was inserted into the starting lineup. I would stay there for a good stretch, playing well, chipping in seven to ten points a game, until I severely strained my hamstring in the middle of a game. The injury was bad, not just a tweak or stitch causing some discomfort—it hurt to walk, and I couldn't bend my knee without serious pain. Basketball, a game of quick bursts of speed, requires having two functioning hamstrings to generate the explosive muscle twitches every player needs to compete. It was the kind of injury that could only be remedied with rest, so I sat out for the next week or two, waiting for my leg to heal. I spent practices in the training room receiving treatment: icing followed by electrotherapy via ultrasound stimulation. When I'd injured my knee the previous year, I felt despondent about the thought of not being able to play. However, this time as I lay there on my stomach, the trainer spreading the clear ultrasound gel over the back of my leg, I felt relief. In ways I was only starting to become conscious of, I was leaving the game.

A distance had grown not only between me and basketball but between me and my friends and teammates as well. In my brief time playing ball in college, I had quickly established myself as something of a weirdo. With my burgeoning interest in school and the arts in particular, I was the guy on the team bus reading Kafka as others watched *Pulp Fiction* on the screens above our seats. When guys talked about going home to see their families, I would recount my trip to Lincoln Center to see *Don Giovanni*. While they listened to *All Eyez on Me* before games, I listened to *Kind of Blue*. I don't mean to suggest I was ostracized in any way. I got along well with everyone and was included in everything. In fact, a lot of the guys seemed to like the idea that I was a "serious" person, an impression I encouraged and a demeanor I was increasingly willing to affect. When we would party in the dorm, as guys crushed thirty-packs of Natty Ice, I would be sipping red wine from stemware. I remember once doing just that when a guy on the football team who was known affectionately as Timmy Triceps looked at me, drunkenly amused: "Drew, you look like Dracula over there, drinking blood and shit." If not a totem, I was certainly a beloved novelty.

Of course, some of this was a nineteen-year-old's attempt to distinguish himself from the pack—to say: *I'm different*—but it was also a way of distancing myself from my teammates and thus the game, to say: *I'm not you*. And while there were the occasional absurdities of my intellectual pretension, they were not entirely disingenuous; in fact, they were born of an earnest desire to learn.

While English had been about the only tolerable class in high school, in college the written word came alive for me in a way it never had before. Perhaps the most significant event in this regard happened in my spring semester of freshman year. While I was completing the second half of my remedial freshman composition class, through a serendipitous mix-up at the registrar, I found myself signed up for a senior-level class on post-Vietnam fiction. The professor, Dr. Hagan, was a veteran of that war, but he had also been a baller back in the day. He had grown up in New York City and played against Lew Alcindor ("Lewie," he would remember him fondly) and Jim Carroll ("He couldn't go left"). Perhaps because of this, he tolerated me and let me stay in the class. Somehow I had navigated high school without encountering much contemporary literature. I'd never heard of any of the writers we read, but being introduced to people like Tim O'Brien, Louise Erdrich, Tobias Wolff, Bobbie Ann Mason, and Andre Dubus was a revelation. There was something about their stories, told in voices not so dissimilar from my own—not the ornate, purple, antiquated language I had associated with "fine" literature—that elicited a depth of feeling over a range of emotion that felt alchemical. I began to chase that feeling in everything I read, all the while harboring a desire that I might learn to be someone who could evoke it in others. I sought Dr. Hagan out after class and in office hours and sometimes we would talk about basketball, sometimes literature. One day I showed up with something I had written of my own, a handful of pages that were pure O'Brien ripoff, and asked if he wouldn't mind looking them over. To my surprise, he agreed, and thus began the period when I would periodically show up with my first fictional failings and he'd read and critique them, and, despite that, still somehow summon the grace to encourage me to keep at it. It was an amazing act of generosity, and I have often wondered whether I'd be a writer today if he had said what would have been most convenient for him: "I'm busy, kid. Aren't you late for practice?"

All of this was happening as I was recovering from my hamstring injury. By the time I was healed we were deep in the conference season. Kevin had found his stroke and had moved back into the starting spot at shooting guard, and I resumed my role coming off the bench. I was less effective than I had been earlier in the season, in part because the injury left me tentative and in part because my heart wasn't in it. I remember one of our assistant coaches coming up to me in the locker room after a game, asking what was wrong. "You look hesitant out there. You look lost," he said. He was trying to motivate me, but as is often the case in player–coach dynamics there was a subtext of threat to it, that I was getting passed by, as well as shame, that I wasn't the player they had expected me to be. *We actually thought* you *were too good to play for* us? I shrugged and shook my head, said I was just getting my feet back under me after the injury. I didn't have the courage to tell him the truth, that I looked the way I did because I didn't want to be out there anymore.

We finished the regular season in the middle of the pack of the Little East Conference, but we went on a run in the conference tournament, winning it all and earning a berth in the NCAA tournament. Only forty-eight teams made the D-III NCAA tournament at that point, so it was an exciting time for us. We won our opening-round game before losing in the second round to the number-one team in the country, Connecticut College. I remember feeling relieved that the season was over, but as we sat in the locker room after the loss, Coach Campbell made it clear that while we had played our last official game of the year, the basketball season never really ended in college. The team might not be able to hold official practices, but we would meet with assistant coaches individually to work on our game in the morning, hit the weight room in the afternoon, and run pickup ball against each other in the evenings. Basically, little would change. When summer break came, the coaching staff sent each of us home with personalized workout and dietary plans to stay in shape, as well as developmental goals to meet before returning to school in August, but I hardly touched a basketball all summer.

When I arrived back in Danbury for the start of my sophomore year, I played exactly one game of pickup before leaving the court to find Coach Campbell to tell him I was quitting. It was impromptu. I didn't know I was going to do it until I was sitting in front of him with tears in my eyes telling him I didn't love it anymore. I was burnt out, I needed to focus on my studies, I wanted to become a writer. Coach Campbell and I had always gotten along. He liked my off-court interests and we would often discuss foreign films and books after practice. Of course, I'd also seen him fly into many object-throwing halftime rages, one of which had a water bottle coming within an inch of my head. I worried how he would react to my speech, but he seemed to know there was little he could say to change my mind. He gave me a hug and wished me luck. I walked outside and felt an intense rush of relief, not because I had worked up the nerve to quit but because I'd finally unburdened myself to someone. That was the thing: I hadn't talked to anyone about what I was feeling, not Chief or Nutso, not my girlfriend, not even my mom or brother. I had bottled it up, and now I was in a curious position. I'd resigned from the team, but no one close to me even knew I was considering it. Why had I withheld my feelings? I have often wondered. Why was it so hard for me to acknowledge? The only answer I can think of is that my identity up to that point was so intertwined with basketball that to reject it felt in some sense like rejecting who I was. I was ashamed not to love what I was expected to love, because for so long I had.

That evening I called a roommate meeting. We had a three-bedroom apartment in the athletic dorms, and I lived with Chief and Nutso and two other guys named Lenny and Hondo. I made a big show of needing to tell them something important, and I could see the nervous confusion in their eyes as they entered the room Chief and I shared. When everyone had taken a seat, Nutso asked what was up. I took a deep breath and gave them a less emotionally spastic version of what I had told Coach Campbell earlier. They took it in, looking at the floor, nodding occasionally. Chief said that he thought I would regret it, but that he supported my decision. They all did. I was a little surprised, had expected more resistance. As we walked out of the room to have dinner together, Nutso patted me on the shoulder and said, "I thought you were gonna tell us you were gay, Drew."

Life at WestConn without basketball was both exciting and lonely. I wanted to transfer, but figuring out where to go and completing the procedural work meant sticking around Danbury for the rest of my sophomore year. I remember walking out of my first class after leaving the team and instinctively thinking I needed to get to practice before realizing I could do whatever I wanted. How strange that felt. How wonderful to realize I didn't have every hour of every day planned for me by the coaching staff. How novel to be able to experience college like a normal student. And yet I was still living with Chief and Nutso, still staying in the athletic dorm with all my old teammates, and they were a constant reminder of what I had left behind, the parts of myself I had rejected and forsaken. I fixed my schedule so that I had to be on campus only three days a week. I spent long weekends back at home in Avon with my girlfriend, who was still in high school, and my brother, who had recently returned from living in Chile. Once I remember upbraiding my roommates for not cleaning up after themselves and Chief shot back: "What the fuck do you care, Drew? You're never here. You've already left us." I imagine my interests and behavior that were so endearingly odd when I was on the team had now come to feel like a rebuke, which, in some sense, I suppose, they were.

I continued to focus on my classes, continued to meet with Dr. Hagan to talk about my stories. That summer, as I worked through a reading list of his suggestions, I had begun notes for a novel that was very much about someone like me doing very similar things as me. It would be wonderful and important. It would say profound things about masculinity in a post–Vietnam America. My goal was to finish it that year at WestConn before transferring to the University of Arizona, where I could attend tuition-free because my dad taught there. Of course, what I mostly did was get high and think about how wonderful and important my novel would be. More than anything, this—smoking impeccably rolled blunts with another former player and not actually writing—made me feel like a writer. Eventually that would become boring, and I would learn how to spend hours at the keyboard working over sentences, but my aesthetic awareness had been sparked, my engagement with the arts initiated, and thus my intellectual awakening had begun. I was becoming an adult, something that at that time seemed to necessitate leaving basketball behind.

That summer before I moved to Tucson, my old friend from Lawrence, Todd, came to live with my family in Avon. Both of us were going through major life changes and it helped to be around each other. He joined the house-painting crew I worked on with Chief and Nutso and he fit right in with the guys. Todd was playing basketball at South Dakota

State University then, and after a day of work all of us would head to the gym and play pickup. It was the first time I had played in almost a year and I was surprised to find little dropoff in my ability. The first game we played, Todd and I were on the same team, and we ran the court undefeated for the next two and a half hours. From then on, the ballers from Kansas would be placed on opposite teams, while everyone else shot free throws to decide whether they would be on Todd's team or mine. I remember once being at Chief's house and overhearing him in the kitchen talking to his mother about me. "He's still better than all of us," he said. That made me feel good, but it didn't make me regret my decision. During those summer evenings playing ball with my friends I wouldn't say my love of basketball was rekindled so much as it was recalled. That is, I remembered what was fun about playing a game when it was allowed to remain a game, when it didn't dominate every second of my waking life.

I did not play for seven years after that summer, not until I was in graduate school at the University of Iowa. I was studying fiction writing at the Writers' Workshop, and there was a longstanding game of Saturday morning pickup that was mostly a way to detoxify yourself from all the booze you drank on Friday night. One night out at the bar, I mistakenly bragged that I'd once been very good at basketball and the Saturday morning regulars tried to get me to come out and play. I declined, but they pressed and I declined and still they pressed. When I finally accepted the invitation, I tried to temper expectations, telling them I never played anymore and wouldn't be very good, and compared to my old self I wasn't. But though my stamina and fitness were weak, the more skilled aspects of my game—shooting, passing, dribbling, moving without the ball—had not fully deteriorated. I wasn't half bad. In fact, there were occasional flashes of what I had once been. Of course, a crushing blow to the ego of many a former athlete would be spared if they could return to the game alongside a motley crew of hungover writers.

The first twenty years of my life were bound up in the body, in the physical, driven by the desire to play basketball, while the last twenty years have been bound up in the mind, driven by my desire to write and read books. For a long time these two halves of my life seemed to have little to do with one another, and only in the last few years did I realize how connected they are. There is the obvious: to do anything well requires a lot of hard work, and all those years of training and practicing for basketball taught me the discipline it took to spend long hours at the writing desk, trying to get a little bit better on the page each day the same way I used to on the court.

Less apparent to me, however, was how similar the actual experience of playing basketball and writing are. On the one hand, playing ball requires preparation and forethought and concentration that is intensely mindful and conscious. On the other hand, when players are at their best they slip into a certain level of unconsciousness—what's called being in the zone—that is instinct guiding a well-trained and prepared mind and body. Playing the game is about negotiating the vacillations between these two extremes of consciousness, mindfulness and spontaneity, and much of the beauty as a fan is bearing witness to it. The only thing I can compare the experience to is writing. Most days I sit down at the desk with a strong sense of what I want to write about and the hope is that in doing so at a certain point I will slip into a level of unconscious thought—what's called being visited by the muse—that can't be planned for, that opens up new doors in my writing the same way a lane to the hoop would suddenly open up on the court and I was at the rim before I even knew how it had happened.

A few years ago, I was pleased to come across some scientific backing that supported what had always felt to me like an odd and personal hunch. An article by Carl Zimmer called "This Is Your Brain on Writing" that appeared in the *New York Times* on June 20, 2014, begins: "A novelist scrawling away in a notebook in seclusion may not seem to have much in common with an NBA player doing a reverse layup on a basketball court before a screaming crowd. But if you could peer inside their heads, you might see some striking similarities in how their brains were churning." The article cites the research of a group of neuroscientists in Germany, led by one Dr. Martin Lotze, who studied the brains of expert writers at work and found that the area of the brain called the caudate nucleus became animated. Explains Zimmer:

> The caudate nucleus is a familiar part of the brain for scientists like Dr. Lotze who study expertise. It plays an essential role in the skill that comes with practice, including activities like board games. When we first start learning a skill—be it playing a piano or playing basketball—we use a lot of conscious effort. With practice, those actions become more automatic. The caudate nucleus and nearby regions start to coordinate the brain's activity as this shift happens.

These days I make an effort to feel present in both my mind and body. I meditate and work out at the gym. I have even returned to playing the occasional game of tennis, but I never play basketball. Somehow the burnout that began twenty years ago has lasted to this day, though I watch basketball constantly. I continue to follow my Jayhawks obsessively. I absolutely love the game, but I feel no desire to play it.

For a long time after I quit, my excuse when someone invited me to play was that I did not want to see myself become bad at basketball. There was a sliver of truth to it, but it was also a narcissistically backhanded way of conveying to the person that I had once been really good—so good, in fact, that I couldn't disrespect the memory of my greatness by deigning to play a simple game of pickup against lowly you. I wanted the person to know that I had been a certain caliber of athlete without the burden of having to prove it, when I should have just Bartlebyed the truth: I would prefer not to. As I've said, the few times I did play since quitting I played pretty well, and it was pleasantly surprising that I still had some court skills after such a long absence. The last time I played a game of basketball, however, was the first time I saw that I bore no resemblance to the player I'd been. I had become, as long feared, bad at basketball.

It happened one winter when I was back visiting my mother and brother in Connecticut over the holidays. As I always do, I made a point of meeting up with my friends who still live in the area, many of whom I played ball with. Chief was the one who told me that our old high school was having an alumni game—former players taking on the current team—as a fund-raiser of some sort. I told him I hadn't played in years, that I had no shoes or shorts, but he said it would be okay, that I could borrow gear from him. I tried to decline but he pressed, and finally, weak-willed or simply curious to see if I still had it, I agreed.

I showed up at Avon High with Chief, feeling slightly clownish in clothing meant for Chief's six-six frame (I'm six one). We made our way into the renovated school. Much had changed; the town had grown. They had built a new gym and used the one we'd played in as a practice facility. We joined Biff and Nutso, who were sitting in the stands, as was Coach Taft, who had retired several years prior. We caught up for a few minutes as people filed in and took their seats. Hanging on the walls above the new basketball court were banners celebrating conference and state championships. The thousand-point banner with my name still hung, joined by a few new names, as did the one honoring our 24–0 conference season.

I did little right during the game. I lost my dribble, missed a shot, and mistimed my jump so that I got out-rebounded by a smaller opponent. My lungs burned and I regretted my decision to play, to look so feeble in such a public way. Things only worsened after our alumni team beat the current team. Avon had won the state title a handful of years after our class graduated and one of the running debates, so I learned from Chief, was over which was the greatest Avon team: the state title team with a less gaudy record, or our 26–1 team that lost in the Final Four? In the locker room there was all sorts of trash being talked so we made a bet—winner buys the other team's beer at the bar later—and played an impromptu game of pickup in the old gym, which Coach Taft let us into. Our team won, but, again, it had little to do with me, and, again, I regretted having agreed to play. It was tough seeing that I was no longer good, that I no longer derived pleasure from playing even the occasional game of basketball, and I told myself I wouldn't play again.

This happened in December 2010, the year after Kansas's loss to Northern Iowa, the event that sparked this recollection and assessment of my relationship to the game. Just as I was beginning the process of trying to understand why I love the game the way I do, I was also making the decision to give up experiencing it as a player and participant. From then on I would only ever enjoy basketball as a spectator, as a fan. Of course, I could change my mind at any moment if I ever felt the desire to play again, but in the nine years since then I haven't, and I think it is unlikely I ever will.

After that trip to Connecticut, I returned to San Francisco. H had spent the holidays with her own family, and we were at her apartment, catching up after being apart for a week or so. At one point I told her about the alumni game, how I had played basketball with my old friends for the first time in a long time, and she wanted to know how it went. I told her that we killed the current team and then won the showdown against the state championship team. And how did I play, she asked then.

There's a line from the T. S. Eliot essay "Shakespeare and the Stoicism of Seneca" that has stayed with me ever since I read it many years ago as an undergraduate: "Humility is the most difficult of all virtues to achieve; nothing dies harder than the desire to think well of oneself."

H waited for me to answer and I only shrugged, giving her a sheepish smile to indicate that I had played well.

"Were you still the best?" she said.

Finally, after a lengthy pause, I told her yes.

Mama, You Been
on My Mind

Though I generally consider the three weeks of the NCAA tournament to be my High Holy Days, I don't suffer from the somber day-after-Christmas malaise when it ends. The tournament in all its agony and glory frankly doesn't feel emotionally sustainable after twenty-plus days; there is a kind of mercy when it ends. After Kansas was upset, ruining half the country's brackets and sending me into a downward spiral, I pulled myself together enough to hate-watch the rest of the 2010 NCAA tournament, a childish and invidious act the basketball gods repaid by making me bear witness to Duke—*fucking* Duke—win the title. I remember watching Coach K smile smugly as he handed off the championship trophy to his players and thinking, *I know all about the Faustian bargain you struck long ago, and, brother, I promise you this: When Mephistopheles comes to collect, I will be there, and I'll be the one smiling.*

The sting of KU's loss hung around for a while, but the season was over, and I didn't have the opportunity to let myself get caught up in the game. Sure, there were the NBA playoffs, but those I could watch and appreciate more impartially, purely for the beauty and drama of the game and without all the emotional baggage. I went back to work on my collection of short stories about Kansas, and I continued to work my two jobs, teaching at the day program for adults with developmental disabilities and "coaching" the JV tennis team. However, the writing fellowship that had brought me to the Bay in the first place had ended and without that monetary support my financial situation fell into a different economic quintile of shitty. I could no longer afford to live in the apartment in Bernal Heights, so that September I gave up the lease when I lucked into a housesitting gig in Berkeley. The house belonged to family friends of H, professors at the university, who were sympathetic to my predicament and generously allowed me to stay essentially rent-free in exchange for looking after the place while they were away on sabbatical in Boston until December. The move to Berkeley left me logging a lot of time in the car, driving northwest to my teaching job in Novato, then south over the Golden Gate into San Francisco to see H, and then east over the Bay Bridge to check on the house and water the plants, but I didn't mind. I felt lucky to be getting by in a place that seemed to actively dissuade such foolish hopes with its astronomical cost of living.

One evening in early October of 2010, I started to drive from Berkeley to Sacramento. I had lost track of time and jumped in my car unshowered, goopy-headed, wearing flip-flops and the shirt I slept in, hoping to beat rush hour traffic. It was a warm evening and I drove for ninety minutes, watching the views of a road I had never taken unfold under the ache of that wonderful California light, still impressive to this midwesterner.

There are few things of less import in the world that come readily to mind than a preseason NBA game, and yet there I was making my way to the capital city to watch the Sacramento Kings play the Phoenix Suns in the first game of the NBA preseason, and all because Darnell Jackson had been traded from the Milwaukee Bucks to the Kings in the off-season. It had been six months since my beloved and number-one-ranked Kansas Jayhawks were upset in the second round of the NCAA tourney, six months since I held the corpse of the 2009–2010 Kansas team in my arms and whispered, "Why can't I quit you?" and there I was, loyal as a beaten dog, making the drive to that unfamiliar city to watch a game I did not really care about just so I could pay respect to my favorite Jayhawk of all time.

I Want to Take Your Pain and Put It Inside Me

Like most squads, the KU basketball team celebrates Senior Night on the final home game of the regular season. Before the game, the seniors walk to center court with their families to be introduced and acknowledged by the crowd as the cheerleading squad showers them in red and white roses. After the game, each senior makes a speech, a chance to thank fans, teammates, the community, his family. Darnell Jackson gave his Senior Night speech in early March of 2008, a month before Kansas would win the NCAA title against Memphis in one of the more memorable finals of the last thirty years.

The speech is a little over four minutes long, the first half of which Darnell thanks his teammates for helping him when "he was going through all that stuff." Afterward, he acknowledges the crowd: "I know everyone here knows what I was going through with my family and friends." He's right. There are few things more important than basketball in Lawrence, Kansas, and anyone able to get a ticket to Senior Night in Allen Fieldhouse knows what he is referring to. For the rest of you, what he means is this: during his four years of playing at Kansas, Darnell lost his grandfather, a close cousin of his was murdered, as was a childhood friend, his uncle was beaten to death with a hammer, and his mother and grandmother were hit by a drunk driver in an accident that killed his grandmother and left his mother in chronic pain. After the accident, Darnell returned home to Oklahoma City to grieve with his family and nearly quit the team. Head coach Bill Self flew there and talked him out of it, something Darnell acknowledges in the speech as well, referring to Coach Self as a "father figure" (Darnell's father was shot to death by police when he was thirteen).

Around the two-minute mark of the speech, Darnell waits for the crowd to stop applauding and looks up to where his family and friends are sitting. A sly smile on his face, he whispers into the mic: "Mama, stand up." The Jumbotron flashes a picture of his mother, Shawn, putting her head down, embarrassed, before finally standing as the crowd erupts again. Darnell takes a few steps back, smiling, letting his mother take in the ovation, then says: "You had me at sixteen. We had our fights, wrestling in the living room. Only thing I can say is that I love you. You're an amazing person, fighting through what you went through, and you were there with Grandma." He acknowledges a few other family members and after a brief pause, staring at his mother, finishes: "I don't know what else to say. It hurts so bad, because I wish I could take your pain away and put it inside of me."

I find myself watching and rewatching this speech from time to time, first a version I found on YouTube from a shaky handheld camera and then later a professionally filmed version I discovered on a Kansas basketball website. I was drawn to it for reasons I didn't fully understand, other than that it moved me, as it did the August before this trip to Sacramento, when I was in New York with H. We were staying at her godmother's apartment in Morningside Heights for a few days, seeing friends and family. I was sitting at the dining room table watching the speech on my computer as she packed her bags a few feet away. When she heard me sigh, she looked over and asked what was wrong. I took out my earbuds and put them on the table. "Darnell's Senior Night speech." She had heard me talk about it before, knew it held some strange private meaning for me. "Can I listen?" she said. So she came over and the two of us listened to it together. Afterward, she walked away and resumed packing. "Why does it move you so much?"

"Because he's been through so much shit," I said. "And the way he talks about wanting to put his mother's pain inside himself is sad and beautiful. And he's my favorite player. It's just . . ."

"Why is he your favorite?" she asked, and I thought for a few moments, mouth open, trying to figure out how to answer.

Parking Lot Sunset

After I pulled into the arena complex and parked, I made my way toward the main entrance, where a line of people were waiting. It was ten till six and the game didn't tip until seven, but I had come early because I wanted to catch some of the warmups, hoping to get close to Darnell. As a journeyman bench player, he was unlikely to see much game-time action. The people around me, a racially diverse mix of middle-aged men and their special lady friends and children, wore Kings jerseys, hats, T-shirts. Lots of team propaganda. Purple and silver everywhere. I spotted a blue-and-white oversized number-one foam hand with Hebrew scrawled across the knuckles—a tribute to Omri Casspi, whom the Kings drafted in 2009, making him the first Israeli to play in an NBA game—sucking up the entire arm of a young boy who could barely hold it up.

When we gained entrance, everyone rushed courtside. Tyreke Evans and top draft pick DeMarcus Cousins were out early warming up, shooting languid jumpers. Assistant coaches fed them balls and applied soft mock defense. There was no sign of Darnell, no sign of anyone else on the team but these two young stars. It was wonderful being ground level. Only there could you appreciate the size and strength of professional athletes. It was the opposite of those stories we've heard where a friend spots a movie star in an airport or restaurant and reports back how small and unimpressive he or she is—how disappointingly *normal* for a person we are used to seeing on movie screens to appear. What's striking and beautiful about professional basketball players is how wonderfully abnormal they are, how gloriously mutant. Not only their height, of course, but their size, speed, strength—all the attributes that seem black-and-white in the abstract but that bound to life in garish Technicolor when you actually witness them. It was amazing to see a group of people so mindfully present in their bodies in a way that was not about—in fact, was the exact opposite of—stillness. I was trying to take it all in, scribbling in the notebook I always bring with me everywhere, which drew looks from the people around me who were hollering for autographs and taking pictures.

I recognized one of the assistant coaches as Mario Elie, who won two titles with the Houston Rockets in the mid-nineties during the first Jordan sabbatical. He was decked out in Kings practice gear, like the other assistants. A bit overweight, a step slower, they were all former players, and you could see how much they still loved being around the game. When Evans and Cousins headed back to the locker room, the old-timers hung around, dribbling, laughing, challenging one another to shooting contests.

After a while, men with collared shirts and lanyards approached, telling those of us standing courtside that we needed to leave, so I followed the rest of the groundlings to the concourse, where I wandered around from one concession stand to the next. I considered buying a $9.75 Premium Draft Beer, but passed it up when I laid eyes on the Royal Wine Cellar, a plasticky wood hovel made up to look like the tasting area of a winery. I approached the bartender, who was carefully arranging cocktail napkins in flared stacks before a few bottles of low-end wine. I ordered a seven-dollar cabernet and moved over to a window to catch the last bit of an achingly gorgeous sunset through trees that had been installed to mask the miles of parking lot. There at that window, in the odd world of fandom, where grown men wear jerseys bearing the names of other grown men, I told myself there was nothing weird about me and my notebook, my wine and my sunset. Nothing at all.

Larry K

We moved—my mom, brother, and I—to Lawrence after my parents divorced. They had been married for fourteen years, part of that time as Peace Corps newlyweds in Liberia, part of the time in Columbus, Ohio, where my dad was in graduate school and my mom worked for the state, and part of it in Lexington, Kentucky, where they had met at the University of Kentucky and where my father later became a professor. My mother needed to escape Lexington and the life that no longer existed for her there, and she applied to graduate school at the University of Kansas. I was three when we arrived in Kansas.

I remember the day we arrived in town and pulled up to the house we would rent, a yellow split-level across the creek from the trailer park in a neighborhood of working-poor families. In my memory of that distant time, it seems like the second we pulled onto the street every kid on the block could smell our arrival, Brint and me, newbies to befriend or beat up on, and they streamed out of each house on the block, running alongside our truck before it could even stop. Afterward, Mom was always tickled that we had made friends immediately, a testament to the decency of the Midwest, the solidarity of our economic class, but I don't remember us making friends right off the bat. I remember them inspecting us, watching us unload the belongings we had brought from our old house and intended to put inside our new one. Sometimes when I think of this it's happening at night and sometimes it's happening in the bright of midday summer. I see kids standing all around us, looking on until it is time for us to go indoors. Some leave without words, others say, "See you tomorrow," and one says, "Welcome to Larry K."

"Who's Larry K?" I say.

The East End Party Zone

I found my seat in the second-to-last row of the arena, in a section unironically called the East End Party Zone. I had bought the cheapest ticket I could find, so I had some sense of the degree of nosebleed, but any farther away and I could have shared my Dippin' Dots with a Martian. I hadn't brought binoculars, but having seen Darnell play so many times over the years I knew I would be able to spot him. As I watched the leisurely gait of the players warming up in layup lines, however, I didn't see his familiar stride.

Other East Enders filed into our section, squinting to read ticket stubs, fumbling over leg and step, and by the time we stood for the national anthem about three-quarters of our section was filled. Soon began the familiar *unts-unts* of NBA arena music, a John Teshian techno beat that might have been commissioned for a drug-free rave. Then the lights went out and there were various explosive sounds as a voice-of-God announcer asked us if we were ready to meet our 2010–2011 Sacramento Kings. Apparently our clapping wasn't convincing enough, because suddenly bright colors started lightsabering through the darkness, and several hype men sprinted out in silver warmups and purple headbands and wristbands, with telemarketer-style mic gear strapped to their heads, shouting, "Stand up!" before sprinting to another corner and demanding that we let them hear us roar. Most of the lower levels complied—whether out of fear or excitement was unclear—but we were a safe enough distance away just to observe the madness.

I was having the first inklings of the ill ease that would characterize much of my NBA experience that night. The harder they tried to get me to care—"they" being whoever the hell in the Kings corporation is responsible for the presentation of all that nonbasketball extraness—the less I did. They were telling me I was having fun, but I wasn't because they were so insistent that I was and did so in distracting ways that had nothing to do with basketball. I just wanted to see Darnell play and watch the greatest athletes on the planet compete, and they wanted me to go on the kiss cam and get excited about some person on a unicycle flipping bowls onto her head at halftime. It's not that the college game didn't have similar kinds of inanities and timeout buffoonery, but somehow it seemed so different in the NBA. A strange inversion was taking place, by which basketball became secondary to all this crap, whereas in college the sport was the point and everything else ancillary. It felt like a bait and switch: we had purchased a ticket to watch a game but had actually been brought here to witness this tawdry and tasteless spectacle. Furthermore, part of my aversion was that their actions didn't even seem sincere. They did not really care whether I was having fun, any more than they cared whether I watched the game or considered it more than just entertainment. What they really cared about, I understood, was whether they had seduced me into feeling good enough to spend ten dollars on a beer, six more on an Omri Casspi Hebrew foam hand, and a hundred on a jersey before making my way home. I felt lost in the not-so-funhouse being built by the marketing team of the modern American corporation, obvious and overdetermined, staggering in how little respect it gives us. Whatever its virtues, there is nothing that capitalism can't debase, and seeing art so crudely and desperately peddled for profit accounted for the hollowed-out feeling I would have at the end of the night.

Heart

Darnell was one of Coach Self's first recruits after taking over as KU's head coach in 2003. He was slow to adjust to the college game his first couple of years, but the potential was there, and by his senior season, 2007–2008, Darnell had moved into the starting lineup and was the team's leading rebounder while also contributing eleven points a game. It was an incredibly balanced team that included five players who would be drafted into the NBA after the season and two more who would follow later, and while there was no single star upon whom the team's success depended, I would argue that Darnell was the most important player on that team. The team was full of very talented but very quiet, almost aloof, players like Brandon Rush, Mario Chalmers, Darrell Arthur, and Russell Robinson. Vocal and animated, Darnell was the exception. He was to that team what Draymond Green is to the Golden State Warriors, and just as the Warriors' present dynastic reign in the NBA would fall apart if Green were traded, I feel certain that the 2008 KU basketball team never would have won the title if Darnell had opted to quit the team after his grandmother was killed. More than his rebounding and scoring, he brought heart.

It's said so often—*He plays with a lot of heart*—that it has become a sports cliché, dead language, ennobling shorthand for saying that someone displays effort on the court. And effort is an important part of it, surely, but playing with heart is also about energy, attitude, toughness, leadership, hustle, and support, as well as a seriousness with which one accepts the tasks before them, the sense that the game really matters. That was what Darnell brought to the game. Watching Darnell, I suppose I felt something akin to what John McPhee wrote of watching Bill Bradley compete in his classic book *A Sense of Where You Are*: "His play was integral. There was nothing missing. He not only worked hard on defense, for example, he worked hard on defense when the other team was hopelessly beaten. He did all kinds of things he didn't have to simply because those were the dimensions of the game." Darnell's contributions did feel integral, which made his presence in the game not only important but consequential.

"It seems like one of the things you like about Darnell is that he loves his mom," H had said that blistering August day in New York when I tried to talk about why Darnell was my favorite player. She said this after I went on and on about how Darnell played with heart and what that meant. I grimaced, and then she added, "And that he seems like a nice guy." While I love my mother very much and do value kindness, I didn't want to believe that character traits and personal demeanor factored into the hard science of my player-love for Darnell. It simply could not all boil down to "He's a nice mama's boy like me," and it didn't, but I realized in retrospect that H was right, or at least in part. There was no denying that that was some of the missing calculus I needed in order to understand why I found myself pulled toward Darnell more than any other player before or since.

After the car accident in which his grandmother died and his mom was seriously injured, Darnell began thumping his chest three times after a big play or before a free throw attempt. He explained to a reporter that one thump was for his grandmother, one was for his mother, and one was for a family friend. "I do it to let 'em know I love them. If they are watching the game, they know they are in my heart." It's not the all-eyes-on-me bravado of many players who make a great play and beat their chest. To me it always looks like he's reminding himself: *This is my heart. This is it, right here.*

Per Aspera

I was born in Lexington, Kentucky, and raised in Lawrence, Kansas. I sometimes have to explain to folks who are unfamiliar with college basketball that it's like being able to trace your matrilineal line directly back to George Washington and your patrilineal line directly back to Lincoln. They are home to the two winningest programs in the sport, after all, and I feel confident in asserting that were I not to love the sport, a majority of both populations would see cause for radical reeducation, if not outright banishment. Hunter S. Thompson hardly exaggerated when he said: "I am more than just a serious basketball fan. I am a lifelong Addict. I was addicted from birth, in fact, because I was born in Kentucky and I learned, early on, that Habitual Domination was a natural way of life." Lawrence, however, has none of the battling for its soul the way my birth town— pulled between horseracing and basketball—does. Since 1898, when James Naismith became the University of Kansas's first coach, basketball has been the only game in town.

Having spent most of my youth traveling between two basketball-crazed towns, my brother and me going to visit our dad on vacations and returning to live with our mom during the school year, I realize that my love of basketball is undoubtedly influenced by place, the context in which I was exposed to the sport; however, I think my love is also inextricably bound up in place in ways that have little to do with basketball and more to do with connection to and identification with Lawrence and what it meant to our family—specifically, what it meant to our family's new configuration as a trio instead of a quartet. The Kansas state motto is Ad Astra Per Aspera—"To the stars through difficulty"—and in Kansas we did struggle. We had little money and Mom drank for a while. Throughout the marriage she had largely put her own career on hold to raise us boys so that my dad could forward his. In Lawrence she enrolled at KU, not in the art history she loved but in accounting, which was a more employable degree. She went back to school and through it all managed to give my brother and me a childhood far happier than any combination of graduate student stipend and child support should have allowed her. She had escaped to Lawrence, fallen into a hole for a short time, and emerged from the darkness stronger, clean, confident in herself and in her abilities to mother. And as struggle tends to do, it bound the three of us close, gave us an esprit de corps, united us in the common purpose of being a family undestroyed.

Mom found ways to do fun and interesting things on the cheap: camping, community theater, libraries, town-league athletics, potlucks, and hootenannies with other former hippies who had resurfaced in Reagan-era America lost, divorced, recovering. Basketball had been an important part of it, too. Since she was a student, she occasionally got inexpensive tickets to games in Allen Fieldhouse—not an easy thing, given the demand of the rabid fanbase—where we often sat high in the rafters and watched, learning the rules of the game, learning to love our Jayhawks. After the game was over, we used to make Mom wait with us until everyone had cleared out, and then Brint and I would walk through row after row of the fieldhouse, picking up empty plastic soda cups. We would compete to see who could collect the most. Finally, after a while, Mom would say enough, and we would leave. Stacked high in the air like soda pop tributes to the Tower of Pisa, the cups leaned as we made our way to our VW camper bus, which was affectionately known as Shirley, a familial pun on the phrase "surely she'll make it," something we'd taken to saying every time we set out to drive somewhere because the VW was always breaking down. There inside Shirley, our hands sticky with fructose, we'd count cups and talk about basketball, recounting our favorite plays of the game.

Halftime

It was nearing the end of the second quarter and I had still seen no sign of Darnell. I cursed myself for not having checked to see if he was on the injured list, let alone whether he was even still on the team. A player like Darnell, a basketball vagabond, could sign with an NBA team one day and wind up playing pro ball in Kazakhstan a week later. I'd barely watched the game, distracted as I was by the varied strangenesses of the preseason NBA experience. With about a minute before halftime, Phoenix called a timeout and music blared as the hype men reappeared, sprinting to their respective corners of the court, assailing the crowd to *Stand!* They were followed by several men carrying colorful bazookas that launched T-shirt salvos into the upper reaches of the arena as the announcer started with the giveaways, calling out seat numbers of fans who would receive future game tickets, jerseys, gift certificates, Blu-ray disc players, etc. Many in the crowd seemed to love this part. They stood. They danced. They tried to draw the camera's attention so they would show up on the Jumbotron. They shouted bestially at the announcer, whom no one could seem to locate, which created a general hysteria of whirling and hand waving, and from my crow's nest the whole spectacle seemed to take on the appearance of a gone-awry Be-In. Why was I the only one who found this horrifying? Why were so many fans able to muster this kind of energy for timeout foolishness but not the actual game? The second the game breaks were over the crowd went back to sleeping through the action or doing what we all do when bored: play with our phones. I wondered why they had even come.

It all made me feel depressed and I seriously considered leaving at half-time, but then, as the teams broke from their huddle after the timeout, I saw him. Darnell. He was in street clothes, jeans and a stylish khaki blazer. He walked away from the huddle, whispered something to a Kings min-ion—one of the many people dressed in black pants and Kings polo shirts who scurry around the bench during timeouts, handing water bottles to players, chucking towels, and wiping down wet spots on the court, all with an urgency and seriousness that is vaguely military—then joked for a mo-ment with another bench player, slapping hands, laughing. As he walked off the court, I understood why I hadn't seen him. He wasn't sitting on the sideline, where the team bench was, or in the row right behind the bench, the way most players do when injured or unavailable. He was sitting along the baseline, something I'd never seen before. Next to him was another player, Samuel Dalembert, who was the Kings' highest-paid player, a real salary black hole, the result of being almost seven feet tall in a league where true centers had become mythopoeic. In a matter of seconds the halftime buzzer sounded—Suns 58, Kings 51—and the teams headed for the locker room. Darnell walked toward the tunnel, stopping to let his teammates go first, giving them five as they passed, until the last player had left the court, and then he followed his team inside.

As the teams broke for halftime, I felt a rush, a renewed sense of purpose, that even though he wasn't playing Darnell was there and all was not lost. I stretched my legs, successfully navigated the gauntlet of men and boys lined up waiting to pee, and stopped by to see my friend at the Royal Wine Cellar so I could fuel up for the second half. I switched from red table wine to a crisp pinot grigio, that's how fucking fired up I was.

For Deyonta B, Who Is Focusing on the Here and Now

When I took my seat, shortly after the start of the third quarter, I found that the seats directly behind me, *the* last row of the arena, which had been empty in the first half, were now occupied by three young people: two boys, black and Latino, and one girl, white. *Who are these urchins and where have they come from?* I wondered, but I couldn't give the matter too much thought because I had basketball to watch. By which I mean I had a man to observe as he watched basketball. Which is what I did. I became fascinated watching Darnell watch the game, studying the way he reacted to plays, wondering what he and Samuel Dalembert were saying to each other when they leaned over to whisper. Unlike Dalembert, who sat back in his seat, Darnell seemed invested in the game. He leaned forward at attention, clapping. When Evans hit a three, he stood and applauded, took a moment to urge on the crowd. He joined his teammates during timeouts. You could sense he wanted to be with them. After one break, he lingered by the bench when someone vacated the last available seat. He appeared to ask the guy in the neighboring seat, Luther Head, if he could sit there, and Head waved Darnell on. But before he could sit down, someone else slipped in and nabbed the spot, so Darnell went back to sit on the baseline and the whole thing left me feeling a little sad.

I realize I've given the wrong impression of the crowd. I have not been fair. Not everyone was hibernating until the next break in action, when whatever nonbasketball excrescence appeared. There were people, particularly up where I was in the outposts of civilization, for whom the game seemed to mean a great deal. This became apparent when the kids behind me began shouting, "You suck!" every time someone missed a shot. That was when I first really took notice of them, these other people, these Men Who Care. They were entirely adult males, mostly white, mostly lone wolves gone rogue in the Party Zone, all of whom actually seemed very invested in the game. They were easy to miss because theirs is a species that bleeds into their surroundings, sporting chameleons. They were unassuming in their glasses and ballcaps and zipped-to-the-neck windbreakers. These jock-sniffers had programs they'd budgeted five dollars to purchase as well as teachable moments and strategy from their time playing JV ball twenty years ago. Cartoon thought bubbles hovered next to their heads, packed with stats they had memorized, sports-talk radio theses they would deliver tomorrow on their commute. There was an angst about them that was familiar. The foot tapping. The missed-shot "goddamnits," silenced by a fist closed so tightly it could bend a penny. They seemed unable to enjoy the game because they were so invested in it. Unlike the kids, whose jeering was mostly an effort to weather the longueurs of a preseason game, these men were impassioned and serious. They chastised the players for not *concentrating*, for not playing the *right* way, for not practicing *hard* enough. Both were unpleasant, though it's hard to blame the kids' battle against boredom when I was writing down every movement of a player not even playing. But it was the adults I loathed, and to do so was to despise the part of me that is them, that is self-conscious about the power something like

Kansas basketball holds over me, that is embarrassed by the fact that I feel a sudden desire to defend my fandom, to hold it up as somehow different, more noble, and thus superior to theirs.

Midway through the quarter, one of the kids tapped on my shoulder. I turned to take in the three of them, putting faces to the assailing voices for the first time. I wouldn't get the names of the other two, but the guy who got my attention was named Deyonta. He pointed at the notebook in which I had been furiously scribbling notes and impressions most of the quarter. "You a writer?" he asked, and I told him yes.

"I'm a writer," said the girl. "I've basically written three books."

"Cool," I said.

The other boy had his arm around her and wore a white headband far back on his skull so that it pushed up his short black hair. I asked if they were in high school and Deyonta and the girl nodded just the littlest bit. "Cool," I said again, and the conversation went cold for a few seconds. In an attempt to rekindle our bond, I asked the girl what her books were about. "Everything," she said. "They're fantasy. They're really good." The boy with his arm around her looked past me, watching the game, and pulled the girl closer to him. He made a sound like he was spitting through his teeth out of the corner of his mouth, and I understood that he would like me to shut up and turn around. So I did, but Deyonta kept talking to me. "What are you writing about now?" he asked.

I told him that I'd come to see Darnell play, that I was working on a "piece" about him, as if I were there in some official capacity, a reporter chasing a story. At the moment it was a complete lie, in part to account for why I had brought a notebook to the basketball game and in part because I was embarrassed about having identified myself as a writer when the young girl behind me seemed to have done more to warrant the title. She had basically written three books, after all. All I had were some short stories about Kansas. What the hell was I doing with myself?

"Don't know Darnell Jackson," Deyonta said.

"He's new to the team. Traded from Milwaukee this summer." I asked him if he came to a lot of games and whether it was always this dead-feeling. He said he did, and that it wasn't. "So a regular season game is different than this?"

"Most definitely." He saw me writing down his answers and leaned forward, away from his comrades. "You know, I got me a scholarship."

"Really?"

He nodded slowly, chin out, like he was working over a wad of chew the size of a softball. "Got me a connect with the Miami Heat too, so I think I'm gonna go pro. Team up with LeBron and D-Wade in South Beach. Win us a championship."

To understand the degree of lunacy within this statement, perhaps a visual might help: Deyonta was about sixteen, I would say. He was Plastic Man skinny, with a chest the size of a Cornish hen. It was tough to tell sitting down, but later, when I saw him stand, I would guess he was about five six, maybe five eight with inserts and an expensive pair of Nikes. And while it shouldn't bear upon the likelihood of his playing prowess, there was the faintest hint of cheesy mustache germinating across his upper lip that, more than anything else, seemed to expose the ruse.

I told him that I played ball for a year when I was in college, but that I was nowhere near good enough to play in the League. He didn't say much after that, and his story quickly fell apart under my high-pressure questioning, such as when I asked, "So what school recruited you?"

"I don't know," he said.

"I thought you just said you had a scholarship?"

Slowly, he turned his attention from the game to me and nodded, a sudden pensiveness about him. "I just gotta focus on the here and now, know what I mean?"

I told him I did.

Of course, I can imagine how I must have seemed to him. We were keepers of each other's illusions. He was letting me feel like a reporter, despite the fact that I was sitting in the second-to-last row of the arena "covering" a player not even playing, and I was letting him feel like a kid on his way to the NBA with a scholarship to some as-yet-unnamed university that would be decided upon when he was done living in the here and now. There was both kindness and meanness in what we were doing.

I asked for his name and wrote it down as he spelled it out.

"I'll keep an eye out for you," I said.

"You do that."

Mother's Day

Of the handful of websites I make sure to check every day, one is the sports page of the *Lawrence Journal-World*, KUsports.com. More specifically, the men's basketball page of the sports page of the *LJW*. During the season, it is where I read recaps of KU's games and interviews with Coach Self, and find updates on current player injuries as well as on what former Jayhawks are up to in the NBA or otherwise. In the off-season, it is where I track who our coaching staff is following on the recruiting trail. It's my one-horse daily racing form. That previous March I had come across a small article reporting that Darnell's mother, Shawn, had passed away. It was brief and contained no details, and I remember mustering only a callous of-course-she-did shrug, because it seemed everyone in Darnell's life was destined to perish, and most to perish tragically, horrifically. A religious man, he would never see it this way, but I felt certain that if there was anyone from whom God had turned away it was Darnell, though perhaps it would be more appropriate to view his misfortunes within the tradition of Job.

The news of her passing came only a few days after the Northern Iowa upset, when I was in the throes of myopic despair, and Shawn's death seemed only part of the pall I found myself trapped beneath. About a month and a half later, I came across another article on KUsports.com titled "Dearly Missed: Jackson Opens Up about His Mother's Tragic Passing." It ran on Mother's Day and in it Darnell talks about his mother's death, which turned out to be a suicide, an overdose on pain medication. Apparently in the five years after the car crash that took her mother's life, Shawn was in great distress, relying on pills to deal with the physical pain from multiple surgeries as well as the mental pain. She was crippled by guilt and the sense that the accident was her fault, though it wasn't; her car was hit by an eighteen-year-old drunk driver. In the interview, Darnell's tone vacillates. While it's a tribute to his mom, he is also critical of and angry with her, as suicide tends to leave those left in its wake. One moment he says, "What we had was magical. There's something with my mom . . . I'll never have it with anybody else," and another, "Every day that I think about her, I'm pissed off. I'm mad. Some days I want to blow up and go crazy. The other day I broke down while working out. It hurts. It hurts a lot because she was always there."

In an article over four years earlier, written when Darnell was a sophomore at KU and receiving little playing time, Shawn talks about her son and the car accident:

> This has all been so hard for me. It's so hard for him. . . . You must real-ize, I had Darnell when I was 16. With her [Darnell's grandmother] gone and what I'm going through mentally and physically . . . I thank the Lord he is doing so well. He may not finish on top of all the statistical catego-ries at KU, but he will go down in history one of the beautiful men who played for KU.

Darnell seemed to bring out the poet in her. She continues, saying of her son: "We've had a cloud over our family. He is bringing a light." Later, she talks about the drunk driver who hit her car when she and her mother were visiting Las Vegas. "I just want to talk to him. He lives out there. . . . I tell people my mom is in a better place, but I think about him and his family. He was 18 at the time of the wreck. He will get time. I'd like to talk to him, see what was going through his mind. I will tell him I forgive him and pray for him." I don't know whether she got the chance to do so, nor do I know whether Darnell, or anyone for that matter, told him that two people—not one—ultimately died as a result of that accident.

On the Mountain

We were driving to see my mom's cousins in North Carolina. Brint was in the front seat and I was in the back of the old silver Dodge—we hadn't trusted Shirley to complete this kind of trek—that had been passed down to Mom from her father. It was the kind of car that looked like the past's conception of what might be stylish in the distant future. It looked like a Transformer that never transformed into a cool robot. When I see the scene in my mind's eye all these years later, we are on a two-lane mountain road and the car is slaloming across both lanes, getting dangerously close to the edge each time. It feels the way it does driving along Highway 1 in Big Sur, where the edge of the road gives way to a sheer drop that if transgressed would disappear you from the continent. I'm not sure if I knew what it meant to be drunk, but I knew something was wrong. So, too, did my brother. None of us were speaking, but the car was electric with the tension of all the things we weren't saying. Brint would tell me later he had his hand on the door handle so he could army-roll to safety if necessary. (We were midwestern boy-children of the early 1980s, a specific niche in the history of our species that might accurately be catalogued "the GI Joe generation," and there wasn't much trouble a well-executed army-roll couldn't get you out of.)

Somehow my mom made it off the mountain—thankfully a car never passed us in the opposite direction—and took the first exit she came upon. We went to grab something to eat, so that, I understood later, my mom could sober up. Afterward, we were walking around this nowhere town and had gone into a clothing store of some sort when the police arrived to arrest her. Someone had seen her driving and called in a description of our car. What I remember after are details, elliptical and random: the AC freeze of the dark room at the police station where Brint and I were taken, given a blanket to share, and told to get some sleep; the oddity of walking past women in cages; the empty, waterlogged package of Marlboro Reds that was stuck in the corner of the basement shower where the two of us stood naked under the stream of cold water; that old-style, black AT&T rotary phone that could double as an anvil, with which we spoke to our dad to tell him to come get us; the pale yellow corn kernels on my mom's tray as she sat on a picnic table outside the jail in her orange jumpsuit when we finally got to see her.

My dad arrived in North Carolina accompanied by my stepmother's father, whom we called Colonel Ellis because of his years in the air force. I recall little of that drive, except that I had my pet rabbit, Joey, with me, sitting on my lap. Joey was the sort of animal who could have inspired a comic book franchise about a rabbit that accidentally hops through toxic waste and suddenly grows into something Mothra-ish. When Colonel saw Joey, he said in the most dispassionate of tones, "I believe that's the biggest rabbit I've ever seen." For three months we lived with my dad and step-mom in Lexington, a strange, sad time filled with the unspoken awareness that Mom had messed up. After the fall, my dad let us go back to her, a kindness on his part, because though we received much love and care from him and our stepmother we wanted so badly to return to Lawrence, to Mom, to what had—after our exile from Kentucky—become home.

While that incident in North Carolina is the only time I remember my mother visibly drunk, the specter of her drinking haunted much of my early childhood: the orange juice she drank from wineglasses, the tonic she drank neat, the parking lots outside churches where Brint and I played while she met with her new community to accept her disease, tell its narrative, and pledge to stay clean one more day. And given a second chance with us, she excelled, remarkably so. To this day she has never had another drop.

How do we ever make sense of why one thing happens and not another? How impossible to reason why a drunk kid in Las Vegas T-bones Darnell's mother's car while our silver Dodge made it off the mountain without a scratch? God and chance console some, but they are more mysterious and unknowable to me than anything else in human experience. So I'm left resigned, trying, as so often I am, to make peace with not knowing.

The Sublime

By the end of the third quarter it was 80–80, a surprisingly good game. My young comrades took off without so much as a goodbye, leaving me feeling mighty lonely in the Party Zone. While the teams huddled to talk strategy for the final twelve minutes, we were told by the Jumbotron and the hype men to GET LOUD! Then suddenly "Welcome to the Jungle" began to blare and people across the arena moved to stand. With the game close and W. Axl Rose working his banshee voodoo, I began to feel something. I stood. I even began to clap. For the first time I felt like I was part of the crowd, that we were all invested in the common pursuit of an outcome desired: a Kings victory in the first game of the preseason. Finally, there was actual momentum. Finally, we all cared about basketball. Finally, there was the sense that all this mattered. We had somehow transcended the abject reality of the situation and found meaning in the meaningless. We had flung doo-doo at a canvas and made art. But then the G'n'R faded out and everyone went quiet, calmly taking their seats and playing with phones, as the "*clack-clack*-defense" chant soon gave way to the anesthetizing organ of NBA arena Muzak and once again I felt numb.

I tried watching the game, but my eyes always drifted to Darnell, wondering what he was up to, though he was always pretty much doing the same thing: clapping, supporting his teammates, talking to Dalembert. *Perhaps I'm too far away*, I wondered. Maybe the experience of the game and my investment would change with proximity to the court. So with three minutes left I steeled myself with a final swig of pinot and descended from the heavens. Thinking maybe I could slip into a vacant seat, I headed to the lower-level entryway after I hit the ground floor. When I reached the threshold, I saw several open seats ahead, but as I moved forward an usher pivoted around and asked to see my ticket. She was in her late sixties, I figured. Her auburn hair ponytailed out the back of the purple Kings ballcap she wore, the brim of which did nothing to dull the sweetness of her eyes. I explained my situation, tactfully hinting at standard stadium protocol that allows us rafter peons to occupy empty premium seats at the ends of games, but she didn't budge. She was following orders, she said. I considered trying my luck at another entrance, possibly drawing an usher of a generation with less reverence for authority, but there were only two minutes left, so I stepped back into the tunnel, that liminal spot between the lower level and the concourse, and I watched the rest of the game from there. And what a sight it was. I had a good angle on the action, a direct line of vision slightly to the right of the baseline corner where Darnell sat.

The Kings had stretched a small lead into double digits, and with thirty seconds left the beat-the-traffic morons began rushing out into the aisles. I saw my opportunity and dove in, swimming salmon-like against the current. I thought I heard the usher lady call after me but whatever sound she could have made was muted by the frantic crush of people exiting. Those remaining in the crowd stood and clapped as the Kings dribbled out the last twenty seconds of a 109–95 victory. I moved as far forward on the stairway as I could until I was standing at a rail, not twenty feet away from Darnell. That part of the arena, the baseline section, didn't lead right on to the court the way the sideline sections did. It dead-ended above the court, so that the cameramen and cheerleaders had space to move around near the action. So I was perched a few feet above him, looking down on Darnell, who, like everyone else, was standing and applauding. When the final buzzer sounded, players shook hands, and many ran toward the locker room. The stars hung around on court to give interviews. The two young players I had watched warm up, Tyreke Evans (twenty-six points) and DeMarcus Cousins (sixteen points, sixteen rebounds), were the most in demand. Evans put on a headset and planted one butt cheek on the scorer's table as he talked to local radio, and Cousins answered questions about his impressive rookie debut before a cameraman clad ankle to neck in denim.

Darnell and Dalembert hung around while all this postgame media was going on. They sat in their seats talking to a third man who had come over to them, a trainer or team handler, I suspected. Even that close, however, I still couldn't make out the discussion. Audible but indistinct, a verbal white noise of sorts. I remember Darnell remarking in an article once that he has a great smile and he's right. I had seen it a hundred times on the court as he embraced a teammate or celebrated a play. He smiled now at Dalembert and the other man as they talked, but it was a different, softer smile. A pleased half smile, slightly sly, like he was listening to a funny joke he already knew the punchline to.

Some part of me must have sensed that I would eventually want to write about Darnell and this was as close to him as I would ever get, that after this season he would end up playing ball in Ukraine and later in China, the NBA development league, and the Philippines, because my mind was racing, trying to figure out how to draw his attention, how best to interrupt his conversation. I didn't know then that all of my attempts in the coming months to pester the Kings media relations people into granting an interview with Darnell would go from probable to naught. "Darnell doesn't want to talk about the past," I would be told, even after I said I wouldn't ask about his family, even after I'd written an achingly sincere letter for the media relations man to pass on to Darnell explaining why I wanted to talk to him.

There I was, mind reeling, not realizing that this was it. But I couldn't find the words. For a moment I thought I'd scribble a note on a piece of paper from my notebook and throw it at him, but what would the note be? What would I write? *You're my favorite player of all time. . . . I love the way you play the game. . . . The NBA doesn't deserve you. . . . You seem like a good and kind man. . . . I was raised by a single mother too. . . . How have you encountered such unfathomable sadness and not let it swallow you?* Now was my chance to confess all of that, all of my respect and admiration for him that had to do with basketball and all of it that had nothing to do with basketball. Finally he stood and with the others began to walk toward the tunnel to the locker room. I moved along the rail, slowly following them, until they turned left off of the baseline and started down the tunnel. Above them I joined all of the fans shouting for autographs. Darnell was just below me, the caramel of his clean-shaven head eclipsed by the arena lights it reflected. *He is bringing a light.* I started to say his name, *Da—*, but it caught in my throat. He slapped hands with a fan across from me and disappeared out of sight as I was still turning it over. *What do I say to a man like him? What do I say?*

Yankee Town I

What does it mean to say that I love basketball? It sounds like a facile question, and yet it's one that I have found myself pondering with some regularity over the last few years. First and foremost, of course, it is a love of the sport itself, its dimensions and rules that are so simple and perfect. It is a love that such a game even exists. It is a love of dramatic competition and artfulness, the spontaneous beauty making of both individuals and a collective. There were so many things I loved about playing basketball, but now that I no longer do they are only memories. As a spectator, I love that I can have very different experiences watching a game. Sometimes I get so caught up in the action that I lose myself. Literally. I mean to say that I forget I exist; I shed my ego and become an anonymous quasi-being that subsists only within the context of the game being played. Other times, of course, I watch and I'm all ego, certain that the events unfolding on the court are only about me, a reflection upon—a validation or rebuke of—me, the Ptolemaic Earth at the center of basketball's universe. And there are still other times when I can watch a game in the same serious manner in which I go to a museum or watch a play or attend a concert. That is to say, I can experience it in the same thoughtful way I experience and appreciate art, in a way that makes me thankful to be alive to witness it. I love that the game can make me both insane and highly rational.

But there is more to it than that. As often is the case with our affections and adorations, my love for basketball is highly subjective and idiosyncratic. Strangely, sometimes it seems to have nothing to do with the game. Sometimes when I say I love basketball, what I'm saying is that I love a place, and often that love for the sport, which manifests most acutely in my love for the Kansas basketball team, functions as synecdoche for my love of Kansas, the state, and in particular Lawrence. And loving Lawrence is about not only my personal history there but the deep history of the town, which is a history worth learning or remembering, whichever may be the case.

In 1896, five years after James Naismith invented the game of basketball and two before he arrived in Lawrence to coach the University of Kansas's first team, a book called *The Gun and the Gospel* was published and promptly forgotten about for most of the twentieth century. Written by Reverend H. D. Fisher, a longtime resident of Lawrence living in nearby Topeka at the time of publication, the book would fall out of print and only reappear ninety years later through the persistent efforts of his great-granddaughter. I was fortunate to chance upon a copy while visiting the Watkins Community Museum of History in Lawrence one cold afternoon some years ago.

Of the book's many virtues, its most important is the insight it provides on the complexities of Kansas's fractious birth by one who was not only witness to but protagonist in the events. I doubt any state could make a stronger claim than Kansas as being more integral to the history of our country while at the same time occupying less space in the cultural imagination. It is fitting that Kansas is the geographic center of the United States, because its settlement—by white Anglos, anyway, not the many native peoples and tribes who had, of course, long been settled on the land and who were subsequently forced or bought off their land or expelled to "Indian Territory" (now Oklahoma), as the case may be—presaged the crossroads the country was at in the mid-1850s.

A CliffsNotes sense of US history is helpful in contextualizing Reverend Fisher's account: the Missouri Compromise of 1820 was supposed to mitigate the growing tension between slave and free states fighting for congressional dominance by allowing that while Missouri and Arkansas territories would be slave states, any new territories in the unorganized Great Plains would remain free. Thirty years later, as conflict between the free and slave states increased, when those Great Plains territories wanted to organize, the Missouri Compromise was repealed by the Kansas–Nebraska Act of 1854. Forwarded by Democrat Stephen Douglas, this act introduced the notion of popular sovereignty, or "squatter's rights," in the words of Reverend Fisher; the people of the territories would decide for themselves whether the new states would be free or slave. This was seen as a betrayal by free state advocates, a concession to the slave state power in Congress, a guileful way to ensure Kansas would become a slave state—given that the only state it shared an eastern border with was proslavery Missouri, whose citizens could easily flood in to settle the territory—under the guise of true, bottom-up democracy. Reflecting today, it seems fair to say it was both.

While the deck was stacked for slavery, Kansas's fate as a free state was won not simply through the barrel of a gun but through persistent and difficult work by abolitionists who saw this not as an issue of increasingly incompatible economic systems or political philosophies but as the crucial issue for the young country's soul: slavery was a moral wrong, a sin against God and man. This is the way in which to begin to understand the seven years between settlement and statehood that have come to be known as "Bleeding Kansas," which is also to understand why, with good reason, many make the claim that the Civil War began in Kansas.

What was intended to be a sure thing—Missourians going over the border to settle Kansas as a slave state—was challenged by a surprising countervailing rush of emigrants from the East Coast, mostly Massachusetts, as well as from the Middle West, particularly Iowa and Ohio. While the settlers from Massachusetts—Eli Thayer's famed New England Emigrant Aid Company—are better remembered by history, their numbers were few in comparison to the Iowa-Ohio contingent. Part of the reason the New Englanders are better known is that they provided the capital and the leadership that would shape early Kansas history. The state's first governor and senator, Charles Robinson and Samuel Pomeroy, respectively, were originally agents for the New England Emigrant Aid Company.

There is an unseemly side to this that gets at the root complexity of the free state coalition. Before being turned into something on the order of a benevolent society, Thayer's Company was originally founded as a speculative profit-making enterprise. It had less to do with stopping the spread of slavery than with trying to capitalize on antislavery sentiment by sending New Englanders to Kansas to develop the state and send profits back to East Coast investors. In fact, it was an early platform of the company that Kansas would enter the Union as a free state but that blacks would be barred from settling there. Huh? Many people involved in the company were very committed to the antislavery cause, but being antislavery was not the same thing as being an abolitionist like Reverend Fisher, which was a far more radical position. The two are often conflated. As Robert K. Sutton writes in his recent book *Stark Mad Abolitionists*: "Generally, abolitionists demanded that slavery in the United States should end immediately, no matter the cost, whereas antislavery advocates . . . wanted slavery to end but they begrudgingly were willing to accept slavery confined to the states where it already existed." And there were still others in the coalition who identified as a certain kind of free-stater, who wanted not so much a state free from slavery but free soil, meaning land they could develop for themselves instead of for proslavery southerners looking to expand their plantations.

They wanted to break the South's dominance of agricultural production. The fusion of these free-staters with mostly well-meaning eastern capitalists like Thayer and radical midwestern clergy like Reverend Fisher may seem like an odd alliance, but it seems certain that no branch of the coalition could have triumphed without the other.

Hugh Fisher was born in Steubenville, Ohio, in 1824, "by a long line of Teutonic extraction." His mother was sickly and his father ran a general store and ferry near the Ohio River. Young Fisher was a voracious reader, so much so that the family apparently had to bring in a physician to scare him into easing up, "lest I should ruin my health." He felt the calling early on, something that was by turns excruciating and ennobling:

> My soul thirsted for knowledge that I might be qualified for usefulness
> as a preacher of salvation. Often I went under the river bank into coves
> washed by the eddying waters of the beautiful Ohio, and imagining the
> stream a congregation of sinners I would preach repentance, faith and sal-
> vation, weeping at the story of the cross while my soul was moved with a
> desire to do good. There were times when the sense of responsibility upon
> me was so great that I prayed in agony of soul to be released and have
> another called in my stead.

Fisher attended a local Sabbath school, whose leaders were primarily Presbyterian, Episcopal, and Methodist. Despite the quaint image of a one-room schoolhouse conjured by the name, these Sabbath schools were essentially small colleges—Fisher describes his as having forty-four teachers—where students not only studied scripture and learned to sermonize and lead meetings but were trained to go into communities and start new, or rehabilitate faltering, churches. It was there that Fisher met the woman who would become his wife, Elizabeth Acheson, and it was upon graduating in 1847 that he began what in most situations would sound like a hard-luck fate: he set out on what he refers to in the memoir as "my itinerancy."

Circuit rider was the name given to clergy members who traveled by horseback to mostly rural or unsettled locations to preach and organize. Like Fisher, most of these traveling ministers were Methodists, and they were given their assignments by bishops at a yearly conference. Each preacher was appointed a circuit, which typically was a large area containing at least two churches, so they were constantly moving. They had no say in the matter of where they went and their appointments tended to change from year to year. It was difficult and tiring work, but Fisher remembers the experience fondly, noting that the itinerant life was "so full of incident, interest, fact and history that volumes might be written before the whole could be exhausted and recorded." Which, after reading the memoir, strikes me as not entirely hyperbolic.

One of the pleasures of *The Gun and the Gospel* is hearing Reverend Fisher recount his variously sad, funny, and moving experiences with the folks he met on his circuits, which took him mostly to rural areas of Pennsylvania and Ohio. In Marleborough we see him encounter an itinerant Quaker preacher, sizing him up as if he were a benevolent Martian, and afterward, impressed by this stoic Quaker, inviting him to preach to his congregation in a touchingly awkward instance of early interfaith unity. Less productive is his encounter with Spiritualism in Stark County, where he attends a séance full of "moral cripples" with "peanut-shaped craniums." Bedlam breaks out when the spirit rappings start—the source of which is a cat with a stick tied to its tail, the prank of local youths—and everyone stampedes for the exit, knocking over the candles and nearly burning the meeting hall to the ground. There is the deathbed encounter with a repellent bounder in Salem named Carter—"a profane and violent infidel [who] would take his little son on his knee and teach him to swear, giving him money to induce him to excel in profanity"—whom Fisher is called to visit as the man dies an agonizing death, and for whom Fisher laments, earnestly it seems, that his "prayer was unavailing—the pitying heavens seemed to be closed." In Annapolis, "a resort of wicked men and drunkards," he takes up the cause of temperance, and as he preaches on the matter a fortuitous lightning strike punctuates his sermon, granting him the requisite pomp to scare the town sober. Accompanying him on one circuit is a black man he calls Uncle Jimmie Armstrong, who assists him in meetings. One senses Fisher's depth of feeling for his "old friend" when he describes Armstrong singing a hymn: "He sang as only he could sing. Under an inspiration every heart was moved. The whole company was swayed by this grand old hymn and tune sung by this dusky son of Methodism, as by the magic of a master."

In 1851, several years into his circuit riding, he received a telegram, "the first in my life," telling him that his father was dying and he should come home to Steubenville immediately. He and Elizabeth made it in time, and his description of his father's last moments is unqualifiedly beautiful: "His sight had evidently failed for he asked, 'Who is in the room? Are you all here?' My oldest brother answered, 'We are all here, father. Do you want anything?' He answered, 'No.' Then raising his hand and passing it over his sightless eyes he said: 'It is dark here, but glory is bright.' And the weary wheels of life stood still."

For ten years Fisher rode circuits across Ohio and Pennsylvania, and during this time he and Elizabeth had three children. He expected to continue church building in this same general area, but when Conference—the yearly meeting of bishops that determined where ministers were sent on their next circuit—met in 1858 he was appointed to Leavenworth, Kansas. "I could not have been more surprised if it had been proposed to have me sent to China." But as his family made its way by steamer to Kansas he grew excited: "Here I was; I, an outspoken abolitionist, en route and nearly to Kansas in the year 1858! . . . I was sailing up the river to my future field more and more ready and primed to engage in the encounter already so long waged on that soil between liberty and bondage." That enthusiasm was quickly tempered by his arrival in Leavenworth. Not only was it a pro-slavery stronghold in the middle of the turbulent Bleeding Kansas years but he was expected to build a church and support his family based solely on congregant donations, which turned out to be a very small well from which to draw. Oh, and there were drought, conflagrations, tornados, and grasshopper invasions within his first few years as well. Which accounts for why, only a page after his encomium to Kansas on the steamer, he is despondent: "I wept because it seemed to me that I'd brought my wife and three dear boys away out to Kansas to starve them to death." He left his family and headed east to Baltimore, Philadelphia, and New York to raise money for the church. He was gone six months but secured the funds. How poor Elizabeth got by with no money and three children is left unstated, Fisher remarking only that they "had a very hard battle with poverty."

The Fisher family stayed in Leavenworth for three years, and there Fisher built a successful church, agitated against the "pro-slavery whiskyite" mayor, and helped slaves elude the Fugitive Slave Act by sneaking them north to Canada. There is a great account of how he and Elizabeth helped a man named Charley Fisher (no relation) out of town. "We concealed the poor fellow, hunted like a wild beast, until the next day, when my wife and Mrs. Weaver dressed him in women's clothes, but unthinkingly gave him a pair of my hose." A cherished pair of monogrammed socks was lost, but Charley Fisher was able to blend into a wedding party making its way to Lawrence, leaving Leavenworth in broad daylight right before the eyes of a sixty-man posse. He would be caught making his way to Canada and forcibly returned to New Orleans, but a few years later, after the war, he would come to Lawrence to thank the Fishers, who had moved there after the Leavenworth appointment was finished.

Each roughly forty miles from Kansas City, Leavenworth and Lawrence were towns settled early in Kansas Territory, and because of their proximities to the city and major rivers they became competing centers of their respected causes. Outliers in Leavenworth, the Fishers found their moral, political, and spiritual ilk in Lawrence. Founded in 1854 by members of the New England Emigrant Aid Company, the town took its name from one of the company's key financial backers, Amos Lawrence. It quickly became the center of the free state abolitionist movement in Kansas and took on the sobriquet "Yankee Town" for the number of New Englanders arriving in town, accompanied by loads of Sharps rifles packed into crates stamped BIBLES so as to go unsearched.

In the seven years leading up to statehood in 1861, the fight for Kansas's fate was fought on two main fronts that often overlapped, the political arena and the battlefield. While the electorate worked to sort out the po-litical realm—various constitutions written, fraudulent elections held, each side declaring victory, competing capitals founded and then dissolved and moved somewhere else—a guerilla war was being waged on the border between proslavery Missourians and Arkansans, called Bushwhackers or Border Ruffians, and radical free-staters, called Jayhawkers or Red Legs af-ter the scarves they tied to their boots. The fighting was as opportunistic as it was ideological. For every John Brown believing blood alone could end the abomination of slavery, there was a Red Leg or Bushwhacker who was in it for plunder or spite, the chance to get one over on those bastards across the border. And I suspect that often these motivations were nonexclusive. The same man who burned the home of a Missouri family suspected of aid-ing the Border Ruffians might also loot that family's home of all its worth and lead their slaves to freedom across the border.

Of course, the North-South proxy war in Kansas would soon expand to become our country's Civil War. Shortly before Reverend Fisher arrived in Lawrence, Kansas entered the Union on January 29, 1861, the thirty-fourth star on the flag. Just over two months later the first shots were fired at Fort Sumter. Fisher was appointed chaplain of the 5th Kansas Cavalry and served under James Lane, one of American history's most fascinating and forgotten demagogues. A congressman from Indiana, Lane came to Kansas Territory in 1855. Depending on how the political winds blew, he was at various times pro- and antislavery. He was elected Kansas's first senator, and when the war began he became the only man to simultaneously hold the rank of senator and general. He was both opportunist and partisan, leading brave and vicious attacks on Confederates and noncombatants alike, as in the infamous Sacking of Osceola.

After the war, Lane became embroiled in financial scandal and was viewed as a traitor when he abandoned the other Radical Republicans advocating for Reconstruction to go further, or as Fisher says more kindly: "In an unfortunate desire to control presidential patronage he found himself as United States Senator supporting the president, Andrew Johnson, in his opposition to Mr. Sumner's civil rights bill, thus antagonising the very sentiment which in Kansas gave him such victories and honors." Though reelected, he grew depressed and returned to Kansas, where he entered a sanitarium in Leavenworth. He tried suicide, shooting himself in the head, though he lived a few more days before passing away. There is a moving account of Fisher's visit to Lane during this time: "Though fatally wounded he regained consciousness and at times was able to recognize his particular friends and members of his family. I was called by telegram to his dying bed and as he took my hand in his and placed it upon the site of his wound he said plaintively, 'Bad, Bad,' and soon afterward died." Preaching Lane's funeral sermon was "the most trying ordeal of my ministerial life."

Though a chaplain and postmaster during the war, Reverend Fisher impressed Lane with his fortitude and forbearance in battle. The memoir recounts several skirmishes with lots of strategic debate, but increasingly, as the 5th Kansas moved through the Midwest they picked up more and more "contrabands," or black refugees. Some they armed and trained—the first blacks to fight in war—but as the numbers of nonfighting refugees in their camp grew, Lane had to figure out what to do with them. He called on Fisher, who advised that they be sent to Kansas and given homes and employment to relieve the labor shortage with so many men away fighting. Lane agreed and charged Fisher with the task of leading the group to Kansas safely. "Such a caravan had not moved since the days of Moses," he writes. "When we reached Kansas I halted my command, drew them up in a line and, raising myself to my full height on my war horse[,] commanded silence, and there under the open heavens, on the sacred soil of freedom, in the name of the Constitution of the United States, the Declaration of Independence, and by authority of General James H. Lane, I proclaimed that they were 'forever free.'" It was September 1861; the Emancipation Proclamation was issued in January 1863.

As the superintendent of contrabands, Fisher secured homes, jobs, and passage for thousands of formerly enslaved people throughout Kansas, Illinois, Iowa, and Ohio. His church-building experience came in handy. In several places he and the contrabands constructed large buildings that would serve as a church and school for all comers. He notes, "I believe these were the first free schools in the state of Arkansas, where all colors and classes attended together." But Fisher's abolitionism does not always sound so radically progressive. As one might expect in writings from the time, he is paternalistic and head-patting when he talks about his friend Uncle Jimmie Armstrong while they are on the circuit, as he is with the contrabands. About a black man named Uncle Moses White he says, "His name and soul are white though his skin was very black." Sometimes, as in the quote about Arkansas above, he makes a case for total equality. Other times he seems to advocate a separate-but-equal position, "knowing they would be happier and more contented in a society by themselves." On one occasion his "feelings of Christian equality" are so outraged by a pastor who holds two services, one for whites and one for blacks, that he tells the black congregants to start their own church, which while invigoratingly self-deterministic nonetheless sounds like solving a separate-but-equal problem with a separate-but-equal solution. But, of course, it is a mistake and morally anachronistic to hold the past to the same standards as the present, especially with an issue as thorny as race in the United States. When the first black man was elected president of the country in 2008 and reelected in 2012, the ideas and language from 1861 should sound regressive and troubling if we have made any progress at all.

By mid-August of 1863, Fisher fell sick and returned to Lawrence to recover. "It thus happened that I was there, an invalid, at the time of the most fearful and barbarous occurrence of the War of the Rebellion, the massacre and pillage of Lawrence by Quantrell and his murderous band." Fisher's rhetoric sounds grandiloquent but with good reason. Quantrill's Raid is the most significant moment in Lawrence's history, the event that everything prior presaged and that has colored everything since. Whenever Kansas and Missouri play in any sport, especially basketball, it is rehashed to stoke a rivalry that needs little provocation. You can't spend time in Lawrence, let alone grow up there, and not know the story. And before you know it, you've likely heard the name so many times that Quantrill has taken firm root in your unconscious. As a young kid, I remember walking along Massachusetts Street—the main thoroughfare in town in Quantrill's time and now—and stopping to scavenge the dank stalls of Quantrill's Flea Market for comics and baseball cards. Later there were commemorations and school field trips to the Citizens Memorial Monument in Oak Hill Cemetery, a massive granite tribute to the victims of the attack that was dedicated in 1895—thirty-two years after the attack—at which Reverend Fisher gave the opening prayer.

William Clarke Quantrill was born in Ohio in 1837. He got around, living in Illinois, Indiana, Utah, and Missouri variously. He is hard to pin down: on the one hand he seems to have been a sensitive and well-educated young man—he wanted to be, and did become for a time, a schoolteacher. Yet biographies like Duane Schultz's *Quantrill's War* also detail his mean-spiritedness and love for torturing animals as a boy. He was at times an ardent antislavery Republican and at others a recalcitrant proslavery Democrat. For a while his main political commitment seemed to be cynical opportunism. Perhaps these are the normal fluctuations of taste and personality, especially in the charged antebellum period he came of age in, but whatever the case, by 1859 he was living in Lawrence—the town he would burn to the ground four years later—where he taught for a spell but grew restless when the school closed. He took on an alias, Charley Hart, and in addition to cattle rustling he infiltrated groups of Jayhawkers, tagging along on stealthy nighttime raids into Missouri to free slaves. After the slaves were brought to Kansas and freed, he would soon recapture them and return them to slave owners to collect the bounty. He ran this racket for a while, until people caught on and a warrant was issued for his arrest. This seems to be the point at which he fully committed to partisanship and became an active participant for the South. He studied guerilla tactics of the Cherokee while visiting an acquaintance in Texas. Afterward, when war broke out, he fought for a time in the Confederate Army before abandoning the regiment and becoming an "irregular" along the Kansas-Missouri border. There he assembled a group of men that would include notables like Bloody Bill Anderson, Cole Younger, George Todd, and Frank and Jesse James. Unlike the Bleeding Kansas years, this phase of regional conflict was taking place within the context of a national war, which made the fighting in Kansas and Missouri schizophrenic, by turns guerilla and traditional, regular and irregular, ordered and chaotic. Quantrill's Bushwhackers retaliated against Jayhawker raids and provoked crackdowns from Union troops stationed along the border.

It was one such instance that either incited or expedited Quantrill's attack on Lawrence. A few weeks before the raid, Union general Thomas Ewing ordered the detention of a group of Missourians suspected of giving aid to the Bushwhackers that included several women who were relatives of men in Quantrill's band. They were taken to a dilapidated jail in Kansas City that collapsed on August 14, 1863, killing four women, including Bloody Bill's sister, and injuring many more. As Lawrence was the symbolic center of abolitionism in the state, it is quite possible that Quantrill had a plan already in the works, but the jail collapse did nothing to tarry its execution.

Lawrence, "the citadel of free-state thought and sentiment," in Fisher's words, had been attacked by proslavery men in the Bleeding Kansas years, and the citizens had long suspected an attack from the Missouri guerillas now that the country was at war with itself over the same issue. After the jail incident, they had stationed guards outside of town, keeping watch through the night, but precautions went lax after a succession of false alarms and eventually the watches stopped altogether. This was part of Quantrill's strategic cunning. He did not lead the raid immediately after the jail collapsed. He waited over a week, letting the townsfolk think they were in the clear. Lawrence had a population of roughly two thousand in 1863; however, the number of people in town on the morning of August 21, when Quantrill's band arrived, was considerably smaller because so many men were away fighting in the war. Reverend Fisher wouldn't have been in Lawrence if he had not fallen ill. Also present were Jim Lane and Charles Robinson, the governor of Kansas. These three men, along with Mayor George Washington Collamore, were at the top of the death lists Quantrill passed out to his men as they looked down on the sleeping town from Mount Oread, the hill where the University of Kansas now resides.

The jail collapse had outraged many in Missouri and the number of men in Quantrill's group swelled to 450. They blew across the border in the middle of the night, catching the troops at Union checkpoints unawares. Everyone knew they were headed for Lawrence, but Union leadership was slow to react and would only mobilize troops as Quantrill's men were nearly finished with Lawrence and readying to make their way back to Missouri. To make matters worse, as a safety precaution Mayor Collamore had recently issued an order that no one within city limits could be armed and mandated that all the government-issued weapons used by the Kansas militia and army recruits be kept in the armory, so the town was nearly defenseless. It would be a turkey shoot.

Quantrill's raiders split into smaller groups of four to six and descended on the town in the predawn, setting fire to homes, looting stores, searching for the people whose names were on their list but content to shoot just about any male, man or boy. Though they had received information on the location of particular homes, they were unable to catch the men they most wanted to kill. Lane, in nothing but his sleeping shirt, made a dash out his back door and through a cornfield. Governor Robinson hid in his barn. And although Mayor Collamore did die, it was not by Bushwhacker hand; he died of asphyxiation while hiding in his well.

Reverend Fisher was awoken by his wife around four thirty in the morning. She was readying to take their boys wild grape picking when she caught sight of the raiders. Fisher went to the window in time to see his neighbor shot while milking his cow. After an aborted attempt to escape to Mount Oread with his two oldest sons, William and Edmund, Fisher, weak from his illness, was unable to keep up and returned home. The boys, twelve and ten respectively, fell in with friends and survived, but not without harm. William saw his friend killed right next to him, "his brains and blood spattering in Willie's face, frightening him almost to death and so terrorizing him that he has never fully recovered his nervous vigor." Back at his home, Fisher sneaked into the cellar, while upstairs Elizabeth waited with their two youngest boys, Joseph, seven, and Frank, a baby. Within minutes a quartet of raiders was at the door demanding that Elizabeth tell them where her husband was. Fisher was below the front hall and could hear the exchange. She told them he had fled when the raiders first arrived in town. One of the men called her bluff, suspecting Fisher of hiding in the cellar, and Elizabeth said they were free to search the cellar. She even offered them a lamp so they could see, and when she went to retrieve it, she handed her baby to one of the guerillas. It was all part of Elizabeth's shrewd psychological play to gain the raiders' trust and save her husband. As the raiders descended the stairs to the cellar, they could not see that Fisher had positioned himself on a bank between the limits of the cellar and the foundation walls. He lay flat on his back, his left foot shaking so intensely that he had to still it with the other. "Every act of my life came before me like a panorama. I lived but did not live. I died but did not die." He describes his brush with death:

> The ceiling was low, and as the man who held the lamp in one hand,
> a cocked revolver in the other, stepped to the floor he was compelled
> to stoop to keep from striking his head against the joists. In stooping he
> brought the lighted lamp directly under his face, and the heat and glare
> caused him to hold it to one side, the side on which I was lying within
> a few feet of him. This threw the shadow of the bank of dirt over me
> and they did not see me. . . . I could see them plainly, could even have
> reached over and touched the leader on the shoulder. But they did not
> see me and I was saved.

For the time being, anyway. Upstairs the Bushwhackers set fire to the house and as they left, the one Elizabeth had handed her child to earlier stayed behind, asking if there was anything she wanted him to help her save. She begged him to help her put out the fire, but he said it was no good—the house was marked for ruin by Quantrill himself. This did not deter Elizabeth. She put out the fire but soon another group of raiders arrived and set fire to the house again. As the fire continued to spread, she had to find a way to get her husband outside before it collapsed. By this time a neighbor was helping her remove belongings from the house, so they draped a heavy carpet over Fisher and sneaked him out from the cellar. Before the watch of several Bushwhackers they dragged the carpet—Fisher underneath, crawling on the ground—to safety.

Fisher lay hidden for several more hours, listening to the destruction, and by 11 a.m., six hours after he went into hiding, Quantrill's men left and he ventured out to survey the horror.

> Upon recovering our self-control we went down town to find that more than one hundred and eighty of our citizens had been killed and many of them burned until they could not be recognized. The whole business part of our town was in ashes. Eighty widows and two hundred fifty children were in indescribable grief! Crushed and grief stricken we returned to our own desolation, and remained about the ashes of our home until four o'clock.

A sense of the scale of loss is illuminating: the nearly two hundred lives lost during Quantrill's Raid is the same number killed in the seven years of Bleeding Kansas fighting. Because Quantrill and his men were technically not part of the Confederate Army, it can be argued that Quantrill's Raid was one of the deadliest acts of domestic terrorism in US history.

Though the Union leaders in Kansas finally mobilized forces—including an ad hoc militia raised by Lane after he fled to a neighboring town in nothing but his nightshirt—they were still a day's ride behind Quantrill's men. They tried cutting off the raiders' escape route but were unsuccessful and Quantrill's band crossed into Missouri unharmed and then went south to Texas. Things would fall apart there. Dissension set in and the men divided, taking up with Bloody Bill or George Todd, or returning home to Missouri. Though his followers dwindled, Quantrill continued to fight his guerilla war on several fronts. He went to Kentucky with a small band of men and led raids throughout the winter and spring of 1865, telling his men they would continue on to Washington to assassinate Lincoln. When news of the president's death reached him in April, he is said to have re-marked, "Good, now I am saved the trouble." In May of 1865, a month after Lee surrendered at Appomattox, Quantrill was shot in a Union ambush. He was paralyzed and brought to a military hospital in Louisville, where he succumbed to his wounds the following month. General Lane and General Ewing responded to the attack on Lawrence with General Order No. 11, a vicious depopulation of civilians living near the border that forcibly removed several hundred Missouri families from their land, their homes burned to the ground.

For two weeks after the raid, the Fishers slept in the hayloft of their barn as the town slowly began to rebuild, receiving help and provisions from sympathizers in Ohio, Pennsylvania, and New England. Fisher went back to his work as superintendent of contrabands and chaplain for the 5th Kansas, and after the war he served as a presiding elder and pastor in nearby towns. After Lane's death in 1866, Governor Samuel Crawford appointed Fisher to fill the vacant seat in the United States Senate, but he declined, citing his inability to give up the church in favor of the state. Thinking back on this at the time of writing thirty years later, Fisher was still wrestling with the decision. There is regret for what could have been. He quips: "I have thought to title this book 'How I Hit it and How I Missed It,' weaving into my story circumstances and opportunities like these to justify the title. Perhaps I missed it in not engaging in a political instead of a spiritual life." But he had seen the importance of his church-building work, had witnessed its positive effects firsthand, so he returned to it, uncertain he could do the same in the political arena. "I might have attained honor; but I might have obtained dishonor."

His work continued to separate him from his family. While they stayed in Kansas, Fisher went west to Utah and Montana. Like his early circuit-riding experiences in Ohio and Pennsylvania, there are hilarious scenes from his "Bible Work Among the Mormons" that I will not detail here.* He returned to Kansas after two years and never left again. Though they settled in Topeka, the Fishers returned to Lawrence often, as they did in 1896, the year the memoir was published, for the commemoration of the monument to the victims of Quantrill's Raid.

I admit that, on the surface at least, the history of abolitionism in Kansas and the fight to make it a free state may seem to have little to do with my love of basketball and obsession with the University of Kansas team. However, in the year after KU's loss to Northern Iowa, I was starting to realize that it actually has quite a lot to do with it. At the time, as I've said, I was working on a book of short stories that were rooted in different points of Kansas's 150-year history. As I researched by day, poring over books and essays about the history that would inform my fiction, by night I was often tuning in to watch the Jayhawks play, and soon it dawned on me, something so obvious, really: Lawrence is basketball crazed and history

---

*However, the time a Mormon bishop presses Fisher about his feelings on polygamy seems worthy of a footnote. The bishop's wives are serving them dinner and Fisher tries to tactfully sidestep the question, but when the bishop won't relent, Fisher says, "I think you are living in a rascally way!" which cracks the bishop up. He tells Fisher: "You are a Yankee, sure enough."

haunted, and when your love of a game is also a love of place, the history of that place matters because you feel it, consciously and unconsciously, in everything.

I spent the first twenty-five years of my life unaware of a lot of this history, while the last fifteen I've been steeped in and fascinated by it, and as such the experience of following KU basketball has become multivalent. Now the game invokes not only the sport's history, which is especially significant at Kansas, given that the inventor of the sport was the school's first coach, but the deep history of America. I don't mean to suggest that I sit around reciting history lessons during KU games. Like most ardent fans, I get caught up in the drama of the competition. For better and worse, part of loving the game this intensely means blocking out a tremendous number of things that might otherwise make claims on my attention. However, sometimes there are incredible moments, temporal wormholes, during games when history seems to assert itself and ask me to remember, which I think is important because most of the time we don't, and we have all been warned, fairly and amply, about what happens when we don't remember the past. It might be something as simple as seeing the school mascot scrambling around the court during a timeout and recalling that "Jayhawk" is not just the name we have given to an innocuous, imaginary blue bird but is derived from the most militant free state fighters from two centuries ago. The German philosopher Walter Benjamin had a wonderful word for this phenomenon I'm talking about: *correspondences*. "The *correspondences* are the data of remembrance. . . . The murmur of the past may be heard in [them]," he writes in his essay "On Some Motifs in Baudelaire." Furthermore, he argues, these correspondences aren't occasioned so much by chance but by ritual, and it seems to me that few things could be more ritualistic than organized sporting events, where players and fans alike gather in tribal clothing on particular days in particular seasons and whose conduct is governed by a set of rules and ceremonial procedures.

In the ritual we call college athletics, rivalries matter, and given the history it is unsurprising that up until 2012, when the University of Missouri left the Big 12 to join the Southeastern Conference, KU versus Mizzou was one of the best and most enmity-infused in the country. A couple of incidents in the rivalry, known as the Border War, speak to the issues of history and remembrance I've raised here. In 2007 a controversy developed around a T-shirt made by a Missouri alumnus in the leadup to the annual KU-Mizzou football game. The front of the shirt depicted the 1863 burning of Lawrence underneath a Mizzou logo and on the back a quote from Quantrill: "Our cause is just, our enemies many." They could have found something better than an overt endorsement of slavery, but I remember admiring the moxie and the invocation of history, a history many in Kansas and Missouri knew but that most of the country seemed to have forgotten, a fact that must have accounted for the number of national news stories about the shirt. For their part, Kansas students responded wittily with a shirt depicting John Brown over the tagline "Kansas: Keeping America Safe from Missouri since 1854."

A few years before the T-shirt incident, in 2004, the name of the rivalry was changed from the Border War to the Border Showdown. Actually, it was changed to the M&I Bank Border Showdown. The addition of corporate branding to the historical amnesia of the soporific new name was particularly offensive. The KU athletic director at the time, Lew Perkins, explained, "We feel that in the aftermath of September 11, 2001, and ensuing events around the world, it is inappropriate to use the term 'war' to describe intercollegiate athletic events." In part he's right—it is absurd—though it's a fairly minor one on the vast spectrum of sporting absurdity. Unsurprisingly, there was bipartisan consensus on the stupidity of the name change. Everyone knew what was being erased was not the un-PC invocation of war but a history that helped explain where these two states had come from and what they had come to be.

The oft-quoted line from William Faulkner's *Requiem for a Nun* comes to mind: "The past is never dead. It's not even past." That may be true, but while the past is not dead it can be edited, erased, obscured, and forgotten. One of our most important tasks, as I see it, is to remember, to seek correspondences wherever we can find them, even in basketball.

Stay Black

A little over a month after my trip to Sacramento to watch Darnell Jackson watch a basketball game, I was sitting at a bar in the San Francisco International Airport waiting for my friend Kevin's plane to land. A writer too, he was in town to give a reading, but all we had been talking about in the phone calls leading up to his visit was basketball. He was to arrive on the first day of the college basketball season. The plan was to pick him up and drive straight to Berkeley, where I was still housesitting, and set up shop at Looney's, a barbeque-and-beer joint, where we would gorge ourselves before ESPN's twenty-four hours of basketball tipoff coverage.

Kansas wasn't playing that day, but for a hoop junkie like myself there was still plenty to feast on. I arrived at SFO an hour before Kevin's plane was scheduled to land, so that I could catch the first half of the Kansas State–Virginia Tech game. Both teams were ranked, a sexy opening day matchup. When I answered the bartender's question about who my favorite team was, he said, "Kansas," almost ruminatively as he set a tallboy before me. "Sure thought they were gonna win it all last year." Flashbacks to the Northern Iowa loss rose slowly from the depths of my traumatized psyche like the carbonated bubbles in my beer. I said nothing, focusing on the pregame prattle. A little while later, coming back from commercial break, there was a shot of the Virginia Tech team in the tunnel, getting ready to run out onto K-State's home floor. The guys were pumping each other up, pushing each other around, yelling, beating on their chests, and then one teammate, who was black, moved to the center of their huddle and began to dance. The other players clapped, getting fired up. I was reminded of the pregame ritual from my own playing days, the way nerves and excitement manifested in all sorts of odd and humorous ways. "That boy's gonna regret dancing like that when he sees himself on TV later," the bartender said. "He'll never do that again." I looked at him—*boy?*—but he was just looking up at the television, shaking his head.

Growing up, I mostly saw my dad in the summers. To keep me occupied during the day while he worked, he often signed me up for basketball camps that were usually run by college coaches or former players. Depending on where he was teaching or where his research took him, I got a good geographical sampling of these kinds of camps, from Rick Pitino at Kentucky to Jim Boeheim at Syracuse, Gary Williams at Maryland to Lute Olson at Arizona. But here I'm not thinking of those fancier camps so much as a low-budget camp my dad signed me up to attend at the downtown branch of the YMCA in Tucson one summer.

I must have been ten or eleven, a white boy from Kansas surrounded by black and Latino kids, and it was one of the earliest times I remember being really aware of race, of my difference from those around me, the reality of having grown up in a state that is 91 percent white. Anyway, there was a kid there named Gerald, whom everyone called Gerry. He talked a lot on the court, but he was able to back it up. I remember battling hard against him in one-on-one drills and in games and doing well, though I knew he was better than me. Mostly I disliked him because of the trash talk. I was an oversensitive kid, practically mute, and I wasn't used to it, thought it was showy and stupid and mean-spirited, not realizing it was a canny tactic, and I was unprepared for the effect it is intended to have on an opponent: to get inside his head and throw him off his game. Which is exactly what happened. I got flustered during games against him and silently seethed afterward, cursing the braggart. One day at the end of camp my dad picked me up as usual. My brother or my stepmom must have been in the front seat because I was riding in the back alone. We were stopped at a light in front of the Y and I saw Gerry, leaning against the building, standing in the shade as he waited for the city bus. I watched him a few seconds before he saw me, and when he did, he jutted his chin at me as if to say, *What's up?*

Nigger, I thought, then said, "Sorry."

The light turned and my dad started to drive, Gerry shrinking behind us in the distance. My dad said, "What are you sorry about, Andy?"

Kevin is one of my closest friends. We met in graduate school at the University of Iowa, where we both studied fiction writing. He was a year ahead

of me in the program, but we shared a workshop his last semester and became fans of each other's work. Soon we were playing Saturday morning
pickup at the rec center or watching pay-per-view boxing at his place,
Kevin patiently explaining the intricacies of a sport I knew little about. He
left Iowa City for Madison after graduation, and I followed him there a
year later. I was living in Madison before I moved to the Bay and missed
having my friend nearby. The two things we talked about most were books
and basketball. It seemed only fitting that he would arrive in town to read
from his first book on the day the college basketball season started.

After his plane landed I drove us to Berkeley, and we arrived at Looney's
in time to catch the last half of the K-State game. We watched them pull
away from Virginia Tech as we ordered an ungodly amount of ribs and
drank a pitcher of cheap beer. Then we decided to switch venues for the
next game, which was the marquee matchup of the opening day: Florida
and Ohio State, both teams ranked in the top ten. This was the game we
really wanted to see. But after we made our way to Kip's, a sports bar near
Telegraph Avenue, we lost track of the game, only occasionally remembering to check the score because we were busy talking, catching up.

In the summer of 1993, I was thirteen and my dad was living in Maryland,
doing research and policy work in DC. He had managed to finagle my
brother a job interning at the White House. Bill Clinton had just come into
office and my brother was on a team of mail readers, filtering out the crazies
from the sane. At night over dinner he would entertain us with stories of
all the letters he'd read that day. That was the summer of terrible flooding
in the Midwest, and I recall one in which the writer had composed his letter along the outside borders of a sheaf of notebook paper, the mad scrawl
of his red pen slowly working toward the center with each revolution, as
he informed the president that he had the power to stop the flooding but
would only do so if Clinton outlawed abortion.

I wasn't doing anything quite so interesting or unique as my brother.
For me it was camp, as usual. I went to Gary Williams's basketball camp at
the University of Maryland, and when that was over, I went to a YMCA
camp in Silver Springs. One day I was playing pickup with other campers
when a man walked past the court and stopped to watch. Afterward, he
approached me, said he coached in a local summer league, and that I should
come practice with his team. I agreed and arrived at practice later that week
to find I was the only white player on the court. I did well enough at that
practice to be asked to join the team, and I arrived at the first game to find

that not only was I the sole white player on my team, I was apparently the only white player in the league.

My dad likes to tell the story of showing up at the first game—they were held outdoors in a public park with packed silver bleachers on one side of the court—when one of the other parents came over to introduce herself, saying, "You must be Andy's father."

"How did you guess?" I'll hear him howl when he tells the story to someone now, all these years later. It's amusing, sure, but it's also meant to convey how good I was to the listener, a validation of sorts. I was certainly aware of this, because when school started back up, I told anyone who would listen about my summer in Maryland balling in the city league. The only white player in the league. *That's how good I was*, is what the story was meant to convey without saying so.

Just like I'm doing now.

Kevin is from Puerto Rico, where he is considered white, his roots in Spain's colonial past. When he steps off the airplane in the mainland United States after visiting friends and family in PR, he suddenly becomes a minority. He is Hispanic. He is Latino. He a person of color. I couldn't wrap my head around this the first time he told me. Race, so arbitrary, so absurd. When I asked him whether he thought of himself as white or brown, he said, "I think of myself as Puerto Rican."

By high school, as college neared, I spent less of my summers at basketball camps than I did playing in summer leagues and on Amateur Athletic Union travel teams. The summer before my senior year was particularly important in terms of drawing the attention of scouts and college coaches. At this point I had been living in the suburbs of Hartford, in the Farmington Valley, for five years, missing Kansas terribly, and that summer I was on an AAU team made up of four of us from my high school team and a handful of the best players from nearby schools. We were, with the exception of one guy who only played with us a short while, all white.

We traveled around the northeast playing tournaments, but the biggest event that summer was a massive tournament in Las Vegas. Only seven of us were able to raise money to make the trip and we went out there a bit ragtag. Our players came from towns with much privilege, but the team itself was more of a DIY project. We had no sponsors, no flashy uniforms.

Our coaches weren't wealthy boosters with connections in the circuit. We went around to local businesses and to the rotary club, trying to raise money for travel expenses. We weren't the most physically imposing bunch. Our center was six two. We were guard-heavy, so much so that I often left my natural position at shooting guard and played down low at power forward. (When I think of it now, we were twenty years ahead of the game, presaging the small-ball court-spreading that so characterizes the current NBA game, and increasingly colleges as well. But of course, this was no visionary strategy on the part of our coaches; we were simply making do with the players we had.) The teams we played against, conversely, were much bigger and deeper, mostly urban black and Latino, sporting bright matching warmups, uniforms, and sneakers. Our first game was against a team from Compton and we blew them out by thirty, starting a run that would take us all the way to the finals, where we would lose an overtime heartbreaker to a team with several D-I commits.

Crowds really loved us because we subverted their expectations. We looked so overmatched that people scoffed at and condescended to us initially, but by the time it was the start of the fourth and we were up twenty on a team wearing Nike across their chests most folks in the stands were cheering for us. *Hoosiers* it wasn't, but we earned a lot of respect for our style of play, which was characterized by a weird kind of flashy unflashiness built on up-tempo full-court pressure, precision passing, off-the-ball movement, and deadeye shooting. And we loved it, of course. Because while basketball may have been invented by a white man it had long since been revolutionized and perfected by the black man so his approval meant everything to us.

It felt good to have spectators of all colors cheering for us, but it wasn't always easy to understand why. I assume they liked cheering for the underdog, liked seeing the game played well, but I also think of the middle-aged white man who came by the pool of our hotel where several of us were relaxing after a day of games. He said he had seen us earlier, that he had enjoyed watching us play. We thanked him and chatted a while, and then he said, "I like seeing them get their own, you know," and walked away, calling over his shoulder that he would be sure to follow us.

A few years before that night in Berkeley, Kevin and I were at a house party in Madison. It was a Saturday night and we showed up late because we had been watching a fight on pay-per-view. Plus, it was February, and though the party was only a few blocks away, there is serious cost-benefit analysis one must undertake when considering whether to venture outdoors in the Wisconsin wintertime. Eventually we made our way over.

The woman throwing the party was also a writer and she and I cofacilitated a weekly writing group for incarcerated men at a nearby prison. The house where she lived was a co-op of social-justice-minded folks and anarchists. Music was blaring when we arrived, and people were either dancing or having very earnest conversations about revolution. I traded small talk with people as I maneuvered around the packed house, but eventually I wound up outside where I met a guy who was young and black, vaguely hipstery-looking. I don't recall his name. It was miserably cold, but better than enduring the human panini press going on indoors. We talked a bit. He was still in school, he said, studying film.

Before long, Kevin joined us on the porch and as the three of us talked. At one point the guy mentioned that he liked to freestyle and Kevin challenged him to prove it. The guy was standing on the front porch steps, feet on different levels. He pushed his skullcap back, thought a moment, and then unleashed a verbal flow so intensely dark and funny that Kevin and I were bent over at the knees laughing. The three of us hung out for a while, eventually making our way back inside when it became too cold.

Later, when the party was winding down and Kevin and I worked up the nerve for the walk back to his house, we bumped into the freestyler again. He was back on the porch, smoking. We said we were out, shook hands, and as we started down the sidewalk Kevin called out, "Keep up that black shit." The guy had to have heard, but he didn't say anything. I looked at Kevin. He didn't seem to think there was anything strange about what he had said, but when I asked why he said that, he threw his head back. "Oh shit, I meant black *humor*," he said. The guy's rhymes, as I said, were darkly funny. Apparently, while I was inside, he and Kevin had had a long conversation about black humor in the films of Todd Solondz and Neil LaBute. "I can't believe I just said that. Should I go back and apologize?" Later we laughed about it and to bust his balls I sometimes tell him to keep up that black shit when I'm trying to tell him I love him.

At WestConn, every guy on the team had a nickname, even our coach. We called him Soup because his last name was Campbell. One of our assistant coaches had eternally bad breath and this earned him the name Coach Hal, short for halitosis. Mine was one of the less creative ones. The guys mostly called me Drew, though sometimes they would riff on my last name: Millstone, Mil-world. As previously mentioned, I was battling for a starting spot with a guy who, like my writer friend, was named Kevin. This Kevin was from Ossining and had been a hell of a cornerback in high school but decided to play basketball in college instead. He was funny and chill. I liked him, everyone on the team did. Kevin went by the nickname "Black." I never got the exact origin of the name—I think it was a hold-over from his high school days playing football—and have no idea if it was related to the fact that he was black or not, but it was what he went by so that's what we called him. At some point during that season, probably as I was trying to play my way into the starting spot Kevin had rightly earned, I started telling him to "stay black" as a way of saying goodbye. For example, if we were all hanging out in a dorm room and he got up to leave, I would say something like, "Take it easy, stay black." In my mind I was telling him: *Be yourself, do you.*

At the time I thought my pun on Kevin's nickname clever, unable or unwilling to see its racist passive-aggressiveness. The first few times I said it, he grinned and said, "All right, Drew, peace," and went on his way. One time, however, I remember coming home from an away game, another game in which Kevin had started ahead of me. It was late as we got off the team bus in front of our dorm and unloaded our things. We were all tired, sore, ready for bed. Class the next day. We were trudging into the building and as we parted ways to head to our respective dorm rooms, I told Kevin to stay black. He stopped, just stood there looking at me, no grin, until I shouldered my bag and continued down the hall.

Long after the Florida-OSU game had finished, Kevin and I left the bar and headed for the house I was looking after. My housesitting job was up at the end of the month, and I was trying to figure out where I would move come December, how to live in a place that made it so hard to do so. There were no clear answers. Kevin and I walked along Telegraph past homeless peo-ple sleeping under copies of *Revolution* newspaper in dark storefronts, then were asked for money by the gutter punks and hippies whose homelessness was a lifestyle choice. A man with what would seem to be mental health issues stood before the giant mural that adorns the outside wall of Amoeba Music, screaming at one of the people in the painting. Kevin was looking at the madness around us, amused. Never seen anything like it, he told me. "Berserkeley," I said.

Back at the house, I showed Kevin to the room where he would crash. We were tired and ready for sleep. I was leaning against the doorframe and he sat on the bed, staring at his bag on the floor like it was going to be a hell of a chore to open it and dig out something to sleep in. It had been a long day but a good one. It was great to see my dear friend again and I dreaded the thought of him leaving. I told him we should get some rest so we were fresh for his reading the next day. He said goodnight and I said the same, adding as I walked down the hallway: "Keep up that black shit." He conceded a weary laugh and I heard him lovingly mutter, "Motherfucker" before I closed the door to my own room.

Tradition

The first time I saw the 2010–2011 Kansas basketball team play—the first time I was able to watch a complete game, anyway—it was early December, a couple weeks after Kevin's visit to the Bay, and I was hunched over my small netbook in the kitchen of H's studio apartment in the Mission. My housesitting gig in Berkeley had just ended and I was staying with her temporarily while I figured out something more permanent. It worked much better when I had my own place and was just a tourist swinging by to have dinner or hang out. There was the vague sense that come the New Year I would find a new place to live. It wasn't the only reason, but the living situation certainly contributed to the fact that H and I were having occasional state-of-the-union conversations about our four-year relationship that seemed to be leading toward breaking up.

But I wasn't thinking about any of that then. That evening I came home from a day that started at 4:30 a.m., so that I could get a few hours of writing in before going to work to help my students with their own stories and poems. The thing I wanted now—more than sleep, even—was to watch my Jayhawks play as I ate a couple of warm pepperoni-and-onion slices from Deja Vu, the pizza joint down the block.

The expectations for the squad were lower than the previous year's bunch, but it's Kansas so there are always expectations and they are always high. We had lost two lottery picks in Cole Aldrich and Xavier Henry, as well as the heart and soul of the team in Sherron Collins, to the NBA, but we returned the Morris twins, junior forwards Marcus and Markieff, as well as Tyshawn Taylor, also a junior. We had landed one of the top recruits in the country in high-scoring guard Josh Selby, but he had to sit out the first nine games for allegedly receiving improper benefits to the tune of

75

$4,607.58 from a family friend who oversaw his recruitment process. Other contributors included sophomore power forward Thomas Robinson, who had the body of ancient Greek statuary but was just starting to learn how to use it, as well as three senior role players: Tyrel Reed, Mario Little, and Brady Morningstar.

Coming into this game we were 6–0 and ranked number four in the country, and while UCLA was 3–3 and unranked, it was a matchup of two of the most storied programs in college basketball history, so there was a buzz about it. At sixty-three consecutive wins, our home-court winning streak was the longest in the country by an insane margin. It was also the longest in school history, which is saying something for a place commonly acknowledged to be one of the two or three toughest venues for visitors to play in the sport. (For perspective, Kentucky's Rupp Arena and Duke's Cameron Indoor Stadium, the two places routinely compared to Allen Fieldhouse, were at the same time in the low twenties, and second longest active home-winning streak behind our sixty-three was Xavier at twenty-seven.) And you could see why. Even on the tiny screen of my netbook, Allen Fieldhouse was large in its presence and raucous atmosphere. My sense memory of attending so many games came to life, and I felt the pleasant percussive drive of "Rock Chalk Jayhawk" in my chest, the leg of a neighboring fan against mine in the packed bench seating, the anticipatory electricity shooting through the fieldhouse as the ref readied to jump the ball at center court, and suddenly the 1,469 miles between San Francisco and Lawrence shrank a millimeter or so.

Filling in at the two for Selby until he became eligible was Reed, who had a huge first half, dropping fifteen points. The Morris twins looked improved, as they should—this was supposed to be "their" team, as the saying goes—though they were being eaten alive in the post by UCLA's three-hundred-pound freshman center, Josh Smith. The game stayed tight throughout the first half, and I took it all in from the uncomfortably functional IKEA kitchen table under the evening glare from a window that looked down on bustling 16th Street. I wore earbuds so as not to distract H, who sat just around the corner on the couch, preparing for the writing class she was to teach the following day.

At halftime, with KU leading 42–39, I watched UCLA coach Ben Howland walk off the court and recalled the time I took a recruiting trip to Northern Arizona University, where he was once head coach. It was 1997, the fall of my senior year, and I drove to Flagstaff from Tucson, where my father and stepmother lived. The three of us made the journey north and toured the campus, sat in on a practice, and met with Coach Howland in his office. I'm making it sound more official than it was. At the time NAU was quite good, coming off a Big Sky Conference championship the previous season, and that March they would earn a trip to the NCAA tournament, where as a fifteen seed they put a real scare into number-two Cincinnati, falling just barely 62–65. I wasn't a recruit Howland desperately wanted. He wasn't even offering me a scholarship—just the promise of the opportunity to earn one if I came and proved I belonged.

I remember sitting in a chair watching the team practice, wondering that very thing: Did I belong with these faster, stronger players? Could I hang with them? Maybe. I didn't know. I sat there feeling awkward and self-conscious in my baggy jeans and Doc Martens, my glasses and yellow sweater. One of the guys on the squad came over on his way to the water fountain and whispered that he wished I came to visit every practice because Coach was going easy on them with visitors present. I remember little else from the trip—not what Coach Howland and I talked about, though I am left all these years later with the impression that he seemed like a good guy. What I remember most was being alone in the hotel room next door to my dad's that night, trying to read William S. Burroughs—that unlikely inhabitant of Lawrence, Kansas—before getting bored and ordering an adult film on pay-per-view and praying Dad wouldn't read the hotel bill too closely the next morning. I suspect Burroughs is one of the few writers who would have understood and likely taken this as a compliment of the highest order.

Soon after my recruiting trip, Coach Howland's success at NAU would give him the opportunity to become the head coach at Pittsburgh, which he rescued from obscurity and turned into a winning program. If I had gone to play for him at NAU, he would have left at the end of my freshman season. His ensuing success at Pitt led to his position at UCLA, one of the five or six unturndownable, Holy Grail coaching positions in the game. And there his success continued, taking the Bruins to three straight Final Fours. All of this in almost thirteen years to the day between when I sat in the gym watching him coach practice and when I sat watching him hold his own against Bill Self and KU in Allen Fieldhouse.

And UCLA did more than hold their own. They kept the game close, thanks in large part to Smith's seventeen-and-thirteen night down low and Tyler Honeycutt's thirty-one from outside. We could never quite pull away like everyone expected. It was one of those games we had controlled throughout, but the Bruins stayed close enough to steal if we made mistakes, which we did. With 19.6 seconds remaining we were up three and Marcus Morris was at the line shooting the front end of a one-and-one.

It was an important free throw because it would make it a two-possession game. He missed, but fortunately we got the ball back on a possession-arrow tie-up. We inbounded the ball to our best foul shooter, Reed, who inexplicably lost control of the ball, which ended up in Honeycutt's hands and with five seconds remaining he did what he had done to us all night: net another deep three to tie the game.

It felt like we were conspiring in our own demise, trying to see if we could lose the game in the most improbable of fashions, and I yelled something to that effect at my computer as I pulled out my earbuds in frustration, shattering the silence of the apartment. I heard H stir in the other room, asking what was wrong. I didn't respond and she went back to her work. Then, as I was mentally preparing for an overtime in which anything could happen and which could cost us our home court winning streak, Mario Little, a sparingly used small forward, attempted to catch a pass so he could put up a final desperate shot and was fouled, allegedly, by a UCLA defender. It was a suspect call, especially under the circumstances, something I could recognize even in the depths of my blind allegiance to KU. I would have been enraged if it were the other way around. But as it was, Little went to the line with 0.7 seconds remaining, hit the first free throw, and intentionally missed the second so that UCLA had to heave up a near impossible full-court shot. Kansas won, the winning streak preserved, but it felt a little muted.

ESPN continued to show the foul over and over, debating whether it occurred and if so whether the ref should have called it in that situation. Howland was livid, red-faced, giving Coach Self an icy fly-by handshake before trying to catch up to the referee in question, who couldn't get off the floor fast enough. I felt for Coach Howland and it made me wish I had gone to play for him at Northern Arizona so I could send him a text, something sympathetic or good-naturedly ribbing. *Tough call, Coach.* Or: *Got hosed!* Or: *You know better than to try and beat my 'hawks in their house.*

Basket Ball

A week after the UCLA game, I came across an article in the *Lawrence Journal-World* titled "Booths Purchase Original Naismith Basketball Rules at Auction for More than $4 Million." The exact number was $4,338,500. In the same Sotheby's auction, a copy of the Emancipation Proclamation that was signed by Lincoln and owned by Bobby Kennedy went for $3.7 million. David Booth grew up in Lawrence, graduated from KU, but now lives in Austin, Texas, where he is chairman and CEO of Dimensional Fund Advisors, a privately held investment firm that manages about $206.5 billion in assets. The Naismith family decided to put the rules up for sale because the Naismith International Basketball Foundation, a charity that promotes sportsmanship and provides service to underprivileged children, was running out of money. Apparently, a rich Duke alumnus was poised to buy the rules and take them to Durham before Booth stepped in to spare KU the embarrassment. Previously, in 2004, he and his wife, Susan, had donated $9 million to build the Booth Family Hall of Athletics in Allen Fieldhouse, and now the rules would be housed there on the University of Kansas campus, where the inventor of the game presided as the coach of the first Kansas basketball team.

It is a familiar enough story, to those familiar with the game, anyway. Basketball's creation myth begins in Springfield, Massachusetts, in the freezing winter chill of 1891. The entire Big Bang can be traced back to one man, James Naismith, a Canadian-born phys ed instructor of Scottish stock, who was given the seemingly inconsequential task of creating an indoor game that would keep occupied the young men of the YMCA International Training School (now Springfield College) during New England's interminable winter months. He thought on it for two weeks and then wrote the rules in one sitting on the morning of December 21, 1891, shortly before the start of the 11:30 a.m. class in which he introduced the new game he called "basket ball" to his eighteen students. He claimed to have drawn inspiration from a childhood game called "duck on the rock," which sounds frighteningly medieval, essentially involving a group of boys attempting to chuck rocks past some poor soul who was forced to stand guard—in effect *trying* to be stoned by his pals—in front of a larger rock, and which to my mind bears little resemblance to basketball, but to each his own muse.

Naismith's primary aims were to create a game that was easy to play and rooted in skill and accuracy rather than force. "Basketball, in my opinion, is one of the few team games that emphasizes agility, speed, and accuracy, and is directly opposed to bodily contact," he wrote in his book *Basketball: Its Origin and Development*. "There is no necessity for the bodily shock that is part of football, hockey, and some of the other games."

Basketball's invention came at a time when the role of sports was changing in American culture. In his book *A People's History of Sports in the United States*, the sportswriter David Zirin notes that prior to the Civil War sports were viewed as wicked, a temptation away from religious devotion, and while it might seem laughably, well, puritanical, today to think of baseball as wicked, there were certainly enough horrors like rat-baiting, cockfighting, and bare-knuckle boxing to bolster the claim. This sentiment carried over even after the war. Naismith recounts the following anecdote of his time playing football while majoring in theology at McGill University: "For seven years I played without missing a game and enjoyed the sport, even though it was not thought proper for a 'theolog.' Football at that time was supposed to be a tool of the devil, and it was much to my amusement that I learned that some of my comrades gathered in one of the rooms one evening to pray for my soul."*

While sports may have long been viewed as a pathway to sin, however, a competing concern among Protestant church leaders in the mid-nineteenth century was that religion was becoming increasingly feminized, the domain of women and effete males. From this anxiety was born a philosophy known as muscular Christianity. In his entry on the topic for the book *Sports in America*, historian Duncan Jamieson writes that "muscular

---

*A sad moment occurs later in the book when Naismith recalls visiting his sister: "I asked her if she had ever forgiven me for leaving the ministry. She looked seriously at me, shook her head and said, 'No, Jim, you put your hand to the plow and then turned back.' As long as she lived she never witnessed a basketball game, and I believe that she was a little ashamed to think that I had been the originator of the game."

Christianity reflected the interrelationship between religion, sports, health and physical fitness, and contemporary changes taking place in Victorian society caused by the industrial and scientific revolutions." Founded in England and imported to the United States, the movement sought to re-brand Christianity by tracing the importance of sport back to the apostles. And it's true. When I break out my old New International Version Study Bible, I find the New Testament peppered with sporting argot: "But one thing I do: Forgetting what is behind and straining toward what is ahead, I press on toward the goal to win the prize for which God had called me heavenward in Christ Jesus" (Philippians 3:13–14); "I have fought the good fight, I have finished the race, I have kept the faith" (2 Timothy 4:7); "Therefore, since we are surrounded by such a great crowd of witnesses, let us throw off everything that hinders us and the sin that so easily entangles, and let us run with perseverance the race marked out for us" (Hebrews 12:1); "You were running a good race. Who cut in on you and kept you from obeying the truth?" (Galatians 5:7).

The goal of muscular Christianity and of its institutions like the YMCA and YWCA was to encourage both physical and spiritual health, while bringing more people into the church. Jamieson writes that "churches, which sometimes had the best recreational facilities in town, built gymnasiums and summer camps for altruistic and practical reasons. Athletics taught young people appropriate Protestant values while reinforcing the image of the body as a temple. In addition to saving city children, gymnasiums and summer camps also attracted members, which improved the church's finances and standing in the local community." Zirin notes that political leaders and ruling elites quickly took notice and saw that sports could be useful in combating their own concerns about social unrest after the Civil War. With the industrial North having defeated the agrarian South, people immigrated to the country in huge numbers, which helped meet the labor demands of the growing economy but also created a host of social problems, like overcrowding in the cities, garbage, poverty, and crime in the streets, as well as the eternal ruling-class fear of what might happen if a large number of highly exploited people get together and try to do something about being highly exploited. The wealthy and powerful saw that sports was a way of assimilating and socializing poor, working-class immigrants into American culture, and they were quick to lend financial support, underwriting and funding sports leagues and institutions like the Y as philanthropic endeavors.

"Muscular Christianity was the intellectual base for the Young Men's Christian Association," writes Jamieson, and with Dr. Naismith having invented the sport in a YMCA, it might best be said that basketball literally came out of that tradition that believed sports were not just salubrious but could teach important values.

Naismith and his wife, Maude, arrived in Lawrence, Kansas, in September of 1898. He had been hired to head up KU's new Department of Physical Education, recommended by a colleague who described him as "the inventor of basketball, medical doctor, Presbyterian minister, teetotaler, all–around athlete, non-smoker, and owner of vocabulary without cuss words." Basketball had gained popularity quickly, spreading throughout the northeast, but was slower to reach the rest of the country, and upon his arrival in Lawrence, Naismith found that the university had no basketball team. He sought to rectify the situation immediately and soon the game caught on.

Naismith would live out the next forty-one years of his life in Lawrence. He is buried in Oak Hill Cemetery, where most of the victims of Quantrill's Raid are buried, and his grave is a popular destination for those wishing to pay their respects to the inventor of the game. Though he would be involved with KU until the end of his life, he coached the basketball team for only nine seasons, the last of which was 1906–1907, when they finished 7–8. He turned the coaching reins over to one of his players, his most gifted, Forrest Allen, who would lead Kansas to winning records the following two seasons before taking a ten-year sabbatical to study and practice medicine. Allen returned to coach KU in 1919, a post he would hold until 1956, when the compulsory retirement age at KU (seventy) forced him to retire just as he had recruited the greatest player ever to play for Kansas: Wilt Chamberlain. During his time, Allen would coach Kansas to twenty-four conference titles, two Helms Athletic Foundation national titles, in 1922 and 1923, and an NCAA title in 1952. Along the way he became known worldwide by his nickname, "Phog."

Phog Allen is often referred to as the father of basketball coaching, and it is easy to illustrate the accuracy of the title. He retired with 746 career coaching wins, a record that would later be broken by Adolph Rupp, who played for Allen at KU, whose record in turn would be broken by Dean Smith, who also played for Allen at KU.* To give you a sense of scale: the three winningest basketball programs in the history of the sport are

---

*The crazy thing is that there were other great Hall of Fame–caliber coaches who played for Allen too, like Dutch Lonborg, Ralph Miller, and Frosty Cox.

Kentucky, Kansas, and North Carolina, and their greatest coaches, Rupp, Allen, and Smith, all played at Kansas,★ with Rupp and Smith learning the game from Allen, who in turn learned the game from Naismith himself. It is a tingly, shivers-inducing thing to ponder if you love the game.

And what is fascinating about looking back at the relationship between these two patriarchal totems of the sport, the father of the game and the father of basketball coaching, is that you see the way Naismith and Allen were in effect debating the nature and purpose of the game, engaging in a veritable Obi-Wan-vs.-Darth-style lightsaber fight for the soul of basketball.

Naismith and Allen were never terribly close, though they maintained a respectful working relationship, which was necessary, since Naismith was the director of the physical education department, a position that was different from what we would call an athletic director today in that Naismith had little role in overseeing or managing the university sports teams but nonetheless meant he and Allen ran in the same circles at KU. Their sense of what basketball was and their vision for what it should be would come into conflict, but their key differences revolved around how authority, competition, and commercialism affected the game.

It is widely remarked upon, usually with a chuckle, that of the eight coaches in Kansas basketball history, Naismith, with an overall record of 55–60, is the only one with a losing record. This had less to do with the fact that he wasn't good at coaching or teaching—he was one of KU's most beloved professors and instructors—than that it didn't interest him, and it didn't interest him because he believed the game belonged to the players, not coaches. What authority he did exercise was less as coach than as referee (he often had to referee his own team's games before the sport got big, exercising a sense of judicious objectivity that surely drove his players crazy at times), trying to enforce the rules and keep the game from becoming too rough and unsportsmanlike. It was the players who would direct the flow of the game and who together would determine the outcome. He writes of watching a game in which players had been "mechanized" through the repeated drilling of a coach to run specific plays: "These players were not allowed to think for themselves." Later in the same game a player on this team stole the ball and scored a layup at the other end of the court. Naismith and the "crowd wildly acclaimed this feat, but the boy was removed from the game for failure to follow exactly the instructions of the coach. . . . It was to practices like these that I objected. Why should the play of a

---

★Rupp and Smith were also from Kansas; that is to say, *Kansans*. Ironically, Allen is the outlier. He was from Missouri, something KU fans prefer not to mention.

group of young men be entirely spoiled to further the ambitions of some coach?"

James Naismith's bottom-up, decentralized approach to coaching was the complete opposite of Phog Allen's highly centralized, coach-as-benevolent-dictator approach, and if measuring success in terms of wins and losses, Allen's approach was superior to his mentor's, though it is obvious Naismith used a different arithmetic to calculate victory. In his biography of Naismith, Rob Rains writes:

> It was obvious that Naismith and Allen had different approaches to their jobs, and a difference in attitude about their work. Allen's most publicized slogan was that he taught his teams to "play to win," while Naismith always maintained that he wanted his athletes to do their best, but it didn't really matter to him whether they won or not. Naismith said often that sports should fulfill three purposes: to play for the fun of playing, to engage in physical activity to aid the overall development of the body, and to learn sportsmanship through being a member of a team. Winning was never mentioned as a goal by Naismith.

There is a story, perhaps apocryphal, that perfectly captures the different stances the two men took toward coaching. In 1906, Baker University, a small college outside of Lawrence, wrote to Naismith to inquire whether his young star Phog Allen, then only a sophomore, would be interested in coaching the team the following year. Naismith called Allen into his office and was apparently amused to inform him of Baker's interest. Defensive, Allen asked what was so funny about that. But Naismith wasn't casting doubt upon his pupil's knowledge of the game. His answer to Allen was simply: "You can't coach basketball, you just play it."

It is necessary to tease out a line of thought on the relationship between winning and competition. Though Naismith did not prize the former, he believed there was a place for the latter. It's an important distinction, one I have often struggled with myself because I have an aversion to competition in most areas of life, and yet it is the lifeblood of sports. Even for a basketball nut like me, it would take an amazing act of self-discipline to watch a basketball game where the players weren't trying and there was no time and score, neither team winning or losing. Time and score are ways of marking the boundaries of the game, giving it shape and structure, but they are also indicators of and incentivizers to give maximal effort, which is to say, to compete. And competition gives the game what my writing instructors used to say that meaningful and consequential conflict gives fiction: stakes, the sense that you're playing for something that matters. The reason it works in sports is that, as in fiction, the stakes are largely an illusion. Unlike most areas of competition in our society, winning a basketball game does not come at the expense of depriving the losing team of something materially significant, like an education or livelihood.

This is not to say that competition in sports can't have negative consequences. Problems and confusion abound when we overinvest the essentially meaningless with absolute and singular meaning, when we trust the reality of the illusion too much, when we insist on turning fiction into fact—which has certainly been encouraged by the ever-increasing commercialism of the game. But before moving on, it needs to be made clear that while both Naismith and Allen valued competition in basketball, they valued it in very different ways. Allen's winning-is-the-only-thing-that-matters take on competition was different from Naismith's, who saw it as a mechanism or trigger that would enable the players and the game to reach its full potential.* Put another way: for Allen you competed to win the game, and for Naismith you competed to play the game in its most artful and meaningful way.

From today's vantage, it is hard to imagine a time when elite sports teams weren't essentially businesses, either nakedly so as at the professional level or as potential revenue makers at the collegiate level. But it wasn't always so, though the transition from sports as purely recreational to professional advanced quickly. Naismith saw what was in the offing, and as early as 1911 he gave an address on the matter. A transcription of the speech was published in the May 1911 issue of the *Graduate Magazine* of the University of Kansas under the title "Commercialism in Sports." It is a well-written and carefully argued polemic about "insidious growth of commercialism" and its ability to "destroy one of the greatest forces of education."

Drawing heavily on the work of E. Norman Gardiner, Naismith opens by going back to "the time of Homer," arguing that the ancient Greeks faced the same problem we would face two and half millennia later. Initially, sports weren't organized affairs, he says. In pre-Olympic times they were

---

*In the last chapter of his book, titled "The Values of Basketball," Naismith gives us a good sense of what full potential might mean, outlining the twelve attributes he believes the game strives to engender: initiative, agility, accuracy, alertness, cooperation, skill, reflex judgment, speed, self-confidence, self-sacrifice, self-control, and sportsmanship.

spontaneous activities of the leisure class and were celebrated chiefly at the funerals of great men. The rewards at this time were given in memory of the dead, rather than for the reward of the victor, and were given to the losing contestants as well as to the winners. The worth of the prizes indicated the amount of honor to the dead and these gifts were in many cases of great value.

From there, he moves to the Olympics, which carried on this spirit through the first several Olympiads but gradually became more popular and competitive, spurring the development of a professional class of athletes that brought with it the simultaneous debasement of the sport and competitors, from Olympians who bribed opponents to lose to the extreme specializations and training that destroyed the body.★ Naismith quotes Gardiner: "'The popularity of athletics, the growth of competition, and the rewards lavished on successful athletes completely changed the character of sport. The events remained the same, but a change came over the attitude of the performers and the spectators.'" That last bit warrants repeating: the sports didn't change, the attitudes toward them did.

Naismith transitions from the antiquity to modernity, drawing parallels between the "evils that wrecked the ancient games" and what he sees happening with sports in the twenty years since he invented the game of basketball. He begins this final movement of his talk by comparing the arguments in favor of commercializing the sport with his own counterarguments. Of the seven "pro" arguments, the two most persuasive, which umbrella most of the others, are that people should have the freedom to "turn skill into coin" and that doing so will raise the quality of play across the board, contentions familiar enough to many of our contemporary sporting debates such as the NBA/NFL draft age limit or paying college athletes.

The sixteen counterarguments that close Naismith's speech are too numerous to quote in full, but among them are concerns that commercialism leads to overtraining and the breakdown of athletes' bodies; it makes work of sport and turns it into a spectacle instead of recreation; it puts the emphasis on winning instead of enjoyment and personal development and thus encourages breaking the rules and stimulates betting. He also says it leads to

---

★"It is said that the diet of Milo of Crotona consisted of eighteen pounds of meat, eighteen pounds of bread, and fifteen pints of wine a day[!] So great were the excesses of the athletes of this time that Galen, the great physician, said that the life of an Olympic victor was five years."

"worship of the dollar" and "class distinction, for when a man is paid for his services in athletics he is on a different level from the man who buys him."

Over one hundred years after Naismith gave the speech, I imagine him going absolutely centrifugal in his grave, given the current landscape of sports, particularly basketball and football, in universities. As William J. Baker writes in his introduction to Naismith's book, "Whatever its later commercial developments, basketball was made for principled play, not for profit. . . . Naismith designed his new game for athletes to enjoy, not for coaches, television networks, or corporate sponsors to control."

Allen, on the other hand, was quick to realize the monetizing potential of the game. One of the issues he and Naismith clashed over was whether tickets should be sold for KU games, which, by the time Allen had returned to coach KU in 1919, had become quite popular. Again, Rains: "Allen wanted to use the strong interest in basketball that was developing on campus to generate as many sold tickets as possible, while Naismith considered selling tickets an exploitation of the student athletes. Allen argued that bringing money in to the university through the sale of basketball tickets would benefit the other university sports as well." There is compelling logic in both positions, but the chancellor agreed with Allen. That same chancellor, Ernest Lindley, demoted Naismith from director of the physical education department a couple of years later. The person he appointed to replace him was Phog Allen. And so, while Allen had consolidated total control of the athletic department, Naismith receded to the background, focusing on his teaching, mentoring, and ministering. There are accounts of Naismith occasionally attending KU basketball games, sitting alone in the stands impassively while the crowd went wild around him.

I do not mean to paint Allen as the villain. The truth of the matter is that even had he shared Naismith's views on the sport, basketball would have ended up where it is today. Simply put, the values and purpose of the game, as envisioned by Naismith, are at odds with the values and purpose of American business. Allen was shrewdly adapting the game to the larger societal forces going on in the world at the time, the explosion of American capitalism and the commodification of our lives in ways never before known. It is for this reason that Naismith was derisively viewed as behind the times, out of step, unrealistic, or simply nostalgic. With every rule change and adaptation, every small step toward commercialism, he would warn not to stray too far from the game and rules he had invented. "It was the best game," he would continue to asseverate, even as he felt it slipping through his fingers.

F. Scott Fitzgerald was right: it's a hard thing to hold two seemingly contradictory things in your head at once. Yet somehow I know that when I'm cartwheeling down the block after a KU victory or pensively staring out a window after a loss, when I'm watching YouTube clips of a player KU is recruiting two years down the line or spending an hour on the phone with Todd dissecting KU's performance against a D-II team in the preseason, I'm swearing allegiance to the game that Phog Allen helped create and perfect, and part of me loves these aspects of the game, the insane carried-away-ness of fandom. But I also know that when I look back on my time playing the game, the thing I most appreciate was not only the fun I had on the court but the values basketball instilled in me, the bullshit platitudes that happen to be true: teamwork, discipline, cooperation, effort, solidarity, commitment to something bigger than yourself. Those were the kinds of values Naismith had in mind when he imagined basketball into existence, and he knew it was the game itself, not coaches, that could instill them in participants.

"Saints should always be judged guilty until they are proved innocent," wrote Orwell in an essay on Gandhi, adding, "but the tests that have to be applied to them are not, of course, the same in all cases." At times I have been tempted to see Naismith in a saintly light, despite Orwell's cautionary bon mot. The truth, however, is that I don't know enough about him to be able to issue an opinion on his case for canonization. But does it even matter? Isn't it enough that there is so much we do know that can be admired?

He refereed some of the earliest women's basketball games and supported women's right to play sports, opposition to which sounds laughable now, but which was a highly controversial notion at the time. So too was his stance on race. He spends most of his book on the origin of basketball detailing to the point of tedium his surprise and pleasure at seeing the sport played by so many different countries, cultures, and skin colors. At home, he was an antisegregationist and enacted those beliefs. Rains's biography devotes an entire chapter to Naismith's mentorship of John McLendon, a black KU student in the phys ed department who Naismith helped navigate through the virulent racism of the time to become a successful teacher at integrated schools as well as a coach. Ultimately McLendon was elected to the Basketball Hall of Fame in 1979. In an interview at the time, forty years after his mentor's death, McLendon said: "Dr. Naismith didn't know anything about color or nationality. He was so unconscious about your economic or religious background. He just saw everyone as potential."

And furthermore, Naismith did his good works without any expectation of reciprocation. He understood that, like a skillful assist to an open team-mate, giving was the gift. He talks about this in his book. Of his younger self, he writes: "For several years I had been wondering what I wanted to accomplish; finally I decided that the only real satisfaction that I would ever derive from life was to help my fellow beings." His personal motto was: "Leave the world a little better for having lived in it." Elsewhere he writes,

> Thousands of times, especially in the last few years, I have been asked whether I ever got anything out of basketball. To answer this question, I can only smile. It would be impossible for me to explain my feelings to the great mass of people who ask this question, as my pay has not been in dollars but in the satisfaction of giving something to the world that is a benefit to masses of people.

I will grant that a lot of that sounds like something you would read on a cross-stitch sampler in the Cracker Barrel gift shop. Naismith's bromides provoke suspicion, sounding like the sort of thing a very calculating person would want remembered for posterity. He is almost so good and humble that you distrust it because it feels like the humility of one consciously participating in his own deification. And I would remain doubtful, cynical even, except that his beliefs are bolstered by fact and action. Consider that he could have patented the game he invented—imagine the boatloads of money—but chose not to because it didn't "belong" to him. Consider that he never really made a dime off basketball, turned down countless endorsement opportunities. Consider that the book in which these quotes appear was written with great reluctance and not as a moneymaker,* but because his children knew the story of the game needed to be recorded and preserved. He and his family bore the material cost of not cashing in on basketball. The Naismiths were not wealthy, but they weren't poor the way many were poor in those years. It is enough to say they got by, at times barely, on his modest professor's salary.

In Lewis Hyde's book *The Gift*, he distinguishes between a market economy, such as our own, and what he calls a gift economy, as one might find

---

*The book wasn't released until 1941, two years after Naismith's death. His son Jack had originally intended to find a publisher for the manuscript after it was completed in 1937, but another book about the origins of basketball had just come out. It was called *Better Basketball* and it was written by—guess who?—Phog Allen. Naismith saw that the books contained a lot of the same information, and like so many disappointed writers before and since, he put his book back in the drawer.

in certain tribal societies. There is much to be said about what distinguishes them, but central to my concerns here is that in a gift economy something is given and accepted as opposed to being bought and sold. A bond is created between people in a gift economy, whereas in the smooth efficiency of a market economy you buy what you want and never have to see the seller again if you don't want to. That is to say, potential bonds are severed or severely undermined in a market economy because it encourages separation, which can be a useful thing at times. Part of the cathartic tension in Naismith's life story is that he was trying to participate in a gift economy right at the time the United States was fully committing itself to a market economy. Naismith never complained about this. He derived satisfaction not from material comforts so much as knowing that he had passed the gift on.

> I am sure that no man can derive more pleasure from money or power than I do from seeing a pair of basketball goals in some out of the way place—deep in the Wisconsin woods an old barrel hoop nailed to a tree, or a weather-beaten shed on the Mexican border with a rusty iron hoop nailed to one end. These sights are constant reminders that I have in some measure accomplished the objective that I set up years ago.

That was enough for him. And yet, in a functioning gift economy, Hyde argues, while something is given without expectation of reciprocation, the gift is passed on and will eventually, likely in some other form and at some unexpected moment, return to those who originally gave the gift away in the first place.

I came across a story in Rains's biography about how Naismith began missing mortgage payments after KU cut professors' salaries when the Depression hit. The bank threatened to foreclose, but someone intervened to make arrangements on Naismith's behalf. That person was Phog Allen, stepping in to offer help when his old mentor needed it. A few years later, in 1936, when basketball was officially added to the Olympics, Allen began a nationwide campaign to raise funds so that Naismith could attend the games in Berlin, a successful effort that afforded Naismith one of his most cherished memories: tossing the ball up at the very first Olympic basketball game. A functioning gift economy the United States wasn't, and certainly isn't in our own time, but thankfully contributions such as Naismith's tend to go noticed.

'08

In April of 2008 I was living in Iowa City, finishing up my last semester of graduate school. When not in class or writing or teaching or hanging out with my friends, I had spent a lot of the last year or so knocking on doors for a young black senator from Chicago in the leadup to the Iowa Caucuses. Strange to think of it now, eleven years later, with all that has happened since. It seems impossible—and quite embarrassing—to admit that back then I was still under the impression his last name was Obamba and would continue to pronounce it so until H, who was also in school at the University of Iowa, finally had to say something. She seemed to find it both disconcerting and endearing that I had been carrying signs bearing the man's name for months and not realized my error. One night when we were out at dinner she laughed when I said his name and asked me why I pronounced his name *Obamba*. Burning in shame, I doubled down on my commitment to the solecism and fired back: "What, is the second *B* silent?" That's one I'd love to have back.

In any case, it was an interesting time to find myself in Iowa City. With no incumbent and two primaries, it seemed you couldn't go to the bathroom without ending up at a urinal next to Ron Paul—or, rather, some dude who *really* loved Ron Paul and wanted to tell you all about him while you pissed. I remember a friend of mine stumbling into the Hamburg Inn #2, a wonderful local diner, in search of a hangover cure only to find Bill Clinton sitting singly at the counter. My friend took the neighboring stool and ended up talking policy for a spell as they each demolished the house specialty: the pie-shake, which is exactly what you're thinking it is. They were everywhere, Democrats and Republicans, stumping, shaking hands, feeling your pain, and beyond them were their minions, asking for donations or for your vote.

It was in this latter category that I found myself, despite my tendency to not be a joiner as well as an aversion to feeling like I'm inconveniencing people. But an adventitious desire to be more than a sardonic bystander had grown in me during my mid-twenties, and I was trying to get past my innate passivity. I had joined the graduate student teachers' union and had become quite involved. I attended meetings where we spent hours debating the language of a couple of sentences of our contract. I had marched and held signs outside meetings of the university trustees, shouting union slogans. My steward appointed me to get more people from the Writers' Workshop to join the union, but trying to organize my fellow writers—cf Orwell: "All writers are vain, selfish, and lazy, and at the very bottom of their motives lies a mystery"—was Sisyphean work. I was an utter failure as an organizer and for a time became someone to be avoided in the halls of Dey House, the building where our writing classes and workshops met: that union guy who was probably stuffing another flyer or membership card in their mailboxes. Regardless of my own shortcomings as an organizer, however, the union won a better contract and it felt good to be involved.

All of which is in some sense to explain how I got to the point where I was willing to trudge through the snow with H, my contact lenses freezing to my eyeballs, sipping from the hot cocoa in our travel mugs, to knock on the doors of Iowans who were either fed up and angry about the incessant propaganda or driven near mad. I can still see the eyes of an older white-haired woman behind a screen door, head trembling as I delivered my spiel, too polite to tell me to fuck off. Those eyes masked a hanging-by-a-thread desperation that said *Just. Make. It. Stop.*

And finally, it did. The night Obama won the caucus was surreal and, up until then, one of the most gratifying moments of my life. The excitement of his underdog victory in Iowa was matched by knowing the tiny hand my friends and I had had in making it happen, and in the days, weeks, and months after January 3, we would gather to watch the returns of every primary, alternately celebrating and sulking. As we sat around waiting for the numbers to come in, eating Pokey Stix and debating the fate of Chuck Todd's hair, our belief in our chosen candidate was tempered by the sinking certainty that the Clinton political machine would find a way to steal it.

After the early March primaries that left Obama clinging to a significant yet surmountable lead came a six-week break before the next primaries in late April. It was a perfect little intermission into which the NCAA tournament fit, a political hiatus so I could fully devote my attention to basketball, specifically Kansas's run. We had a great team that year. Almost everyone was back from the previous season, when we'd gone to the Elite Eight.

We tied Texas for the Big 12 regular season title and had just beaten them in the championship game of the Big 12 conference tournament, accomplishments that earned us a number-one seed in the national tournament. I had been keeping tabs on all of this, of course, watching televised games when there wasn't a primary on, but for perhaps the first time in my life my instinctive commitment to the Jayhawks was trumped by a more mindful commitment to something I knew was way more important. But caring about important things, like who is going to be the leader of the country, was also tiring and stressful, and I was looking forward to just watching basketball and cheering on my team. Then, just as the tourney was set to start, the video of Jeremiah Wright surfaced.

Remember the first time you saw it?

The white-hot intensity of his eyes, the booming delivery, the halting histrionics of a powerful speaker. It didn't matter that his lines had been removed from the immediate context of that particular speech or from the lineage of black liberation and liberation theology to which they belonged. It didn't matter that the sentiment—*God damn America!*—was something I had often felt myself as a privileged white heterosexual male, so I could only imagine the frequency with which the line might occur to people who had not had the country built to benefit their class, race, orientation, or gender. But if Dukakis in a tank and the Dean Scream could instantly derail the campaigns of candidates with a lot less impeding their paths, what the hell would this do to Obama? The news networks would never play the entire sermon—it would be conveniently impossible in the strange irony of our times: twenty-four-hour news channels devoted entirely to sound bites and pundits debating sound bites. Immediately I thought: *The Clintons—they leaked it!* Then I thought, *Fox News made it up!* Then I thought, *The Clintons and Fox News working in concert!* It was over; Obama was done for. No amount of damage control could repair this. I had little faith that the majority of white America would not so much look past the clips but actually look at them and try to understand why a black pastor might be standing before his congregation saying "God damn America." I thought of the words of James Baldwin and how impossible we had made it for people to understand the notion that "I love America more than any other country in the world, and, exactly for this reason, I insist on the right to criticize her perpetually."

I was devastated, and then I felt relief. I didn't have to care anymore. I could sit back and be a passive critic of my country's affairs while devoting my time and energy to basketball with no qualms. And on some level, of course, I must have known that my personal demographic breakdown carried with it an unearned privilege that meant that I would pretty much be just fine, no matter who was elected president, unlike many other Obama supporters. Somehow at that despondent time, nothing more fully exposed the ruse of American democracy than that I could care as much as I did about the NCAA tournament. True, I had pretty much always thought of March Madness as the best three weeks of the year, but now I did so self-consciously, because while throwing myself into the arms of the tournament I was fully aware that behind its back I was furtively flipping off the rest of the country with the petulance of a child playing one parent against the other.

During my time in Iowa City, I lived around the corner from a bar called the Vine, a bar often referenced in Denis Johnson's classic *Jesus' Son*, one of the books that had made me want to become a writer, and since I didn't have a television, I'd spent many a night over my two years slumped in a booth or with my elbows on the rail, watching ball. They brewed a sweet brown liquid called "Vine Ale" that was possible to ingest—for a time, anyway—because a stein of which, a so-called Vinestein, cost only $2.50. In the years since, in certain moments, the phantom taste of Vine Ale will suddenly envelop my tongue and I'll gag, but at the time it was basically grad student ambrosia, and come tourney time the Vine was the perfect place to set up shop on the most perfect four days of the year: the first weekend of the tourney, nonstop basketball games from noon to midnight. If they had let me set up a cot in the back, I wouldn't have even gone home. Over that first weekend, from my booth at the Vine, friends would stop by, watch for a little while, maybe have a drink or order some food, then leave, replaced sometime later by someone else, the only constant me and my Vinestein. Every once in a while, CBS's basketball coverage was interrupted by a news update and I would catch an image of Obama or Reverend Wright's mouth moving—the TVs were on mute because someone was always feeding the juke quarters—and I would head to the bathroom. It was in this manner, in this state, that I watched Kansas ease past its first two opponents, Portland and UNLV, and make its way into the Sweet Sixteen.

The following Thursday I drove the five hours from Iowa City to Kansas City to spend the weekend with Todd. KU was to play number-twelve-seed Villanova, who had upset five-seed Clemson in the first round, and Todd and I went to Lawrence to watch the game with his parents. As we watched KU handle Nova pretty easily, 72–57, we kept an eye on what was going on in the rest of the bracket. The big story in the Midwest region was not KU's quiet efficiency but the run a tiny school named Davidson was making. A ten seed, Davidson had already dispatched of number-seven Gonzaga, number-two Georgetown, and that very day had pulled a third upset, taking out number-three Wisconsin to set up an Elite Eight match against Kansas with a Final Four berth on the line.

But the story wasn't really about Davidson; the person who had captured the media attention was their star player, Stephen Curry. Part of this, certainly, was because after hanging thirty-three on Wisconsin he had become just the fourth player in tournament history to score thirty or more points in his first three games. However, I'm convinced that part of it was also because he looked so unassumingly childlike, and this peculiar quality was as fascinating as his talent. There was something kind of beautiful and doll-like about him, a JonBenét Ramseyness made less tragic by his ability to cross fools up and hit shots that looked like end-of-practice stunts. This was the NCAA tournament where announcers learned and fell in love with the words *pluck* and *moxie* and not a sentence re: Curry could be spoken without their inclusion. The amount of attention he was receiving had become a little nerve-racking and the media's Cinderella narrative now felt overdetermined: Davidson was going to upset number-one KU.

I'd continued my boycott of all things political over the week, but periodically I would catch snippets on TV or receive a text from my friend Ted in Iowa City. *It's not as bad as you think. He can still win.* Something about how Obama had delivered the greatest speech on race ever and that I should watch it on YouTube. But fuck that shit! Unjust as it was, Obama was done, and I wasn't gonna waste thirty-seven minutes watching a dumb speech when I had KU on the brink of the Final Four to worry about. On Saturday, as Todd and I returned to Kansas City, fellow number-one seeds North Carolina and UCLA advanced to the national semifinals, as did Memphis the following day. Now the pressure was really on. With three of the four spots taken, the question was whether Kansas could slow down Curry enough to make it the first time in tournament history that all four number-one seeds advanced to the Final Four. Now, in addition to the David(son)-versus-Goliath narrative, there was the burden of history. There was a reason all four top seeds had never advanced to the Final Four, and it usually had to do with some avatar of Steph Curry crushing your team's dreams.

In my recollections of the affair, it was a real polished turd of a game, something confirmed when I recently went back to read accounts from the time. It was close throughout, but ugly, neither team able to get into a flow. KU was clearly bothered by anxiety as much as Davidson was by the Jayhawks' length and athleticism. Todd had just purchased his first house and we watched the game in his barely furnished living room, which was somehow fitting. To have watched the game in comfort would have felt wrong. We needed to be as bothered physically as we were mentally. We needed room to pace, and those various hazards like unpacked boxes or table lamps on the floor that we could take odd pleasure in the concentration it took to avoid, as well as that blind spot where the glint of light from a nearby window hit the left side of the screen because Todd hadn't figured out the best placement of his TV—that little black hole of athletic drama onto which we could project all hatred and misery and injustice because clearly Kansas was going to be denied the Final Four this day.

And it was all set up to happen that way in the most spectacular of fashions. With fifty-four seconds left and Kansas up five, Curry did exactly what Curry does: hit an absurdly long three-pointer. Leading 59–57, KU used the shot clock to run the game clock down to twenty-one seconds before guard Sherron Collins missed a long jumper. Davidson got the rebound and now the stage was set. Twenty seconds: two to tie, three to win, but everyone knew Davidson would go for the win, just as they knew Curry would be the one to take the shot. Davidson inbounded to you-know-who and Curry slowly walked the ball up the court, guarded by the taller Brandon Rush. A double-team from Sherron, however, forced Curry to pass it to point guard Jason Richards at the top of the key, who let fly a game-winning three that thudded against the backboard.

As CBS continued to alternate between replays of the final ten seconds and the real-time celebration of the Kansas players, announcers Gus Johnson and Len Elmore, already missing lil' Steph, wondered aloud in melancholy tones why he hadn't found a way to take the winning shot. The truth was that there was no way for him to get the shot off, so good was the Kansas perimeter and help defense. And it wasn't just the final play— Brandon Rush, Mario Chalmers, and Sherron Collins had been in his jock all night, holding Curry to twenty-five points it took him twenty-five shots to earn. At the time, Coach Self was often referred to as the "best coach to never reach a Final Four," and there is footage from a single camera focused on him as he crouched on the sideline and watched the final shot miss: lowering his head, patting the floor a few times, exhaling a huge sigh relief, as we all were. It was KU's thirteenth Final Four in school history. The last time we had been was in 2003, when we were coached by Roy Williams, the man whose team at the time, UNC, was both the favorite to win the tournament and our next opponent.

To this day one of the most divisive topics for Kansas basketball fans is how we should feel about Roy Williams. Ol' Roy is a real nasty nest of psycho trauma for a host of reasons. He took over the program at a time when we were under sanctions from the Larry Brown era that included a postseason ban the year after winning the 1988 NCAA title for recruiting violations, the major one being that potential transfer Vincent Askew had been provided a plane ticket so he could return home to see his sick grandmother. After Roy's first year, when we were on probation, all he did was make KU the winningest program of the nineties. There is an impressive list of stats that I could geek out on, but it is enough to say he was—and is—a great coach. He has a humble Huckleberry Hound charm about him that is endearing. He got flak in the media for crying after his teams lost in the tourney, but to Kansas fans like me it was just further proof of what a great coach he was; he loved his players *that* much.

Of course, for all his gaudy success, Roy never won the BIG one. He took Kansas to four Final Fours and two championship games, but never managed to win the title. Much the way Bill Self had been saddled with the "Best Coach to Never Reach the Final Four" tag, Roy was considered the "Best Coach to Never Win the Title" by the end of his fifteen years in Lawrence. This wasn't Roy's real crime, however; everyone knew he would eventually win the championship. The enmity toward him stems from his decision to leave Kansas for North Carolina—or rather, his decision to leave Kansas for North Carolina three years after he spurned UNC when they first tried to lure him away in 2000.

That year, 2000, when Dean Smith's longtime assistant coach, Bill Guthridge, retired, everyone knew UNC would come after Roy, who had been an assistant there before coming to Kansas. Roy loved and idolized his mentor, Smith, publicly stating so numerous times, and everyone assumed he would leave. ESPN and media outlets even ran reports that he had accepted the job when he hadn't. As the days dragged on, with Roy tormented over whether to stay at the program he had rescued from peril or return home when his master called, the mood for Kansas fans was grim. Like most people, I thought he'd leave, and I even understood why. But then, amazingly, he called a press conference in the football stadium where he famously announced, "Well, I'm stayin'," citing a promise he had made to Nick Collison that he would be Collison's coach throughout his years at KU and how he couldn't break that promise to his player. This just confirmed what all of us Kansas fans already knew: Roy was not only a great coach, he was a great man, and we were lucky as hell to have him. North Carolina went on to hire one of Roy's former assistants at KU, Matt Doherty, who recruited a number of exceptional players but ruffled a lot of feathers. After just three seasons he was forced out and once again UNC came after Roy, daring him to publicly reject his mentor/surrogate father one more time.

The rumors were already swirling by the time KU made it to the 2003 Final Four. Earlier in the week, Doherty had "resigned" and as the Jayhawks suited up to face Dwyane Wade's Marquette team, all the media wanted to talk about was whether Roy had been contacted by North Carolina. Even after we put it on D-Wade by thirty-three, more people were speculating about Roy's future than they were talking about whether this would finally be the year Roy won the national championship. The '03 title game is a salty wound for every Kansas fan. We were the better team, but Syracuse—aided by the greatness of Carmelo Anthony, six first-half threes by Gerry Fucking McNamara, historically poor free throw shooting by us, and an injury to Wayne Simien—was just a little better on that night and won 81–78. I was living in Lawrence at the time, watching the game with Todd at his family's house and when it was over we sat around shaking our heads, not saying much, simply taking in the celebration of Syracuse hoisting the trophy that should have been ours.

After the 'Cuse players cut down the nets and before the playing of the tournament's coda, "One Shining Moment," CBS sportscaster Bonnie Bernstein interviewed a teary-eyed Roy Williams outside the KU locker room. In the entirety of the forty-five-second interview she asked him nothing about the game he had just coached. Her first question was what level of interest he had in the North Carolina job. Visibly annoyed, Roy said he could give a "flip"—a classic Royism, the closest he would ever get to swearing was this or a peeved "daggum"—about what people who wanted that answer thought and then tactfully said it wasn't very sensitive to ask that question. Bernstein's response was, "If they offered the job, would you be willing to take it?" Now truly pissed, Roy gave her an awesome dressing down:

> I haven't thought about that for one second, I haven't thought about
> that for one second. The guy in your ear who told you you have to ask
> that question, as a journalist, that's fine, but as a human being, that's not
> very nice, because it's not very sensitive, and I gotta think in tough times,
> people should be more sensitive. I could give a shit about North Carolina
> right now. I've got thirteen kids in that locker room that I love.

It's one of the most underrated verbal nip-slip moments in sports history. I remember clapping as Todd and his family looked at the television, shocked, watching as Greg Gumbel and the rest of the announcing crew awkwardly tried to decide whether to ignore the confrontation or to apologize for the profanity. Not only was Roy correct—she was being insensitive, even if it was her job—it gave me hope that he wouldn't leave. Todd and I had thought that winning the title would make it easier for him to go to UNC in a keep-everyone-happy sort of way: *I'll give you the championship you've been wanting so badly and you don't give me too much grief for going home after saying I wouldn't.* I felt pretty confident that he wouldn't go, the lone solace after the heartbreak of the final game. The next day, all throughout Lawrence, people could be seen wearing T-shirts that said, "I Don't Give a Shit about North Carolina Either." Roy's postgame outburst felt like a blood oath commitment to us Kansas fans instead of the emotional in-the-moment reaction that it was. So when Roy accepted the job at UNC a week later, it felt like a betrayal on many levels.

I remember being surprised that he left, and disappointed, but I also understood why he did. Furthermore, it was hard to be ungrateful, as many KU fans proved themselves to be, for all Roy had done over the last fifteen years. He was in a situation where whatever decision he made would end up hurting the feelings of a lot of people he cared deeply about. If there is a villain in the drama, I've always felt that Dean Smith is the person nobody ever talks about. He knew Roy idolized him, knew what resolve it must have taken for Roy to say no the first time, and yet he wasn't content to leave Roy alone to build a life and program at KU the same way Smith had at UNC. (There is also the double insult that Smith is from Kansas, played at KU under Phog Allen, and still went forward in poaching our coach.) He certainly was aware of the imbalance in their power dynamic, as well as the pressure he was putting on Roy's allegiance and used it to his advantage, knowing his proxies were making Roy an offer he couldn't refuse—not twice, anyway.

Of course, it didn't help the hurt feelings in Kansas that Roy won the title—with Doherty's players—just two years into his Carolina coaching career. That was a little kick in the stomach we KU fans could have done without. The first few years after Roy left were difficult. Illinois's young and successful coach, Bill Self, was picked to replace the man who stood behind only Allen as Kansas's winningest coach. We won a lot of games and got to an Elite Eight Self's first year, but it didn't feel right. It was awkward. Self was trying to win with players Roy had recruited in a style very different from his own. Roy's teams flew up and down the court, a fun fast-breaking continuous motion, equal parts controlled and improvisational. Coach Self brought with him from the Big Ten a more plodding, defense-oriented style of play that players and fans were slow to accept, even as the wins continued to pile up. But over the next few seasons things began to jell. Self learned to loosen up the reins on the offense and fans learned that defensive excellence wasn't incompatible with offensive efficiency and pace. Though Coach Self has completely put his stamp on the KU basketball program and his stature as one of the best coaches in the game is indisputable, there are people who still harbor ill will toward Roy, which is just baffling to me by this point, but which is also to bring us back to the 2008 Final Four and to give some context for what it meant—how pregnant with meaning it was—for Kansas to be facing Roy for the first time in the five years since he left.

There was an excitement about this Final Four, different from the buzz and pageantry of most. Not just that history had been made, but the anticipation of seeing the four best teams all year get a chance to play. Think how often the best teams don't actually win the tournament, or even make it to the Final Four. On one side of the bracket was UCLA, in its third consecutive Final Four, taking on John Calipari's Memphis squad, who had lost only one game all year. On the other side was KU versus the number-one overall seed and tournament favorite North Carolina. If there was a criticism of Kansas that year, it was that we didn't have the star power of the other top teams. UCLA featured Kevin Love and Russell Westbrook, Memphis had Derrick Rose and Chris Douglas-Roberts, and UNC sported a quartet of stars in Ty Lawson, Danny Green, Wayne Ellington, and national player of the year Tyler Hansbrough. Some actually argued that Kansas was too much of a team to win it all. At the point we had Russell Robinson, solid and steady floor general. Elite on-the-ball defense and reliable shooting from Chalmers at the two. At small forward was Rush, considered by most our best player, so quiet and smooth that his moments of brilliance could be easily undone by stretches you forgot he was in the game. And in the post, Darnell Jackson—my favorite—was the constant beating heart and Darrell Arthur the mercurial talent. Off the bench we got energy from a human cannonball named Sherron Collins and a Russian Hulk, commonly known as Sasha Kaun. Of these seven, no one averaged more than thirteen points but none less than seven. Ironic in retrospect, I recall Jimmy Dykes, that happy idiot, opining on the radio before the Final Four: "I have serious doubts about Kansas. I mean who's gonna take the last shot for this team? That's what I want to know. When the game's on the line, who'll take the last shot?"

Having basically avoided all intellectual labor over the last two weeks, the morning after the Davidson game I returned to Iowa City to catch up on work for the classes I took and to prepare for the one I taught. That class was creative writing, a beastly two-and-a-half-hour affair meant to introduce students to the craft elements of writing poetry, nonfiction, and fiction. That I wrote neither poetry nor nonfiction at the time had somehow not disqualified me from teaching the class. It met late on Monday nights, and when I walked in there were grins from several of my students, reminders of how indiscreet I was in my idolatry of Kansas basketball.

As the game against Carolina neared, I felt a peculiar equanimity. I'd guess that in 95 percent of the games Kansas plays, we are the favorite, and with that comes the burden of expectation. Though Kansas had played to their seed in getting to the Final Four—that is, done exactly what they were expected to do—not a lot of people outside of the center of the country were expecting us to beat UNC. I felt the least amount of pressure heading into a KU tourney game I can ever remember. We had done what we were supposed to do, had gotten the Final Four monkey off Coach Self's back, and there would be no dishonor in losing to a team generally considered the best in the country. I suppose in some sense I believed UNC would win, so I went into the game with a playing-with-house-money calm. Imagine my surprise then when KU raced out to a twenty-eight-point first-half lead.

I've since rewatched that first half and it never stops being puzzling, the perfect imbalance of seeing one team play near flawlessly and the other barely able to dribble up the court. Or rather, I had seen such things happen, but they were usually against inferior opponents. I couldn't tell whether we were the greatest basketball team of all time or if the entire UNC team was on acid. I can still hear Billy Packer, that human carbuncle, declare that the game was over when there were still several minutes left in the first half, prompting me to address the television angrily, "Don't you dare fucking jinx us, Billy," which drew a few *Chill, buddy* glances from neighbors at the bar. For all our domination in the first half, we held only a seventeen-point lead at the break, and that was quickly chipped away at in the second as UNC woke up, remembered they were a great team, and made their inevitable run.

I knew this would happen; the earth would right its axis and the game would tighten. But watching it happen was torturous, as all rational thought left my faculties. When Ellington hit a three to cut a once twenty-eight-point lead to five with over nine minutes to play, I was suddenly a paranoid deep in the headwaters of psychosis. It was a conspiracy! Roy was going to break our hearts all over again! It was planned—let Kansas get a big lead and nearly taste the glory of exorcising past trauma only to reopen the wound and wiggle a diseased little finger around in it. No team had ever come back from a deficit greater than twenty-two in a Final Four game and here we were set to make history in the most spectacular and ignominious of ways. I was already worrying about how I would explain it to the poor people whose faces I shoved my love of Kansas into like I was pieing them with banana cream.

Thankfully, however, UNC could never quite get over the hump, and five points was the closest they got. In fact, Kansas didn't just hang on; we built the lead back up to eighteen by game's end. As I made my phone calls to Todd and family members, reveling in the victory, the reality of the situation began to sink in: Kansas would be playing in its first championship game since 2003 for a chance to win its first title since 1988, twenty years before. And they would be doing so on Monday night—and that's when I remembered my class met on Monday nights. The game was set for an 8:21 p.m. central time tip and my class ran from 7:00 to 9:30. Clearly something needed to be done. I made an embarrassing attempt to reschedule the class, citing a "professional" conflict, but failed, so I walked into the room that night at seven and told my students we were going to go hard for an hour and a half and call it quits an hour early. I had already contacted my friend Ted, who had TiVo, and asked him to record the game. I would come over to his house as soon as class finished and we'd watch. I have no idea what we covered about poetic forms that night because at the time I was metaphysically truant; my soul was somewhere up in the ethers above Iowa City making burnt offerings to basketball gods that they might favor Kansas this night.

I was doing a good job of keeping one eye on the clock while pretending to engage in meaningful interaction with my students, moving us through the accelerated schedule of things we needed to cover. When I noticed that it was 8:23 and the game was already two minutes under way, I felt sad. I was missing it as I sat there among my students in the stupid circle I had us arrange ourselves into to show we were all equals. I considered wrapping things up right then, but in an amazing act of willpower I took us all the way to 8:32 and even indulged the after-class questions of one or two innocents who had no idea the emotional Armageddon my placid smile was masking.

When I arrived at Ted's, sprinting from the car and still carrying the bag containing my students' papers, I found him standing in the kitchen, making cocktails of some sort. Chill music issued forth from the iPod.

"Hey, dude," he said pleasantly.

"What's up, Milward?" said our friend Craig, stretched out on the couch reading a magazine like he was waiting to be fed grapes by a togaed nymph.

The whole scene felt strange. I had to remind myself that though they were my friends, this was pretty much a night like any other to them. I half expected to enter and find them watching the game, unable to wait for me to arrive. I looked at my cell phone—it was 8:44, twenty-three minutes into the game. There was also a text from Todd, commenting on the game. I looked away, trying not to register what it said, and turned off my phone. Ted brought over a tray of drinks and offered one to Craig and one to me. I took a seat in a big comfy chair beneath one of the original Shepard Fairey prints of Obama that would soon become ubiquitous but at that point were novel. It reminded me of all I'd blocked out over the past three weeks, and I had a fleeting fantasy of taking it down and turning it around to face the wall, like a photograph of a cheater's spouse during a romantic liaison.

"Shall we start the game?" asked Ted.

"Please," I said.

I have never expressed a truer or more concise sentiment in my life.

For all the athleticism and offensive talent on each team, both Memphis and Kansas were excellent defensively that season, and the first half was tight and unpretty, with KU having a slight edge in control. I would get so into the game that I'd forget we weren't watching it live, and then a commercial break would come and I would be surprised to see the screen suddenly a blur, Ted fast-forwarding right through the ads, breaking the temporal dream of watching it live. It might have been the only time in my adult life when I wanted to watch commercials.

At the half, Kansas held a five-point lead. As Craig was getting up to fix another drink, I grabbed his hand and placed it on my chest. "Jesus Christ, man. Are you all right?"

"I don't know. It always does this when we play."

"Ted, you should check this out," said Craig, staring at his hand covering my heart. "Feels like Milward's all coked up."

During halftime we blazed through commercials and most of the announcers' prattle and were able to catch up to real time. I felt a little relief, back in sync with the universe. One bit of intermission news I did catch was about Roy Williams. He was at the game and sowing discord because he was wearing a Jayhawk sticker on his shirt. I thought it was awesome, but he was already getting called out both by UNC fans for supporting another team and by still-bitter KU fans. I felt sad for Ol' Roy. It seemed his great desire to be loved by everyone and his fate to always be pissing large numbers of people off.

Our modest halftime lead quickly evaporated in the second half, as Derrick Rose and Chris Douglas-Roberts showed themselves to be the

All-Americans they were. Their defense locked down and our inability to score worked in concert with our inability to keep Rose out of the lane, allowing Memphis take control of the game. A certain kind osmosis particular to fandom began to happen, whereby my cheering for Kansas spread to Ted and Craig and now they were really into the game as well, asking questions about strategy, cheering after a much-needed defensive stop and the occasional basket. At a certain point KU switched out of man-to-man defense. Billy Packer was confused, working through his befuddlement before the entire nation: "Now, Kansas is doing something different here . . . "

"It's a triangle and two," I said to the television.

"I'm not entirely sure what they . . . "

"Billy, it's a triangle and two."

Ted and Craig sniggered.

"Some sort of trick defense, I believe . . . "

"It's a fucking triangle and two!" I yelled.

"It's a triangle and two, by God!" Billy echoed. "Kansas has switched to a triangle-and-two defense."

But nothing we did slowed Rose down, and when he banked in a long two as the shot clock was expiring it felt like fate and there was little we could do; even his junk shots were going in. He scored fourteen of Memphis's sixteen points in a run that gave them a nine-point lead with 2:12 left in the game. It was all but over and the three of us went silent. But then, amazingly, in just twenty-two seconds of game time we cut the lead to four after a long Darrell Arthur two and after Sherron Collins made one of the most impressive basketball plays I've ever seen. Darting toward an in-bound pass, he ripped the ball from a Memphis player's hands as he spun in the air, twirling out of bounds, and somehow managed to toss it to Mario Chalmers in the complete opposite direction from which he was spinning, before rejoining the play in time to get back on the court and knock down a three in the corner. The whole sequence sort of defied physics, and the kinetic genius of Sherron in that moment was amazing to behold. Suddenly we had life, and the Kansas fans in the Alamo Dome were roaring, as were the three of us in Ted's living room. Being down nine with 2:12 to go had seemed impossible; down four with 1:48 was doable.

The one universally agreed-upon vulnerability Memphis had that season was foul shooting. Out of 341 Division I teams they ranked 339th with a team average of just 59 percent. Because they had no real other flaws, all season long people asked Coach Calipari if it worried him, and he would say it didn't, that his players would make them when they counted. Coach Self put this theory to a test. Given that we had tried about everything else and been unable to stop Rose, we began intentionally sending Memphis players to the foul line.

When Douglas-Roberts went to the line with 1:15 left and Memphis up 62–58, they had made their last five free throws. They were in the bonus and he missed the front end of the one-and-one. Kansas raced down the court and fed Darrell Arthur in the post, who hit a tough turnaround, the ball deciding to touch every part of the rim before dropping in. Here we were, within two points with exactly a minute left. Now we didn't need to foul, certain that if we could get a defensive stop we'd be assured a chance to tie or win the game. And that's just what we did. Brandon Rush forced Douglas-Roberts into a tough shot that started a fast break toward the other end, but Memphis stole the ball back and we had to send Douglas-Roberts to the line again with just 16.8 seconds left and Memphis still clinging to a two-point lead. It was an emotional swing—from certain game-tying basket at one end to potential victory-cementing free throws at the other—and all in a few seconds.

Douglas-Roberts had missed his last free throw but had made the previous four. He dribbled, right foot forward at the line, dropping his left foot back several inches, and patted the scroll-like tattoo on his arm for good luck, before releasing a shot that was short and ricocheted off the rim to the right. The crowd reacted with surprise and the murmur of intrigue. Douglas-Roberts went through his same routine again and, amazingly, he missed again to the right. I remember feeling unbounded excitement—we had a second chance!—that was extinguished a millisecond later when Memphis forward Robert Dozier grabbed the offensive rebound over Arthur and kicked it out to his guards. By the time we were able to foul, six precious seconds had gone off the clock and we were sending the unflappable Rose, maker of thirteen straight free throws, to the line with 10.8 seconds. Again we had squandered a chance to tie. We used our final timeout before the referee handed Rose the ball to ice him.

Derrick Rose played with an expressionless calm that somehow exuded confidence and maximal effort instead of lack of concern, and as he prepared to shoot after the timeout, he betrayed no nerves. He took several dribbles, released the ball from over his right shoulder, where it went toward the basket in a textbook arc and started to go through the rim, then bounced out and off the backboard and seemed like it might drop back through the rim again but it too missed to the right. Rose was still Rose, however, and calmly knocked down the second free throw.

Up 63–60 with 10.8 seconds, Memphis elected not to call timeout to set their defense or to discuss strategy, such as fouling and sending us to line instead of giving us a shot at a three to tie. Coach Calipari would later say he had told his guys to foul—part of a bad habit he has of blaming his players after tough losses—but there's no evidence of that when you watch him on the sideline during the final seconds. Arthur inbounded the ball to Collins, who held it for a few seconds. Watching time tick away, I remember shouting "Go!" at the television, but I realize now he was letting his teammates get set at the other end. He began dribbling up the court, guarded by Rose, and as he crossed half court, he lost control of the ball. The ball squirted away from Collins and he dove for it, flipping it to Chalmers as he fell to the ground. In doing so, he inadvertently screened Chalmers's man, and that bit of daylight, as Memphis rushed to switch, allowed Chalmers to get off a good but contested look that from the second it left his hand you knew was true. "Mario's Miracle," as it came to be known.

I was kneeling before the TV and threw my hands up, as Ted, Craig, and I harmonized on a spontaneous and collective howl that cannot be rendered typographically. But wary of the quick and incessant vacillations of the game, I realized there was still time—over two seconds—and got to my feet, doing a little nervous tap-dancing jig as Coach Calipari again decided not to call a timeout, and his team was only able to get up a half-court heave. We cheered anew. Ted's girlfriend, Carrie, came out from the back room, where she had been working, wondering what the hell had happened, as the three of us were high-fiving and oh-my-goshing.

"Kansas won?" she asked.

"Well, no," I said. "But neither has Memphis. It's going to overtime."

"Oh," she said, and returned to the back room.

The three of us were still shaking our heads, filled with the dramatic rush of the final play. It seemed both exciting and unfair that we would have to endure another five minutes of basketball, given all that had happened in the final two minutes and twelve seconds of the game, back when Memphis had a nine-point lead and the game was over. Seemed ages ago.

"I need a smoke," said Craig.

"Overtime's gonna start after the commercial," I said.

"We'll TiVo it."

The idea appealed to me now. Filled with the hope of KU's furious comeback, part of me must have been scared that we would blow it in overtime.

"Sure," I said. "I'll come with you."

So I went outside with Craig onto the front steps of the house and stood there as he smoked. Craig was smiling at me.

"Can you imagine if they win it?"

"No," I said, which was true.

I had been eight the last time Kansas won the title, in 1988. We were still living in Lawrence, my mother finishing up her PhD at KU. That team, known as "Danny and the Miracles," had indeed made an improbable run. Given a generous six seed, we'd had to defeat three teams that had beaten us on our home floor during the regular season: K-State, Duke, and Oklahoma. Contributing to the fairytale sense of predetermination was the fact that the championship was to be played in Kemper Arena in nearby Kansas City. My mom's cousin was a trader on the Chicago Exchange and a few of his stockbroker buddies flew in for the game. He invited my mom to come along. A poor graduate student at the time, my mom often recalls what a luxury it was to wine and dine with this high-rolling crew. She had a friend look after my brother and me, the three of us watching in the basement of our home, where I was used to watching cartoons as Mom plugged away at her dissertation. My most vivid memory from the night was after the final buzzer sounded, when I opened the front door to find the sky suddenly lit by fireworks as the jubilant honking of horns sounded all through town.

In the twenty years since then—the period when my basketball consciousness as a fan and player truly formed—I had seen twenty Kansas teams have great seasons that finished short of the title, sometimes in the Final Four or championship game and sometimes in devastating upsets. Having seen so many worthy and capable teams not close the deal, I truly could not imagine us winning it this time, and I was stricken by the certainty that I definitely did not want to watch the overtime. I floated the idea to Craig that I would wait outside and he could signal to me from the window whether Kansas had won.

"What are you, nuts?" he said. "You have to watch."

"I know, but I think it might kill me if we lose."

Mercifully, overtime was a breeze. KU carried over the energy from the comeback into the extra session, and when we scored the first six points there was no doubt that momentum was on our side for good. Memphis fought to stay in the game, but now their shots weren't falling, and their previously impenetrable defense had become porous, hollowed out by the demoralization of certainty made frangible. A couple of minutes before they had been all but champs. When the final buzzer sounded, Kansas winning 75–68, Craig, Ted, and I cheered, once again smiling and shaking heads, high-fiving at the heart attack of it all.

And then, we might say, shit got real, and I was in tears and freaking out my friends because though it was an entertaining game that they had gotten swept up in, it was just that: a basketball game. I tried, but words failed to explain why I was crying. Someone should have just thrown a blanket over me.

It was all very different from the scene six months later, when the four of us would gather on election night to watch the returns. By that time I had graduated and was living in Madison, Wisconsin. To my amazement Obama had somehow weathered the Jeremiah Wright and Bill Ayers miasma, and I had once again been knocking on doors for him in the chilly Madison fall. On the day of the election I came back to Ted and Carrie's house in Iowa City. It was only fitting. Craig came too, and every time a state was called for Obama we took a shot of an alco-concoction we had christened "the blood of John McCain." And when the election was called and the pictures of Harlem and Chicago and Spelman came in, we would all cry and it wasn't the least bit unusual because we had the same investment and because it had come to feel like something we couldn't possibly live to see: a black man in the White House. We hugged and drank a little more blood of John McCain, and then we left the house, walked downtown, and celebrated with the masses who had suddenly gathered in the streets of Iowa City.

One and Done

There was a reason I got out of bed on a cold Saturday morning in late December 2010, and that reason was Josh Selby. Selby, our star freshman who had accepted improper benefits from a family friend, was set to make his Kansas debut. KU routinely lands recruiting classes ranked in the top ten, but until then, with the exception of Xavier Henry the previous year, Kansas rarely scored what have come to be known as OADs, players who are "one and done," off to the NBA after their mandatory year in college or overseas. Coach Self tries to recruit some of these players, certainly, but his real genius is in developing the next tier or two of players who will stay for multiple years before going to the NBA or graduating, like the Morris twins and Thomas Robinson, and more recently players like Frank Mason, Perry Ellis, Devonte' Graham, and Svi Mykhailiuk. That year, however, Self landed Josh Selby, a player who by most accounts was the top recruit in the country and a certain OAD. It had been said several times that Selby was the most talented recruit to come to Kansas since Danny Manning. This was hyperbolic, debatable, and up until then unknowable, since he'd had to sit out the first nine games of the season.

Christmas was a week away, but this was my present: to get to see Selby play for the first time. We were playing USC at home, and the game was set for a noon tip for the East Coast networks, which meant 9 a.m. in San Francisco, something I was still struggling to adjust to. Breakfast and basketball. It had been two weeks since the UCLA game, and we'd improved to 10–0 and a number-three national ranking heading into this game. Again I watched on my netbook, earbuds in, at the kitchen table by the window. Below me 16th Street was quiet but for the one or two people scurrying off to yoga class.

Selby didn't start but came into the game after the first TV timeout and the fans went wild. For weeks they had been holding signs reading "Free Selby" and chanting his name as he sat on the bench in street clothes. We'd all been waiting to see him play, and he did not disappoint. Immediately after checking in he hit two threes. Within his first five minutes of action he had already scored ten points. The fans went bonkers. Selby was a scoring point guard, but Coach Self had moved him to shooting guard so Tyshawn Taylor could remain at the point. He was six foot two and strong for a guard. He reminded me a little of a taller Sherron Collins, and like Sherron he played with the insouciance and arrogance of many of the greats. He was having fun, you could tell, and amazingly he seemed relaxed, as if he were only playing pickup ball with his buddies, but he wasn't; he was excelling against a quality opponent in his first college game and doing so on national television before a rabid fanbase with impossible expectations. There were one or two moments where his perfection slipped—a defensive lapse, a forced drive to the basket that resulted in a turnover—but his excellent play continued throughout the first half. His teammates seemed to realize that something special was happening. They had a tendency to stop when they passed the ball to Selby. Like us fans, they wanted to watch what he would do with it.

When the second half started, USC began chipping into our eleven-point lead. It didn't happen all at once, no big run. Just a patient basket or two here and there that suddenly started to add up. Selby's strong play continued, and it was surprising to find ourselves suddenly in a tie game. It had been so seemingly comfortable because we'd all been under the spell of Selby. But with a minute and a half remaining USC hit two free throws that gave them the lead and suddenly it was a very real possibility that we could lose this game and snap our home-court winning streak, now up to an unfathomable sixty-five games. And it appeared that would happen when Marcus Morris, our leading scorer, shot an air ball. Fortunately, it happened to land in his brother Markieff's hands, and he kicked it back out to Marcus. And then an interesting thing happened. Marcus had been our best player to this point in the season, and as juniors he and Markieff were the team's leaders. It was on his back to take the shot that would win or lose the game. But instead, as the clock ticked down, he deferred, passing to Selby on the opposite wing, who caught it, pass-faked to his right, and rose up to net a textbook-perfect three, putting KU up one with twenty-six seconds left.

When it happened, the headphones flew out of my ears because I shot up from my chair, sending it flying backward, howling, arms waving over my head, and nearly scared poor sleeping H to death in the other room. That there was more game to play hardly registered and is not worth mentioning, except to say that we did in fact hold the lead Selby gave us and win, because in that moment it felt like the rarest of things. The unprecedented hype surrounding Selby was not only justified, it was perhaps too low. Drop a game-high twenty-one and hit the winning three when your team is down two on national TV in your first game and maybe you're not just the best freshman in the country this year; maybe you're the best freshman in years. The AP writeup of the game begins: "Is it too soon to call him the legendary Josh Selby?" It's the stuff of two-out-bottom-of-the-ninth schoolyard fantasy, only it's real.

Only it's not.

What I didn't know in that moment, what no Kansas fan knew, what Josh Selby didn't even know, was that this would be the best game he would play in his one season at KU. It's almost tragic in retrospect, because it really was all downhill from there. He would have some solid and even good games, but he'd also play poorly and unremarkably for long stretches. Despite this, he would declare for the NBA draft and would be selected not first overall as projected in early mock drafts, not in the lottery, not even in the first round, where the money is guaranteed, but in the middle of the second round. He would play in a total of thirty-eight NBA games over the course of two seasons, averaging 2.2 points per game, before going to play in leagues in China, Croatia, Israel, Turkey, and Korea. (I'm not knocking the guy. He made a career out of doing something he loved, worked hard at, and had a gift for; we should all be so lucky.)

Selby's drop in play over the course of the season was mysterious, though it was surely due in part to a foot injury that would cause him to miss some games. But it was also because he couldn't possibly be as good as he made everyone believe he was on that cold morning in December, a performance somehow both illusory and real all at the same time. On that day he *was* the greatest player Kansas has recruited since Danny Manning. On that day he was an artist, he was so damn beautiful.

Yankee Town II

Mary Lease and Charles Langston arrived in Lawrence, Kansas, in 1882, set-tling in a home at 732 Alabama Street. The house no longer exists today—the addresses jump from 730 to 736—but it was situated in west Lawrence, or what is today known as Old West Lawrence, at the base of Mount Oread below the tall buildings of the University of Kansas, which opened in 1866. In the years after the Civil War, there was a great influx of migrants to Lawrence. Some were white farmers from neighboring midwestern states, some were German- and Scandinavian-born emigrants, some were "exo-dusters," the name given to freed people fleeing the terrorism and racism of the South after Reconstruction. All sought freedom, land, and opportunity in this "Eden on the Prairie." Added to the peoples who were already in town—New Englanders, formerly enslaved people, midwestern abolition-ists, and Native Americans—this made for an ethnically diverse population, if still overwhelmingly white in terms of skin color.

Though Lease and Langston were of mixed race—Indian, African, French—their darker skin tone meant that they were understood to be black. Each had been born free and they were part of the radical abolitionist aristocracy. They were among the first group of black students to attend Oberlin College and both became active in the abolitionist movement. Mary's first husband, Lewis Leary, was one of the twenty-one men to take part in John Brown's raid on Harpers Ferry, where he was shot and killed. Langston did not take part in the raid, though he was militant and took part in the well-known Oberlin-Wellington rescue, in which armed radicals prevented the return of an escaped slave to the South. Charles's youngest brother was John Mercer Langston, believed to be the first black man in the United States to hold office by popular vote when he was elected town-ship clerk of Brownhelm, Ohio, in 1855, and who was later the first black congressman in Virginia, a man mentioned in the same breath as Frederick Douglass and Booker T. Washington.

Both widowed, Langston and Lease married in 1869 and began a family in Lakeview, Kansas, the following year. One son was the namesake of the revolutionary Haitian general Jean-Jacques Dessalines and the other of a revolutionary closer to home, Nat Turner. A third child, Carrie, soon joined, and in 1882 the family moved to Lawrence, where Charles took part ownership in a successful grocery store on Massachusetts Street. In addition to his work at the store, he became a prominent man in the community, a regular hummingbird of civic activity. He was elected president of the Colored Benevolent Society, founded the Interstate Literary Society, edited the local black newspaper *Historic Times*, and was Grand Master of the black Masons of Kansas. He considered an appointment as minister to Liberia and a run for lieutenant governor, but ultimately preferred to keep his politics local.

But that such for-the-time racially progressive institutions existed or that a black man could be a small business owner should not obscure the fact that Lawrence was wildly racist and that the situation of the Langston-Lease family was hardly representative of life for most black people in Lawrence. While Charles and Mary lived in a white neighborhood in west Lawrence, "the masses of blacks crowded into diseased and deteriorating neighborhoods in the east 'Bottoms' on the swampish floodplain along the river, or in separate North Lawrence," writes Arnold Rampersad. The promise of Lawrence's free state history belied a counterhistory

> told wherever oldtime black settlers gathered . . . of the steady demeaning of Lawrence into a segregated town. The "exodusters"—the last, the biggest, and the poorest wave of black settlers—met an often hostile white population and an uneasy, ambivalent group of settled blacks. . . . [A]ll blacks were barred from formerly open churches, hotels, restaurants, and other social establishments. In one restaurant, blacks ate at the end of the lunch counter furthest from public view, blocked off additionally by a wooden barrier. At the theater they were restricted to the back of the balcony—"Coon Hill," or "The Buzzards' Roost," or "Nigger Heaven."

Despite Charles's prominence, there was little saved for his family when he died in 1892. The main asset was the house, but it was heavily mortgaged and men from the bank were regular figures to be avoided. But as it was all she had, Mary fought tooth and nail to keep it. It was in that home at 732 Alabama, in the predominantly white neighborhood near the university, that she would raise her daughter Carrie's child, a quiet, sensitive boy who would become one of the most important poets in the history of American letters, Langston Hughes.

Langston Hughes was born in Joplin, Missouri, in 1902, but with his parents separated and his mother's restless wandering he was sent to Lawrence to live with Mary. He writes in his autobiography *The Big Sea*:

> When I was in second grade, my grandmother took me to Lawrence
> [from nearby Topeka, where his mother was living at the time] to raise
> me. And I was unhappy for a long time, and very lonesome, living with
> my grandmother. Then it was that books began to happen to me, and
> I began to believe in nothing but books and the wonderful world in
> books—where if people suffered, they suffered in beautiful language, not
> in monosyllables, as we did in Kansas.

What a wonderful way to describe that initial glimpse of what would become his life's work. Not, "I read a lot of books"—books began to *happen* to him, like some natural phenomenon or stage of development occurring outside his will because he was one of the few destined for it.

Another refuge was the neighboring university. If Quantrill's Raid was the culminating and defining event of early Lawrence's turbulent history, the opening of the University of Kansas three years later, in September 1866, would shape its future. Amos Adams Lawrence, whose financial backing of the New England Emigrant Aid Company had been so generous and essential that the early settlers decided to name the town after him, also provided funding for the establishment of the university. KU eventually became the driving force of the town, but it wasn't initially thought to be so. Many of the city leaders were banking on the railroads turning Lawrence into a major shipping and transportation center, but the Union Pacific chose to locate its offices in Kansas City, and by the time Hughes was sneaking into the morgue at the university medical center to stare at cadavers and attending football and basketball games, the university had become the economic and cultural center of town. In fact, one of the ways Mary staved off the bank was by renting out a back room, or sometimes the entire house, to black KU students.

It needs to be said in a nonfootnoted way that KU was not, and is not, the only institution of higher learning in Lawrence. One of the oldest continually operating Native American schools in the country, the United States Indian Industrial Training School—later known as the Haskell Institute, Haskell Indian Junior College, and today as Haskell Indian Nations

University—was founded in 1884, part of the dark history of Indian board-
ing schools that attempted to forcibly acculturate American Indian youth
to white society by separating children from families, from their tribes,
from their religion, from their language, all in an effort to "save them from
themselves" and assimilate them into mainstream American—that is to say,
white—society. This has all changed over the last century, as the Native
leaders and students of Haskell have asserted their autonomy to shape the
institution and educational mission as they choose. Like the University of
Kansas, Haskell has a proud athletic history. Olympic gold medalist Billy
Mills went there, and perhaps the greatest athlete we have ever known, Jim
Thorpe, attended Haskell for a time and would periodically return to visit.
The fitness center is named in his honor. Haskell sent a number of players
to the NFL, and the football teams of the 1910s and 1920s are legendary,
holding their own against powerhouses like Notre Dame, Oklahoma, and
Boston College, and beating teams like Michigan State and their bigger
neighbor down the road, KU, before a crowd of eleven thousand people
in what was the first home night game in Kansas's history. Phog Allen even
coached the basketball team for a time a decade before he took over the position at KU, and James Naismith regularly went over to Haskell to watch
their team play. In his book on the history of basketball, Naismith lauds
the Haskell players' skill and agility and singles out one particular player for
high praise: "I have often said the most expert dribbler that I have ever seen
was Louis (Little Rabbit) Weller, of Haskell Institute."

Returning to Langston Hughes, in his autobiography he speaks of the
stories Mary would tell him as a boy about their family. "Through my
grandmother's stories always life moved, moved heroically toward an end.
Nobody ever cried in my grandmother's stories. They worked, or schemed,
or fought. But no crying. When my grandmother died, I didn't cry, either.
Something about my grandmother's stories (without her ever having said
so) taught me the uselessness of crying about anything." In August of 1910,
he and Mary traveled to Osawatomie, Kansas, for the dedication of the
John Brown Memorial Battlefield, where she was brought on stage by
Teddy Roosevelt and honored as the last surviving widow of Brown's
Harpers Ferry group. Rampersad writes:

> With the spirit of John Brown at hand, former president Theodore
> Roosevelt delivered his almost radical, celebrated "New Nationalism"
> speech, in which he stressed the primacy of humanity over property rights,
> and called for a powerful central government to curb big business and to
> reform the courts. For Mary Langston, the event was the last, long-delayed

honor of her life; for her grandson, only eight years old and largely unconscious of its meaning, it was an unacknowledged summing-up of the
radical heritage to which he belonged by birth, and a prophecy of his life
to come.

This was a heritage that Hughes became more and more conscious of in
time. There is an interesting account not mentioned in the autobiography
but detailed in Rampersad's *The Life of Langston Hughes* in which Hughes's
seventh-grade teacher made all the black students in class sit in a single row,
away from the white students. Young Langston made cards that read "Jim
Crow Row" and placed them on each black student's desk, an act of brave
defiance that would get him expelled, though he was later reinstated when
members of the black community rallied support. Many years later, well
after Hughes was one of the most famous poets in the world, the teacher
would recall the incident: "Of course . . . that stirred up all the nigger pu-
pils and they went home and told their mothers about it . . . he [Hughes]
was a bad combination—part Indian, part Nigra, and part white."
    When his grandmother died in 1914, the bank immediately seized the
house on Alabama Street and Hughes was taken away from the world of
the university to a black section of town near the train depot, where family
friends took him in. He recalled: "I used to walk down to the Santa Fe station and stare at the railroad tracks, because the railroad tracks ran to Chicago, and Chicago was the biggest town in the world to me, much talked
of by the people in Kansas." He stayed in Lawrence another year before
leaving to join his mother in Lincoln, Illinois. During that time, writes
Hughes, he sold the "*Appeal to Reason* for an old gentleman with a white
beard, who said his paper was trying to make a better world." The *Appeal*
was published out of Girard, Kansas, a tiny town in the southeastern part of
the state, and had amassed a circulation of half a million, the largest of any
socialist newspaper in the country. Hughes's job was short-lived, however,
as "the editor of the local daily told me to stop selling the *Appeal to Reason*,
because it was a radical sheet and would get colored folks in trouble." So
he sold the *Saturday Evening Post* and took a job cleaning bathrooms and
spittoons at a local hotel, mostly to raise money so he could go to the mov-
ies. But Lawrence was growing increasingly segregated. It was no longer
enough to be exiled to "nigger heaven"; now when he went to buy his
ticket, he was met by a sign stating "No Colored Admitted."
    The effect of living in such conditions appears most directly in Langston
Hughes's first novel, *Not Without Laughter.* Published in 1930, it is a semi-

autobiographical narrative about black life in Stanton, Kansas, a fictional-ized stand-in for Lawrence: "Besides, what was there in Stanton anyhow for a colored fellow to do except dig sewer ditches for a few cents an hour or maybe porter around a store for seven dollars a week. Colored men couldn't get many jobs in Stanton, and foreigners were coming in, taking away what little work they did have." The novel's protagonist, a young boy named Sandy, has an acute awareness of skin color, throughout the novel describing black people variously: "an ivory-white Negro child," "the tall good-looking yellow fellow," "a coal-colored little girl," "a slight, clay-colored brown boy," "the fat orange-colored man," "a biscuit-colored little girl," "a slender yellow boy," "a mahogany-brown boy," "a large Indian-brown woman," a "mustard-colored man," a "girl of maple-sugar brown," "a large sulphur-yellow woman," and a "tall young light-mulatto woman, with skin like old ivory." Doggedly, Hughes seems to want us not only to see race but to see the arbitrariness of racial codification. We are not one thing; we are everything. He sensed the mixed-raceness of everyone and lamented that so few others did. Surely influenced by growing up with his "Negro" grandmother (whom he describes as looking like an Indian) in a mostly white neighborhood, Hughes was in some sense always living between worlds. That slippery sense of in-betweenness accounts in part for his extreme sense of isolation as a boy, but also, I believe, his bottomless empathy as an artist.

Here I can't help but think of George Nash Walker, another son of Lawrence who knew all too well the social construction of racial differ-ence, someone who knew how much of it was about performance. Nash was born in 1873. He would leave Lawrence to pursue his dream of acting, signing on with touring vaudeville acts. In San Francisco, he met Bert Williams, and the two took in minstrel shows in which white men painted their faces black and performed stereotyped caricatures of blackness for large, paying audiences. It was offensive, of course, but they also sensed a lucrative business opportunity, and the two men started their own min-strel show where they were billed as "Two Real Coons." They were a hit and the Williams and Walker Company was hugely successful, touring the world, once even performing in Buckingham Palace. Later, in 1902, teaming with Paul Laurence Dunbar, they produced a musical called *In Dahomey*, which was the first all-black show to open on Broadway. Hughes recalled that his uncle Nat had taught Walker music "long before I was born." Walker would return to Lawrence periodically when he wasn't on tour. Hughes saw him only once:

I vaguely remember that he brought to Lawrence the first phonograph I had ever seen, when he came back ill to his mother at the end. He gave a concert at my aunt's church on the phonograph, playing records for the benefit of the church mortgage fund one night. I remember my mother said she had dinner with Nash Walker and his mother, while he was ill, and that they ate from plates with gold edging. Then Nash (George Walker, as he was known in the theater) died and there was a big funeral for him and I got my hand slapped for pointing at the flowers, because it was not polite for a child to point.

That was in 1911. George Nash Walker was thirty-eight years old, dead so young, a victim of prepenicillin syphilis. He was buried in Lawrence at Oak Hill Cemetery. Like Walker, Hughes sought to escape what was demeaning and stultifying about being black in Lawrence, though, of course, that was hardly unique to Kansas. Unlike Walker, he would not return frequently to visit friends and family; he would not come home to die. After leaving in 1915, Hughes returned to Lawrence only three times, once in 1932, when he read for a black sorority on campus; again in 1958, when he gave a reading accompanied by a jazz band; and finally in 1965, two years before his death, when he, perhaps the most famous poet in the country, would be feted by the university in whose shadows he had played while growing up in that house at 732 Alabama.

All Tragedy Is Local

Shortly after the new year, eighteen days into 2011, to be exact, I packed what I could of my belongings into my tiny Toyota Yaris and left San Francisco. My situation there was untenable. Despite working two jobs, I made little money, still had no insurance, was going further into debt, and couldn't afford a place of my own. So when H and I finally managed to break up, the last and most important tie keeping me there was severed, and I had no choice but to leave. Given the research I had been doing for my writing, I'd been steeped in Kansas history, and when it dawned on me that 2011 marked the state sesquicentennial of Kansas, that Kansas Day, as it is known, would be celebrated in just a few weeks, I knew where I would go. It gave me a purpose. It seemed only natural that I be there for whatever the hell happens when a state celebrates its 150 years of existence. I would return to Kansas.

A few days later there I was, back in Lawrence, eating barbeque at Buffalo Bob's Smokehouse on Mass Street—as Massachusetts Street is known in the local idiom—with Todd. It felt good being back home, the first time in two years, with my best and oldest friend. It was bitterly cold; a snowstorm had blanketed much of the region. We scarfed hickory smoked ribs and brisket, sipping light, watery beer. In those days our conversations mostly happened on the phone over the great distances between us, so it was nice to be in the same spot once again. We caught up on family, life, and work, and like always, we talked Kansas basketball. We were both pleasantly surprised by how well the team was doing, though we were troubled that our star freshman, Josh Selby, had been struggling almost ever since his spectacular debut the previous month against USC, a game that seemed likely to be known forever as "the Selby game." It was early in the

conference season, a long way to go, but we were looking like a title con-
tender. The television showed a game between undefeated number-one
Ohio State and number-twenty-two Illinois. We watched with interest
because we—that is to say, the University of Kansas men's basketball team
with whom Todd and I overidentify—were also undefeated, and ranked
number two. Soon Todd and I would make our way to Allen Fieldhouse
to watch our 'hawks take on a very good Texas squad. I was not expecting
to be able to attend the game—tickets were going for $250 on StubHub
when I checked back in San Francisco—but Todd's parents are season
ticket holders and had given us the generous gift of going to see a game
together, like old times.

Outside, Mass Street was trafficked by quick-paced families and individuals clad in various crimson-and-blue winter accessories—scarves, coats,
knitted caps—hurrying somewhere inside to warm up, trying to run a few
errands before the game. Here my fandom was commonplace. I was home,
back in Lawrence, where my obsession with Kansas basketball was not
the least bit odd, was merely a drop in the sea that is Jayhawk Nation. On
our way to Allen Fieldhouse we drove through Old West Lawrence, the
historic part of town, where homes have stood for over a century, some
few even having survived Quantrill's Raid. The entire university flanks the
western side of downtown, and in a few minutes we parked and made our
way past the statue of Phog Allen—which inexplicably manages to make
him look like an immortal basketball deity and an anonymous Munchkin-
land burgher at the same time—inside the fieldhouse.

We came early in part to watch the players warm up, but also because
I wanted to visit the Booth Family Hall of Athletics. I'd never been. Dr.
Naismith's original handwritten rules of basketball that the Booth family
had purchased the previous month would soon be housed there, but on
that day Todd and I walked around the hall, taking in the other exhibits
and memorabilia, the photographs and national championship trophies.

Forty-five minutes before tip, we took our seats and watched the team
warm up in their white shooting shirts and blue tearaway pants. Danny
Manning, KU legend and then an assistant coach, was out there in shorts
and a T-shirt, taking jumpers with the guys. As the fieldhouse continued
to fill with fans, the team went back to the locker room to meet with the
coaching staff one last time before returning around the thirty-minute mark
to stretch, run layup lines, and do half-speed defensive slide drills—mostly
just trying to get loose. At the other end of the court, Texas did the same.
Ball boys and girls rebounded jump shots and wiped down wet spots of

the floor, something Todd did when he was young. It used to make me so proud when I would catch sight of him while watching KU games. I'd point to the TV and tell whomever I was watching with: "That's my best friend, Todd."

We were seated halfway up, right across from the KU bench. There were no actual chairs or seats—just faded numbers on a heavily lacquered bench—and everyone packed in tight. We were all metaphorical family, and like our blood kin we are burdened by the same history. For first-timers used to their personal space it can feel awkward, but it helps account for why it is the best venue to watch a basketball game in in the country—there are this many people willing to endure discomfort and able to channel it into cheering for a team they worship. It was a major reason why at that point we had not lost a game at home in sixty-nine games. That's four years, an insane feat. As the clock wound down and game time neared, the band played "Hail to Old KU" and we wrapped our arms around each other, friend and stranger alike, and swayed, singing the words to the school song. When it was over, we went right into the chilling "Rock Chalk" chant. It starts deep and slow, almost Gregorian chant–like, and progressively builds so that by the end it's near frantic and everyone's shouting, "Rock Chalk Jayhawk KU!" as loud and as fast as they can until it becomes unsustainable and the crowd can only roar and clap its approval and readiness. I felt electric with the shiver of ritual.

Shortly before tipoff, as the teams huddled around the bench, the woman seated next to Todd told us that Thomas Robinson's mother had died the night before. Like many in the crowd who grew up listening to the broadcasts of legendary announcer Max Falkenstein, she wore a radio earpiece in one ear and seemed to have just received the information. Together Todd and I said, "Really?" though we thought she was confused. Robinson, whom everyone called T-Rob, had had an awful month, having lost his grandfather and grandmother in the past two weeks. We suspected this was what the woman was referring to, but then the PA announcer related the same unfathomable news, asking for a moment of silence in honor of Lisa Robinson. There was a murmur through the crowd. Grandmother, grandfather, and mother. All gone within three weeks. I was trying to process the information as the silent tribute segued into the national anthem when I saw him: T-Rob. He was not only present, he was suited up to play. I was shocked. Marcus Morris had his arm around him during the anthem, and I would realize later when I saw the photo on the cover of the *Lawrence Journal-World* that Marcus was crying.

Immediately after the anthem but prior to the announcement of the starting lineup, a pregame video played on the massive Jumbotron showing clips of great moments in KU basketball history set to a "Ride of the Valkyries"–style score that was impossible not to be 100 percent pumped up by. It was an absolutely bizarre flux of emotions. I didn't know what to do with myself. I might have cried or I might have ripped off my shirt and beaten my chest. Perhaps both at the same time. But there was no time to really think, because everything moved so quickly. It was as though a single frame of the tragic had been spliced into a film reel so committed to the nonexistence of such unpleasant considerations that we didn't know how to proceed. We felt its presence, but we certainly couldn't acknowledge it any more than we already had, because to do so would highlight the utter bizarreness that so many of us were there in the first place. The whole house of cards could collapse, but don't dwell on it—hey look, there's a game going on!

Riding high on the emotion, the guys came out on fire. We were up 8–0 practically before the UT starters had taken off their shooting shirts. After the under-sixteen timeout, Thomas checked into the game and the crowd went nuts. There was something awful about it, though. Our cheering for T-Rob was well intentioned, but it also felt like encouragement of an extreme kind of "playing through pain," whereby in its ugliest forms players are shamed, their toughness doubted, if they don't come back on the court after suffering an injury. But here it wasn't an athlete's twisted ankle. It was spiritual and existential. We were talking about his heart, his soul. *Why is he even here?* I kept wondering. "Why is he even here?" I said, but no one could hear because it was so loud.

Thomas had become an important player for us by that point in the season, first off the bench to relieve one of the Morris twins, and I remember hoping that Coach Self had nothing to do with the fact that he was playing in the featured game on CBS against a top-ten opponent expected to be our biggest competition in the league. I felt some relief later when I learned that Thomas asked to stay because, with so much of his family suddenly and irrevocably vanished, he wanted to be with his teammates, his "brothers." It was hard watching him play, though, wondering what was going through his mind. Understandably, he looked lost and distracted. The rest of the team, however, was on fire and we went up 18–3.

If we didn't actually have to stop playing and cheering for halftime—and thus have the dangerous potential to reflect on the sadness and strangeness of the moment—there is no chance we would have lost the game. But after the break we were sluggish, our energy spent, and Texas chipped away at our twelve-point lead. With thirteen minutes left, they cut it to five, finally taking the lead at the 10:38 mark when Cory Joseph banked in a twenty-five-foot prayer as the shot clock expired. At the under-four timeout it was all but over at 63–51. There was the restless frustration of fans feeling it slip away. "Do something!" shouted a guy in a ballcap in front of me. Others, like me, just silently took it in. Across the aisle was a family of Texas fans in burnt orange who respectfully and unobnoxiously clapped for their team, and I remember being glad no one gave them trouble.

With under a minute left, fans began to stream for the exit, but Todd and I preferred to sit and wallow in it, roost in the loss awhile. We were silent. Once most of our section cleared out, he moved a few rows away and stared down at the court despondently. The debris of fandom surrounded us: half-drunk cups of soda, torn newspaper, an errant dollop of nacho cheese, a forgotten ass cushion. The band played the school song, which now sounded funereal. There were others who stuck around. I couldn't tell if they were dejected like us, or whether it was some strategic let-them-fight-it-out acquiescence to the madness of the parking lot. The light darkened in the upper rafters. To me it all looked postapocalyptic, conjuring images of survivors after some great calamity, huddling around burning oil drums in a long-evacuated city, wondering if there are other survivors. Occasional words were exchanged. "Tough one today," a man said to a passing stranger. "Yeah, tough one all right."

Eventually we made our way to the car. As we drove the short distance to Todd's home in Kansas City, we listened to the postgame show on the radio and heard Coach Self say that Thomas had gotten the call at 11 p.m. the night before. The entire team, coaches and players, gathered to be with him, consoling Thomas through the night. It was a moving image and also made sense of the game. Riding the emotion of the situation to a strong start before succumbing to exhaustion in the second half, we played like a team that had been up all night. Coach Self wasn't upset the way he sometimes is. "You know, Pipe," he said, referring to former KU guard turned commentator Chris Piper, "sixty-nine is a heck of a lot of wins. We've done well to not lose a game here in four years."

Four years, I thought, and instantly my mind did a Terminator-style info scroll back to the last time we lost in Allen Fieldhouse. Of course I remembered. It had been early February of 2007 and I was living in Iowa City. There was a party that night I was supposed to attend, but I went down the street to the Vine and watched the game at the bar. It was the featured Saturday night matchup on ESPN and we let slip away a game we had controlled the entire time to a very good Texas A&M team led by Acie

Law. Afterward, I made my way to the party and tried not to let my foul mood ruin my chances with a girl I was trying to impress: H. Four years. I wondered what she was doing that moment in San Francisco. Driving past the snow-covered fields along K-10, it struck me that the entirety of our four-year relationship had been bookended by the last two KU home losses, a strange fact I didn't know what to do with.

Statehood

1.

The first celebration of what has come to be known as Kansas Day occurred in a small Paola schoolroom in 1877. It was 16 years after Kansas became the thirty-fourth star on the flag, 12 since the end of the Civil War, and 101 after the signing of the Declaration of Independence. The students would have known these dates; the class was US history. The teacher, L. G. A. Copley, thought it would be more interesting to study the history of a place on a significant anniversary, so one afternoon in late January he announced that it was Kansas Day and that they would devote the rest of the day to the study of the state they found themselves inhabiting. He would later move to Wichita and become the superintendent of schools and bring Kansas Day observance with him, even compiling a thirty-two-page booklet "giving the concise information about the state, the songs, and sample speeches suitable for the proper observance of the day." This is the language of the *150th Anniversary of Statehood* program I was given on a chilly Thursday, January 27, 2011, two days before Kansas Day.

I was in a large conference room at the Kansas State Historical Society in Topeka, waiting for the unveiling of the first day of issue stamp of Kansas, which was being released in honor of the sesquicentennial. It was five days after the Texas loss, and I had spent the days in between figuring out my Kansas Day strategy, this being the first of several events related to the celebration of Kansas's founding that I was trying to take in over the next three days. It was crowded. The attendees seemed to fall into one of three categories: government officials, media, and stamp obsessives. Of the latter, Orwell's description from eighty-three years ago still holds:

"Stamp-collectors are a strange silent fish-like breed, of all ages, but only of the male sex; women, apparently, fail to see the peculiar charm of gumming bits of coloured paper into albums." Actually, there was a fourth category to which I belonged, comprising people who were none of the above but had decided to come anyway, a motley crew of transients and weirdo lovers of history and spectacle. There were people in blue blazers and lanyards walking with extreme purpose. A nice-looking blonde woman in a blue winter jacket bearing the insignia of her ABC affiliate asked if she could sit next to me and I said sure. She kept looking over her shoulder toward the back of the room and asked why I was here. I told her I didn't know, that I don't even like stamps. "I'm trying to get a few seconds with the governor," she told me. "I can't find my cameraman."

The place went silent when the color guard appeared. They made their somber march toward the front of the room wearing blue Civil War throwback uniforms. Soon followed Sam Brownback, the newly sworn-in forty-sixth governor of Kansas. He looked almost uncannily like the actor Christopher McDonald. If, like me, you came of age at a certain nadir in American cinematic history, that would be Shooter McGavin from *Happy Gilmore*. He was all smiles and had an affability and charm that was captivating, but slowly started to feel insidious because its insistence betrayed how self-consciously crafted it was, how unnatural, how integral it was to the project of conveying a certain image of himself to the hoi polloi. This was just two weeks into his tenure as governor, but there were already troubling signs of what was to come. He had just presented a budget that would so drastically cut education in Kansas that the state would incur a $70 million fine from the federal government. Soon he would attack public sector workers' pensions, Planned Parenthood, and turn down a $31.5 million grant from the federal government to set up an insurance exchange as part of healthcare reform. That May he would defund the Kansas Arts Commission, making Kansas the first state in the country to eliminate its arts agency, and in years to come he would turn Kansas into a testing ground for experiments in radically conservative think tank fiscal policy, all the stuff that has made Kansas look like the meth-lab Winnebago of American democracy over the last decade.

But I didn't know all of that then, of course. I simply knew he was an antigovernment conservative who looked like Shooter McGavin from *Happy Gilmore*. Which is to say, I knew enough to find his remarks that afternoon a bit peculiar, because he kept listing the progressive accomplishments of the state, from his thunderous opening salvo—"The Civil War started in Kansas because the early settlers couldn't tolerate the idea of another human being in bondage"—through giving women the right to vote before most of the country, desegregation, on up to the present, about which he touted all the renewable energy initiatives and Kansas's efforts to "go green." Of course, all of this paled to the irony that he was even there at all, celebrating, as he was, the unveiling of a stamp issued by a federal government monopoly in a building constructed at taxpayers' expense that he would soon work ardently and successfully to cut funding to.

Eventually he stopped telling us how great we were, and with the help of an official from the United States Postal Service he presented an enlarged version of the stamp, propped up on a wooden support. It was a pretty sky blue and wheat yellow with a windmill in the foreground and five wind turbines in the distance. We clapped and oohed. Brownback said, "God bless America," and finished by leading us in the singing of "Home on the Range," the first of twelve renditions I would participate in over the next few days.

Afterward, we filed into the main lobby of the State Historical Society, where there were tables set up for people to purchase the new stamp as well as the first day of issue cover that carried a notarized seal. I bought a few sheets of stamps and then waited in a much longer line to get the first day of issue signed by the governor. When I finally got to Brownback, one of his toady handlers was whispering in his ear, trying to get him to speed things along. I put my first day cover down and he signed it without looking up. I didn't really know what to say. I asked him how he felt, which made him look up, smiling, staring both right at and through me with eyes that seemed to almost sparkle. "I feel great," he said.

2.

In the north-central plains of Kansas, in a town called Smith County, close to the Nebraska border and to the geographic center of the lower forty-eight states, sits a log cabin that has been preserved and maintained because it once belonged to a man named Brewster Higley. Approximately one hundred visitors come each month to enter their names in the logbook and take in the site, perhaps stopping by on their way to the closest competing tourist attraction: the World's Largest Ball of Twine, Cawker City, Kansas.

Higley would have had no sense that a hundred years after his death his home would be a destination. For him it had been a refuge from a life he wanted to leave behind. He arrived in Smith County in 1871, settling near the banks of Beaver Creek. For a time he lived in a dugout—that is, in the ground, essentially—until he could build a cabin. He had come from Ohio, where he'd been an otolaryngologist and a real trailblazer of nuptial discord, his marriage record at least a hundred years ahead of its time. Married five times, it was his fourth wife, apparently quite the harridan, who seems to have driven him—or provided a needed excuse—to flee his home and children, setting off to homestead in Kansas. You can detect a hint of the instability that would drive him to do such a thing in the one photo I've seen of him. He is dressed in a dark suit, his hair combed, his beard mostly trimmed, a stylish concatenated fob hanging meticulously from a vest pocket. But like *American Gothic*, the more you look at it the more Lynchian things become. His is a gentility barely masking an igneous craze—you can see it in the eyes—that drove frontier men to do both the courageous and horrific things they did. *Don't push me*, he seems to be uttering under his breath through the frozen, placid calm of his expression. To me, he looks like he would have been a good eater were he a member of the Donner Party.

But moving to Smith County provided the calm and solitude he seems to have desired. There he pursued his drinking and doctoring, an early avatar of a now familiar Old West type in popular film and literature: pioneer docs, whose professional "training" and proximity to alcohol and other strange elixirs gives them a touch of madness that makes them either benignly dreamy poets or scary-crazy mountain terrorists. Fortunately for his neighbors, Higley was the former. In fact, it was one of Higley's poems that would account for his posthumous semifame. The poem was called· "The Western Home," and it was discovered by a man named Trube Reese, who had taken a friend maimed by gunshot to see Higley. As Higley did whatever an ear, nose, and throat doctor in 1873 did to treat a gunshot victim, Reese waited in another room, perusing Higley's bookshelf. When he opened one volume, a page of longhand slipped from the leaves and fell to the floor.

"The Western Home" is a paean to place, celebrating the new land to which Higley had moved, the new land he had come to love. He admires the wildflowers and antelope. He gives shoutouts to the nearby rivers. He appreciates the white bluffs and wandering buffalo. But this exalted celebration of the land belies what is actually a eulogy for a place that was rapidly changing. It was written in 1873, a few years into the decade of mass slaughtering of the great buffalo herds, first for profit by hunters and then by the government in a systematic effort to eliminate the native food supply so that the Plains Indians would leave their land, a successful strategy that

left rotting carcasses along the prairie as the number of buffalo plummeted from seventy-five million to near extinction by 1890.

The antelope would definitively be gone soon, too. Those wildflowers and the native grasslands were being dug up and plowed under for planting wheat and corn. Some of this was under way in Higley's time, some of it would occur soon thereafter, and it is part of what gives the poem's otherwise joyous tone a sad undercurrent.

While Ol' Trube was no literary critic,* he was taken with "The Western Home" and encouraged Higley to publish it, which he soon did in the local Smith County *Pioneer*. Later that year, Higley took it to a former Civil War bugler named Dan Kelley, who came up with a melody and then passed it on to his soon-to-be father-in-law John Harlan, a local judge and patriarch of a Partridge Family–style music group called the Harlan Brothers Orchestra. Harlan decided it needed a chorus and, after adding one, his band of family members performed the song for the first time in public at

---

*The poem includes such prosody anvils as: "On the banks of the Beaver, where seldom if ever / Any poisonous herbage doth grow" and "Where life streams with buoyancy flow."

a dance, and from then on it would become a local staple throughout the Solomon Valley.

Thirty-five years later, in 1908, the great ethnomusicologist John Lomax, while compiling songs for his first book, *Cowboy Songs and Frontier Ballads*, came across a black saloonkeeper in San Antonio who sang a version of the song. He called it "Home on the Range," a line that never appears in the original Higley poem.

The story of "Home on the Range" is pure folk song. Though birthed by a single hand, it would not have escaped the folds of Brewster Higley's book collection, let alone become what it is today—one of the most American of songs, *the* anthem of the pioneering West—had not thousands of other people had a hand in shaping it, the song genetically mutating a little each time a passing-through cowboy or frontiersman heard it and carried it with him somewhere else, occasionally making a change, accidentally or not—that slow evolution of song leading to a hundred different renditions.

The chorus that the Harlan Brothers Orchestra added to Higley's poem was: "A home, a home / Where the deer and the antelope play, / Where never is heard a discouraging word / And the sky is not cloudy all day." Lines 2–4, the familiar verse about antelope and cloudy skies, were all in Higley's poem, though Harlan made the subtly important improvement on Higley's clunky "clouded," changing it to "cloudy." The important alteration is that first line, that celebratory declarative repetition that renders an exclamation point unnecessary: "A home, a home." It begs to be returned to, sung again. The Harlans knew this, placing the chorus after the first, fourth, and final of Higley's six stanzas. The addition of that single line, as well as the structural improvement of adding a chorus, was the essential change that would eventually lead to the well-known, repeatable-to-the-point-of-madness chorus that the black saloonkeeper sang for John Lomax all those years later: "Home, home on the range / Where the deer and the antelope play / Where seldom is heard a discouraging word / And the skies are not cloudy all day."

The thirty-five-year journey taken to arrive at this point is impossible to trace, every permutation from Harlan to the unnamed man in San Antonio and whomever he learned it from. But one possible clue comes from the Higley original. While the phrase "home on the range" never appears in "The Western Home," Higley does use the word *range* in the second-to-last line of the poem: "I would not exchange my home here to range." It is possible that the switch in usage of *range* from verb to noun worked its way into the chorus as part of a more macro-level ironing out of Higley's capricious sense of metrics over the years, the communal American effort to save the poor man from his own ear. But he had done something right, because Higley's poem exists in chrysalis-like near total in the 1908 version. The only new addition is this stanza that makes explicit who this song was written for: "The red man was pressed from this part of the West, / He's likely no more to return / To the banks of the Red River where seldom if ever / Their flickering campfire burns."

However, this was only one version of what were surely dozens of takes on the song. In fact, Lomax came upon another version that, he notes, "should be sung in an entirely different spirit." As opposed to the slow, plaintive nostalgia of the saloonkeeper's version, this second version should be sung "with a rollicking lilt" and it's not hard to see why, as this version turns "Home on the Range" into outlaw country: "Oh, give me a jail, where I can get bail, / If under the shining sun; / I'll wake with the dawn, I'll chase the wild fawn, / I'll ride with my saddle and gun." Such is the protean nature of folk songs that are of, by, and for the people who keep it alive by singing it and sharing it with someone else, making additions peculiar to time and place. In this way it belonged to everyone, which is a wonderful thing that becomes wonderfully complicated when someone decides he or she is the rightful owner of the song.

Higley, Kelley, or Harlan never copyrighted the song, and it is uncertain whether Higley ever knew the song was much more than a hit at local barn dances. But by the time Higley died in 1911, the year after Lomax's *Cowboy Songs and Frontier Ballads* was published, the song was starting to have a far-reaching impact. As opposed to a bunch of people knowing the song essentially in isolation, sheet music began to appear for several arrangements, and with the development of radio in the 1920s the song became a meme, moving from a regional hit to a national pop culture phenomenon. On the eve of his election in 1932, FDR claimed it was his favorite song. That was likely a calculated bit of pandering to the middle of the country from an East Coast elite, but that he chose "Home on the Range" attests to the reverence large swaths of the population held for it.

The song had been in the public domain for sixty years when, in 1934, a couple from Arizona named Goodwin sued NBC and scores of publishing houses for copyright infringement. The Goodwins claimed they had written the song "My Arizona Home" thirty years earlier. The song was yanked from the air while the lawsuit was adjudicated. The defendants hired an investigator named Samuel Moanfeldt to determine the song's origins.

One can imagine—or, to be more accurate, rather, can't imagine—what Moanfeldt's journey must have been like. Everywhere he went, he found different incarnations of the song: "My Colorado Home," "My Texas Home," etc. But eventually he picked up the scent and enough people told him about this place called Smith County, Kansas. People must have really wanted the song back on the air, because Moanfeldt was receiving letters to aid his investigation, one of which was from a woman who remembered that the song had originally appeared as a poem in the Smith County *Pioneer.* When he arrived, he was put in touch with Trube Reese, who was still alive. Reese told Moanfeldt the story of how he found the poem stuffed inside of one of Higley's books. The final piece of evidence came when he contacted Cal Harlan, one of the original Harlan Brothers Orchestra members. According to Mary Norris, the great-great-great-granddaughter of John Harlan, Cal was eighty-six and nearly blind, but when Moanfeldt asked him if he could play the song, he strummed his guitar and sang the 1873 version word for word, note for note. Moanfeldt recorded him and returned to New York with evidence and affidavits that settled the suit, and "Home on the Range" returned to the radio, where scores of artists would cover it over the years. In 1947 Kansas would adopt it as the state song, claiming its own ownership of Higley's poem.

In the early 1960s, while finishing high school and preparing to attend the University of Kentucky, my mother was a folk singer in a locally popular band called the Tavernier Trio. They played widely throughout central Kentucky, even once opening for Peter, Paul and Mary. Their name was appropriate, playing as they did most often in bars for beer and the contents of a passed hat. They wrote no songs of their own, relying either on interpretations of traditional folk standards or covers of contemporary artists who were part of the period's popular folk revival. They considered making a go of it nationally, but there was college, creative differences, the usual internecine band conflict, so they broke up. My mother fell out of touch with her bandmates, but she continued to play for fun.

Years later, when we had left Kansas for Connecticut, she taught me a few chords and I began writing my own songs. We would often play together, as we still do to this day, the classics from her days as a Tavernier: "Freight Train," "Saint James Infirmary," "Scotch and Soda," "The Seine," "This Land is Your Land," "Nobody Knows You When You're Down and Out," "Don't Think Twice, It's All Right," etc, etc. My stepfather, who was a generation older than my mom, often took in these "hootenannies"—as my mother persists in calling them—with a bemused smile. As a man who grew up on a farm in rural Kansas, he didn't know most of the songs my mom played, but he patiently waited for the moment when she would strum the opening G chord of "Home on the Range." This was

the signal that we had come to the end of the night and would soon retire, and my stepfather would suddenly burst forth in wonderfully joyous, atonal song. We were all a little lonesome for our past lives in Kansas in those days, and singing the song together we'd come to feel a little less so, as one should when singing a good song.

3.

On a wall inside the state capitol, on the second-floor rotunda, is a mural every publicly educated schoolchild in Kansas is familiar with. There are many paintings at the capitol, but this is the one each field trip stops to see and take pictures of before going up inside the dome. *The Tragic Prelude* was painted between 1938 and 1940 by John Steuart Curry, who, along with Thomas Hart Benton and Grant Wood, is one of the triumvirate of great American painters of Regionalism. The mural, one of three Curry was commissioned to produce for the capitol, shows John Brown spreading his arms wide, a bible in one hand and a rifle in the other. Both hands are bloody and behind him are warring and dead free state and proslavery fighters, as well as a tornado and smoke and fire. When Curry presented it to the legislative committee that oversaw the project, they were not

pleased. John Brown has always been a divisive character for Kansans, some thinking him a saint and others an insane terrorist, and the committee did not think it proper to celebrate him in the capitol. They weren't crazy about the tornado either, apparently, thinking bad weather reflected poorly on the state image. (The film version of *The Wizard of Oz* had just come out in 1939 and Kansans were a bit touchy about cyclones.) Curry tried to explain his intent, but he grew angry with the committee's obstinacy and diffidence and stormed out, refusing to sign the painting.

    I went to see the painting for the first time since I was a boy the day after I attended the stamp ceremony at the State Historical Society. I tried to take pictures of it, but the glint of light and reflection kept ruining the shot, so I bought a magnet and mug of the painting in the gift shop instead and then headed outside, where the celebration of Kansas Day at the capitol was set to take place. When I arrived, I found a modest crowd, not nearly the turnout I had anticipated. Yes, it was Friday and thus a work day, but I had expected delegations from every grade school in the state, sick-day truancy from workers with an interest in history or a modicum of state pride. Perhaps the following day's basketball game between Kansas and Kansas State—which I was looking forward to attending myself, thanks to my stepsister kindly giving me her ticket—was more important and pressing to most than Kansas Day at the capitol. Whatever the case, most people present that day were there in some official capacity. There was the Kansas National Guard and the Kansas Highway Patrol. There was the 35th Infantry Division Band, which played "The Star-Spangled Banner" to open the ceremony, and Second Battalion, 130th Field Artillery, which offered a cannon salute at the close. So too were tribal chairs and representatives of the Kaw Nation, the Iowa, the Kickapoo, the Prairie Band Potawatomi, and the Sac & Fox Nation. The then poet laureate of Kansas, Caryn Mirriam-Goldberg, recited a poem titled "Celebrate This Kansas." The majority-minority bigwigs of the state legislature all made the same forgettable remarks, as did a still-enthusiastic Governor Brownback, whose speech was made a touch more compelling by the fact that he did so while being pummeled by a suddenly gusty flag at his flank, somehow shrugging off Old Glory's advances with aplomb. There were also reenactors. Standing on stage beside Brownback were George and Diane Bernheimer, who on this day were better known as Charles and Sarah Robinson, the first gubernatorial couple of Kansas.

I stood in the crowd next to a man who was also dressed in period costume. He was middle-aged, with a long beard (real, I'm confident), brown trousers, and a gray hat. He shook his head, looking at the Charles Robinson reenactor posing for pictures, a man he referred to aloud as "that grand terrorist." For a brief second I feared I was standing next to an audience plant and was about to be sucked into some prescripted Bleeding Kansas shootout at the capitol, but when I inquired, this man told me he was there "unofficially." On the regional reenactment circuit, which is quite lively in Kansas and Missouri, he kept busy, was quite in demand, in fact, playing a Bleeding Kansas–era Kansan named Cyrus K. Holliday. I introduced myself and he said his real name was Ed, but then he turned back into Cyrus and mounted an impassioned and grandiloquent defense of slavery, while highlighting all the atrocities committed by the free state side that never get talked about.* When he had finally worked it out of his system, he could only stare at the Charles Robinson reenactor in the distance and offer a resigned, melancholic: "But to the victor goes the speechifying."

All of this happened after the ceremony had officially ended and everyone was standing around or leaving. Governor Brownback came down off the stage and made his way through the crowd, shaking hands, trading a

---

*I looked up Cyrus K. Holliday after my encounter with Ed and learned he was a railroad mogul who helped found Topeka and used his position as president of Atchison, Topeka & Santa Fe Railway to profit as he facilitated the population of the western part of the state. Ed seemed adamant that his character Cyrus was proslavery, but afterward I found no mention of that. In fact, he was adjutant general of Kansas for the Union during the Civil War, and I even found him listed as a free state candidate of the third district for the House in the supplementary election of 1855. Ed struck me as quite method about his reenacting process, so it seems an unlikely mistake for him to make, but the confusion remains a mystery.

few words. Soon he came our way and I could tell he had no recollection of me from the previous day's stamp ceremony. Then he saw Cyrus/Ed standing next to me in costume and said hello.

"Well, hello there, Governor," Cyrus/Ed said in a theatrically grizzled voice, hopping to with a military salute. I saw the amiable confusion on Brownback's face—the Charles Robinson reenactor he had expected, but who the hell was this outlier and what did he want?—and from this moment forward neither man would be able to decide whether to engage the other as if it was 1858 or 2011. For a while they carried on a bizarre exchange that nearly dissolved the space-time continuum, but finally the performance broke down and Cyrus/Ed asked in what I assumed to be his actual speaking voice, "Do you remember me?"

"I'm sorry, but I don't," said the governor.

"I drove you around for a while in the early nineties."

Brownback went pensive, but still couldn't seem to recall, so Cyrus/Ed clarified: "I was the bus driver who argued with everyone, but I'm behaving myself today." This still couldn't quite jog the governor's memory and Ed turned back into Cyrus and said: "Today I'm Cyrus Holliday, proslavery Kansan!"

"Ah," said Governor Brownback, just kindly nodding until one of his handlers pulled him away.

4.

Selected Notes, Observations, and Musings from KU–KSU Game, January 29, 2011:

- Catch glimpse of T-Rob in the tunnel with rest of team before game, waiting to run out. Fans gather around. Girl calls out his name, says, "I love you, Thomas." He looks up, then back down at the floor, hopping in place a little
- Seats better, closer than Texas game. Baseline view of action
- Pregame pageantry: PA announcer acknowledging Kansas Day, singing of "Home on the Range," the national anthem, and the alma mater
- Girl in white tank undershirt w/ *#0* and *Robinson* Sharpie'd on the back
- Crowd booing KSU furiously
- Fan holds sign with purple wildcat frowning: *From #3 to NIT*
- Q: # of times Erin Andrews sexually harassed by male college students while sideline reporting over the years?
- Intro video is absurdly inspiring: "The Glory, the Power, the History, the Legends!" Feel ready to storm Omaha Beach
- T-Rob subs in at 16:30. Crowd stands, roars. Misses first three shots, incl. dunk that would have taken off the rim had it gone in
- Under sixteen timeout: KU up 10–2
- Crowd apeshit
- Neighbor-fan staring at me as I write in notebook
- Under four: 29–17
- Similar to TX game—up big early, letting State creep back in
- Neighbor-fan finally asks what I'm writing. My answer: It's Kansas Day. I want to remember this. He nods, lets me be
- Frank Martin looks like man who's dedicated life to trying to will laser beams to shoot from his eyes
- Halftime: 37–20
- Halftime: retiring of Wayne Simien's jersey. Max Falkenstein handles the intro. Big Dub's speech: starts nice, pleasant, what you'd

expect. Then takes really religious turn. Says more than points and rebounds wants to be remembered as man transformed by JC. Begins to cry. Says he's laying his jersey at feet of "He Who Has Died on the Cross." People go wild. Here little separation b/w church and b-ball. Same thing really

- Second half: come out strong, increase lead
- Under sixteen: 49–26
- T-Rob gets in groove, hitting three in a row, last of which an eighteen-footer
- Crowd apeshit
- Somebody keeps farting
- Student holding up sign BUCKET but I misread as BECKETT. Possible story idea: Samuel B attends a basketball game. What would he make of this spectacle?
- Selby: first good game in while
- Marcus: solid and steady, as always
- Idiots behind me talking through entire game
- 16,400 mostly white fans shouting at mostly black players. Strange OK-ness of white men chastising black men in sporting arenas. Weird license. Can scream whatever they want
- 6:30 left: 74–45
- Game romp, crowd apeshit
- T-Rob gets T after monster dunk (hanging on rim)
- Lots of T-Rob-centric signs: "Here's to you Mrs. Robinson"
- "Rock Chalk" starts under two min, fans waving the wheat
- T-Rob star of game: seventeen and nine boards
- One min left: Self pulls four starters out. Immediately after calls timeout so T-Rob can walk off court alone. Crowd stands. Teammates stand, clapping, then circle around him, hugging him. Crying, all of us
- Final: 90–66

5.

The Wonderful Wizard of Oz was written in 1900. There is debate about the seemingly allegorical nature of the book. Many see it as an apologue of the bimetallism debates of the 1890s. The People's Party, the capital-*P* Populists, was a true grassroots, bottom–up movement, made up mostly of farmers, which swept across parts of the South, Midwest, and West in the 1890s and made significant gains at the state and national level. Some of what the Populists proposed, deemed too radical at the time, would be enacted by Progressive Era Republicans who had derided it as utopian fancy only years before: a graduated income tax, savings banks, direct election of senators, a more flexible currency. But the Populists also wanted the government to own and operate the railroads and telephone, as they did the postal service, in the interest of the people, as they were public necessities, but that was taking things too far for the establishment politicians. The People's Party faced a tough decision, like so many third parties, whether to remain autonomous or to join a major party in the hopes of influencing it. Ultimately, they fused with the Democrats in 1896, delivering the Populist vote to William Jennings Bryan and a Democratic Party that took up exactly one very small and single plank of the People's Party platform (the free coinage of silver) and thus was born Bryan's famous "Cross of Gold" speech. This was the end of the party. Some gave up politics, some went to one of the major parties. Many became socialists.

In any case, one exegesis posits the *Wizard of Oz* as a political allegory of the Populists. "Follow the yellow brick road" is the Republican plea to uphold the gold standard, Bryan is the cowardly lion on his way to see the wizard (the president), the wicked witches are the coastal money powers of the East and West. And tornado-plagued Kansas is the source of this unlikely insurgent rebellion.

I have never read the book. Like most, I've watched the movie, but it had probably been fifteen years since I had seen it. Earlier in the day I watched Kansas defeat Kansas State in Allen Fieldhouse, and afterward I made the twenty-minute drive to Topeka for this nightcap to my Kansas Day experience. There I was in the last hours of Kansas Day, back at the State Historical Museum, stretched out on the floor of a room surrounded by families for a screening of the film that, more than anything, seems to mean Kansas to the rest of the country. When we moved to Connecticut, it was the only thing my classmates could think to talk to me about after they asked where I moved from. "Hey, Milward. Say hi to Dorothy for me." It was either that or something about basketball. Near the end of the film I heard a line that nicely summed up how I feel about Kansas, which is maybe how many of us feel about the places we're from or have come of age in. Dorothy has just returned to Kansas after her adventures in Oz, and, remembering that garish dreamscape, she says: "Some of it wasn't very nice, but most of it was beautiful."

F.O.E.

The next day, I made my way over to Johnny's West. The original Johnny's is downtown, just over the bridge on the north side of the Kaw River, and is an institution in Lawrence. It's been there since 1953 and has a charming, no-frills ruggedness that is very different from where I was sitting, a strip mall bar in the far western part of Lawrence. But I decided to go there because it was close to my stepsister's house. Since arriving from San Francisco I had been bouncing back and forth between her guestroom in Lawrence and Todd's basement in Kansas City.

Business was slow. The only other customers in the entire restaurant were three men, all black, and we each occupied a seat at the bar. There were the ubiquitous massive flat-screens hitting the eye from every angle. We sat scattered, with two or three empty chairs between us, looking up at a TV showing the Lakers and Celtics game. I listened as the others discussed KU's domination of our rival K-State and the triumphant play of Thomas Robinson. Lawrence had become obsessed with T-Rob's story. There were proclamations of solidarity from the team and fans alike, even a push to raise money for Thomas and his nine-year-old sister, Jayla, who lived in DC. She had been the one to call and inform him about their mother that night before the Texas game because the other adults in his life, Thomas and Jayla's grandparents, had both died in the previous few weeks. Lisa Robinson was only thirty-seven; the cause of death: heart attack. The Morris twins' mother, Angel, was reportedly close to Lisa and had vocally assumed the role of surrogate mother. There was also the recent murder of Josh Selby's childhood friend back in Baltimore, and the team was coming together to unite against the tragic, real-life forces that kept encroaching on basketball.

The players adopted F.O.E.—Family Over Everything—as their mantra and wrote it on their sneakers and repeated it to the reporters who continued to ask how they were handling all this. "We're a family and it's us against the world," the players said, and they channeled their collective energy into basketball to avoid the overwhelming sadness of the real world. This, we fans desperately wanted to believe, was a healthy way of coping with loss. It invested us even more in the game, not that we needed it, and did so safely because it did not raise the real question: Must the game, in fact, go on?

All of this made me more than a little uncomfortable. The day before, after I stood with everyone else inside Allen Fieldhouse to give Thomas a standing ovation as he left the floor, I thought of him running through the tunnel waving to the crowd, then going to the locker room to give interviews where he would be asked to talk about *what was going through your head when . . .* and *what does it feel like to have all this support from the community*, and then having to go back to his dorm room and reencounter the feeling of being orphaned three times over in the span of three weeks—that was when I hated this self-congratulatory healing-through-sports attitude that seemed to have taken over all of us.

Another recent troubling aspect of the story was the from-the-beginning assumption that Thomas and Jayla did not have a father. That was when the push to raise money began and ideas were floated about bringing his sister to Lawrence where she could be cared for by Thomas and, by proxy, all of us. An ugly paternalism was surfacing. It would take a Jayhawk village to raise this child, and we were thrilled to have asked ourselves to take on this responsibility, so long as the unspoken condition be met: the season must continue. But then it turned out that, while Thomas does not have a relationship with his biological father, Jayla has a father, alive and well, who had no intention of letting his daughter travel to Lawrence, and then we all felt a little disappointed. Family Over Everything. Though we fans persisted in believing otherwise, it strikes me now how exclusionary that motto actually was. We wanted to believe we were members of the family, but we were not. We were supporters, we were fans. *This is our thing, our grief, our loss*, the team seemed to be telling us. *Not yours.*

Occasionally, some auto-flagellation streak causes me to scroll through the chat-board commentary of the KU basketball websites I frequent. It's interesting to note how the online community polices itself and what it lets itself get away with. The familiar, cowardly, petty ugliness wrought by anonymous trolling—sometimes subtly, or not so subtly, racist in nature—is mostly fair game as long as it is about the game itself, but when any kind of real-world commentary, especially political, seeps into postings there is instantaneous backlash. They seem to want the game to exist outside of time and current affairs. *You're ruining this for me,* is the subtext. *Go somewhere else—I'm trying to escape all that!* I don't mean to suggest that this is foreign to me; I've felt the same thing myself at times. I remember turning on the television to watch the start of the 2003 NCAA tournament only to have the coverage periodically interrupted by national news correspondents reporting that our military was invading Iraq. And while this was something I had felt passionately about for months as the drumbeat for war grew louder, in that moment what I felt more than anger or sadness was a kind of annoyance that the world wouldn't let me remain in an ignorant cocoon of basketball for the next three weeks. And then I felt ashamed for feeling that way. It's staggering sometimes to consider the sheer number of things we have to consciously not think about in order to make the sport mean as much as it does to us.

But the real world has a way of encroaching on the game whether fans want it to or not, and it's way worse, of course, when the athletes themselves bring the world outside of sports into the arena in any way that is not about patriotism or preserving the status quo. That's when the real vitriol comes out, and it's not pretty. Think of Muhammad Ali refusing to fight in Vietnam and calling for solidarity with the Vietnamese, or John Carlos and Tommie Smith raising the Black Power fist at the 1968 Olympics. They suffered serious consequences for those actions, and there are many other examples. More recently, think of the response to NBA players like LeBron James speaking out social issues, and of course, Colin Kaepernick, blackballed from the NFL for taking a knee during the national anthem to protest racial injustice and oppression.

The stick-to-sports/shut-up-and-dribble crowd have come to the game to escape and don't want to ask or answer difficult questions not related to the game. They are not allowed to be made uncomfortable. They are allowed to express their own political opinions, if they feel like it, but athletes are not, especially not when the game is about to start. Part of me even understands. It's tempting as all hell, that desire to love the game in a particular and unquestioned way, isolated from the complexities of the world outside the sport and willfully oblivious and unquestioning of the complexities of the world inside the sport. But just imagine if sports, which has the ability to be a great uniter of people, could actually be a venue in which we could have these kinds of conversations and debates about social issues and politics, the great dividers of our time. I want to believe that and

yet I also know how incredibly difficult that is. The issues and tensions surrounding the reaction to Lisa Robinson's death were just the sorts of things
I wanted to talk to my barmates about, but I didn't know how to start that
conversation with strangers. So we stuck to what was safe and easy to talk
about: basketball and only basketball.

After we discussed the upcoming road swing at Texas Tech and Nebraska, the man who was doing most of the talking—I would get his name
but forget it before I could write it down—changed the subject, asking
what I did for a living. I didn't tell him I was unemployed and exploiting
the kindness of friends and family who were housing and feeding me. I told
him I wrote, and it seemed to intrigue him. He left his seat at the end of
the bar near the bathroom and took the seat next to me. He wore a fishing hat and looked uncannily like a slightly graying, middle-aged Method
Man, which was fitting because he began telling me about how he used to
be a rapper back in the eighties and how he had been big on the Wichita
scene. I asked what they were about, his raps. He told me one was a public service announcement he wrote to urge people to get tested for HIV.
Without prompting he went right into performing it, struggling to recall
his words initially before finding his flow, a deliberate and slow enunciation
of a sometimes too-obvious rhyme that sounded to my dilettantish ears like
what I had come to think of as early rap. It was good and I told him so. I
asked if he ever recorded an album and he shook his head.

A few minutes later, when he asked me what I write about, I didn't tell
him about the book of short fiction I was writing. I told him I was working
on a nonfiction book about basketball, and KU basketball in particular. I
don't know exactly why I said this because I wasn't writing this book then.
I think part of it was a bluff, something said to a stranger I would never see
again simply to see how it tasted in my mouth. And yet there was something earnest about the declaration as well. I wasn't writing a book about
basketball yet, but I sure as hell was thinking a lot about the game and my
relationship to it. I was in the germinal stages—the sexy ideas phase of a
potential book project—and that was the first time I had consciously artic-
ulated the intent of all my note-taking and rumination on the sport since
the Northern Iowa loss the spring before. It was starting to come together
in my head, though it would take many more years for me to actualize
anything of substance on the page.

"What about basketball?" my neighbor asked.

I told him: "I want to know why I care about it as much as I do."

What I didn't say was that I wanted to know this because the obsession
sometimes embarrasses me, that it feels like a way to avoid thinking about

other, more important or harder things. But I also didn't say that I think the game is beautiful and that I wanted to try and talk about that beauty in a way that would give pause to someone who thinks sports are uninteresting and meaningless. I didn't tell him I had competing theses that were constantly undermining each other.

"You live here?" he said.

"Not anymore," I said, "but I grew up here."

"There's your answer," he said, and took another sip from his pint.

"Gonna be a short goddamn book," said one of the other men, and we were all laughing.

Home

Sometimes I forget that for all my love of Lawrence and identification as a Kansan I was actually born in Kentucky, in Lexington's Central Baptist Hospital, in late November of 1979. A few years ago my mother had to intervene to correct me when she saw that the bio of one of my books listed me as a native of Lawrence, Kansas, not Lexington. My relationship to my birth town has always been complex. I have few memories of the time my mother and father were married and we lived together as a family in Lexington, those first three years of my life, before they divorced. While Lexington was somewhere I returned to often over the years, up until recently it was the place I thought of not so much as home but as the place where a lot of my family lives, which simultaneously breeds a fondness for the city and a strong sense of otherness, an odd feeling of being somewhere incredibly familiar that is also different, strange, and thus perhaps not quite really home. All of this has been made more interesting and complicated by the fact that a year ago I moved back to Lexington for the first time since I was a young boy. I bought a house, which is to say a home, in a place that was once my home and now is so again, facts that prompt the questions: What do we mean when we call a place home? Is it more than where we were born? Is it more than where we grew up? Is it more than where we live now? Can we have multiple places we call home?

I believe the answer to the latter four questions is a fairly simple yes, but they are all subordinate to the first question—What do we mean when we say home?—which is much more difficult to determine. At first glance it seems to have to do with a place in which one has spent significant time and in which one has significant emotional investment. (Love and hate are both significant emotional investments.) And yet when I push on that

145

theory the littlest bit it seems to quickly deteriorate. I lived in Connecticut almost as long as I lived in Kansas and disliked it as a place quite intensely during that time, but I never thought of it as home. Conversely, there are cities like San Francisco, Kansas City, Madison, Iowa City, and Tucson, places that I've loved and lived in for a significant amount of time, but none of which I think of as home. But when I returned to Lexington last year—when I returned there to live and work and make my life, not simply to pass through for a few days to see family—I did have the sense that I was also returning home, the way I feel when I go back to Lawrence.

Before he moved to Arizona, my father lived in Lexington and taught at the University of Kentucky, as I do now, and it is where my brother and I went most summers to spend time with him. Most of his family is there or nearby, and the differences between our life in Lawrence and Lexington were strikingly salient. In Lawrence we got by on my mother's graduate student stipend, child support, and a list of chores that needed to be completed if the household was to remain functional. All of this was necessary so that Mom could retire to the basement catacombs each night to plug away at her dissertation. In Lexington things were different. With my father firmly established in his career at UK and the presence of my well-to-do grandparents and uncles, my brother and I felt like a Horatio Alger–style brother tandem, bootblacks suddenly come into money. We enjoyed big dinners out at nice restaurants, fun and relaxation at a private country club, and we received the not unfrequent "Kentucky handshake" from a kind and generous uncle or our grandmother, who would slip us a little walking-around money before we went out on some adventure with our cousins. And while I think of my childhood in Lawrence with nothing but fondness, I feel the shame now of how disappointed we must have seemed to our mother upon returning home each summer as we descended back to our actually existing class standing, children of the working poor of the intelligentsia.

My mother would find stability and material comfort years later when she completed her PhD and landed a teaching position in Connecticut, but her situation, and thus ours, felt precarious throughout much of my childhood. I was feeling much the same way that winter of 2011. I had two graduate degrees but was unemployed, writing a book of short stories no one was paying me to write, and driving around Kansas doing god knows what for god knows why. I was watching and thinking a lot about basketball, but was my nascent "book project" on the subject just a way to legitimate my fandom? Was I just watching ESPN while my little corner of Rome burned?

Since leaving San Francisco I had habituated to a life of transience, a life characterized by suitcases blocking my sightline in the rearview mirror and bedsheets in the guestrooms of friends and family that still carried their newly washed smell. Before I left the Bay, I had applied for a fellowship to attend an artist residency in Virginia for the month of February and had recently been granted acceptance, so after my return to Kansas for the state sesquicentennial, I once again packed up my car and started to drive. I passed most of my time that month working on my book of short stories about Kansas, keeping tabs on events in the Middle East—the Arab Spring was unfolding—and scribbling notes about basketball in my notebook. Twice a week I sneaked off the isolated mountaintop of the residency quarters to watch KU basketball games in a tiny bar in a tiny, neighboring town. It was in that bar where I watched Kansas lose only its second game of the season, a real blowout at the hands of Kansas State, eager to exact revenge for what we had done to them only weeks earlier at the game I attended on Kansas Day.

After the residency was over, I made my way to that other place, my other home, Lexington, to help celebrate my grandmother's ninetieth birthday. Everyone would be there, a real gathering of the tribe. As different as Lawrence and Lexington are, the one thing they do share, of course, is a fanatical love for college basketball. With all due respect to Bloomington, Chapel Hill, and Durham, they are the two most rabid fanbases in the country, which accounts for why my grandmother's ninetieth birthday celebration, which was originally to occur on the Saturday before her March 1 birthday, had been pushed back to the Saturday after because the original date conflicted with UK's final home game of the season against their hated rival Florida.★

Like many families, we are a big roiling bunch when we get together—all my uncles, aunts, and cousins, who are now themselves married and starting their own families—and the family continues to expand each year, it seems. We are scattered throughout the country, though many remain in Lexington or nearby in Cincinnati. My grandmother was the center, though, the lodestone that had always brought us all back together. I didn't know it then, but that trip to Lexington was one of the last times I would see her alive. She passed away a year and a half later, in August of 2012, a devastating blow to all of us in the family. But the night of her party we

---

★As I write this, my younger brother Bryan has caused a minor family controversy by inadvertently scheduling his wedding on the same day that Kansas travels to Lexington to play Kentucky in Rupp Arena. Apparently not everyone looks at basketball schedules a year in advance when planning one of the most important days of their lives.

celebrated her as she deserved to be celebrated, with love and warmth and good cheer.

The night after the party, my grandmother and I passed a pleasant evening, just the two of us. We talked every Sunday on the phone, but this was one of the last occasions we would have to speak in person privately. I remember sitting at the kitchen table of her condo, me sipping bourbon from one of her polished silver julep cups and her drinking a mug of hot tea. My financial instability and inveterate travels had made getting back to Lexington with regularity difficult the previous several years, but we always remained incredibly close through our letter writing and weekly phone calls. I don't remember how it came up, and I don't know how it had never come up before, but at one point that night at her kitchen table she told me she had been a Spanish major at UK. It surprised me. The thought of my sweet southern belle grandmother chatting away in Spanish was so odd-seeming and droll that I stifled a laugh. She said she had wanted to go to Spain to study abroad but her father hadn't allowed it. "There was all that"—she flicked her hand—"going on over there then, you know." The wave of her hand was a placeholder for either the Spanish Civil War, which had ended a year before in 1939, or perhaps World War II, which was already under way. I asked if she still remembered the language and she thought a moment before saying a few phrases I couldn't translate. She chuckled, tickled that she could still call upon them when asked. She had a gift for memory. I recall her quoting passages of *The Canterbury Tales* back to me when I told her I was studying Chaucer in college.

When I finished my drink, I rinsed the julep cup and dried it. She asked me when I was leaving, and I told her the next morning.

"Where will you go? Back to San Francisco?" she asked.

I hadn't given much thought to that. I might have had no money, but I was totally free. I could go anywhere. But I had a home, not Lexington yet but that other home, and I could return to it again. I had people there who were kind enough to let me stay with them. It was early March and the NCAA tournament was only days away. There was only one place I wanted to be.

"No," I said. "Lawrence."

Lexington to Lawrence, a drive I have made so many times over the years.

"Going back to Kansas," she said and smiled. "Home again, home again, jiggety-jig."

We embraced and said we loved one another, and then I opened the door and left.

First Weekend

Solemn preparation for the sober observance of a religious holiday. That was what the days leading up to the start of the NCAA tournament felt like when I arrived back in Lawrence, and it was a complete ruse. I tried to go about things as normal, which mostly involved spending time at the State Historical Archives in Topeka, doing research and writing, though there were long stretches of ardent study of the bracket, the making of plans of where and with whom to watch the games. There was a heightened sense of *being*—the air gravid with expectation and anxiety—that comes with uncertain proximity to both the elation of winning and the devastation of losing. Many of us KU fans feel this metaphysical burden come tourney time, but none of us wants to articulate it because we can't jinx shit now. We've come too far.

What I believed to be empirically true at that point in the season was that Kansas and Ohio State were the clear best teams in the country, and that OSU was probably a little bit better than us. Like them, we had won our regular season conference championship as well as the conference tournament championship, and we'd done so while accruing only two losses, one of which was the heavily asterisked Texas game the morning after Thomas Robinson's mother died, and which we had just avenged in the championship game of the Big 12 tournament. The Morris twins had become perhaps the best one-two post option in the country, perfect for Coach Self's high-low offense, and Marcus was likely to be a first-team All-American. We were getting good play at the point from Tyshawn Taylor and T-Rob had become one of the best sixth men in the country, though he had been slowed by a recent tear in his meniscus, the same injury that befell me before the start of the state tournament my senior year.

Josh Selby's inconsistent play, due in part to injury and in part to, well, an innate-seeming Selbyness, was troublesome but had been more or less off-set by the solid play of Tyrel Reed and Brady Morningstar, who provided dependable outside shooting, defense, and passing. But all of this meant little in an NCAA tournament that, unlike the NBA's seven-game series format, doesn't all but guarantee that the best teams win. Anyone can have an off night and anyone can catch fire and go on a run. A lot depends, as we're so often told, on matchups, which is why where your team lands in the bracket is important.

Most years when the bracket is released, I spend a good five hours moping over the sins of the selection committee, the myriad ways they've wronged Kansas. That year, however, I was amazed to find that I felt pretty good about our region. It's not that there weren't things that worried me. I wasn't crazy about a tough Louisville team seeded fourth. There was also a potential second-round matchup with Illinois, Coach Self's former team, which would be full of potential psychobaggage, but on the whole it seemed manageable. Notre Dame was the two seed. They were good, but I thought we would match up well against them. The three seed was Purdue, who was very good and would have been seeded higher but one of their key players, Robbie Hummel, had torn his ACL early in the season. I even liked that we were set up on a Friday/Sunday schedule, so that I could enjoy the opening day of the tourney on Thursday without the stress of KU playing.

The first two days of the tournament, when all sixty-four teams are in action, are a glorious marathon. The highlight of the first day of action that year was that number-thirteen Morehead State upset four-seed Louisville, our likely Sweet Sixteen opponent. I watched most of Thursday's games at a bar near Todd's workplace in Kansas City so he could join me over lunch, and when I arrived back there on Friday, I got a few *You again?* eyebrows from the waitstaff.

That night we watched KU's opening game at the birthday party of a friend of Todd and his wife, Rebekah. It wasn't expected to be much of a game, as we were playing Boston University, a sixteen seed; however, for all our success over the previous decade—two Elite Eights in 2004 and 2007, back-to-back Final Fours in 2002 and 2003, and a national championship in 2008—we had had some colossal upsets and choke jobs. Beyond last year's defeat at the hands of mighty Northern Iowa, there were back-to-back first-round flameouts against fourteen-seed Bucknell and thirteen-seed Bradley in 2005 and 2006. And going back to the Roy Williams teams of the nineties we twice lost as a number-one seed in the second round, to the University of Texas at El Paso in 1992 and Rhode Island in 1998, respectively. All of which accounts for the odd inversion of a norm: we tend to play tight against teams we are vastly favored over and loose against the better teams. No one-seed team had ever lost to a sixteen seed, and for a long time, up until Virginia fell to University of Maryland–Baltimore County in the 2018 tournament, my fear was that we would be the first. It would be so us to do that one year and then win the title the next. We're bipolar that way.

And so, predictably, while the other number-one seeds all won their first games by roughly thirty points, we found ourselves up only six at the half. The party was at a restaurant at a trendy bar in the Westport neighborhood of Kansas City, and while the poor birthday girl tried to carry on some semblance of cheer, more and more of the guests gathered around the television in the bar, where Todd and I had long since sneaked off to. It wasn't until the final ten minutes of the game that we started to finally pull away, and while we ended up winning by nineteen, Todd and I were nonetheless annoyed that we tend to play down to our competition.

That night we studied the bracket back at Todd's house. The next game made us nervous. We were hoping for a date with eight-seed UNLV, but they lost to number-nine Illinois, which meant a matchup against Coach Self's former school. In 2003 Self gave the famous not-so-last words that he would never leave Illinois and then did when KU came calling after Roy Williams left for UNC. Coach Self had been successful in his three years at Illinois, taking them to the Elite Eight in 2001 and winning two conference titles. He recruited the players, including Deron Williams, whom his successor, Bruce Weber, rode to the 2005 championship game. One gets the impression Weber has been reminded of this—that his most successful team consisted of Self's players—many times and he carries an unconcealed contempt for Coach Self. You knew he wanted nothing more than to stick it to him and send us home early.

On Sunday I left Kansas City and drove to Lawrence because I wanted to watch the Illinois game at Johnny's. I knew it would be packed, so I showed up three hours early to claim a spot at the bar. I sipped from a schooner and ordered my favorite menu item, the pork tenderloin sandwich. My eyes fixed on the screen showing another game, but I was worrying about the matchup with Illinois in my mind. As game time neared and Johnny's became so filled as to be unnavigable, all televisions switched to KU and the juke cut out, the CBS audio now piping in over the PA. Most people were there with friends, sharing a seat or squeezing between stools at the bar when it became standing room only. I ordered two beers at a time because I knew it was going to be a while before the bartender made his way around again. In fact, there was a general staff-wide work stoppage while the game was on that the patrons respected, but which made the commercial breaks feel like you were on the floor of the NYSE, everyone screaming across the bar or, when verbal communication became impossible, gesturing to someone on the other side of the bar to put in an order. There were occasional outbursts—"Let's go 'hawks!"—that were usually met by an echo from some unseen corner of the bar. Like the TVs—all except the one that had a two-second delay—we fans had synchronized and our individual reactions to the emotional ebbs and flows of the game were parts of the larger whole we had become. We communally cheered and groaned.

Thankfully the game itself eventuated without much drama. After jumping out to an 18–6 lead, we let them back in and were up only four at the half. But in in the second we expanded the lead, firmly in control, and the twins, Markieff and Marcus, dominated the game, combining for forty-one points and twenty-four boards. Final score: 73–59. There was a huge sigh of relief exhaled by all of us in Johnny's, thinking back on the year before, when another top-seeded KU team failed to make it to the second weekend of the tournament.

The thing few of us seemed to realize was that all the real drama of the evening had been happening offstage. Because every TV was tuned to the KU game, it became clear only afterward that major upsets had taken place or were under way in our region. Number-ten Florida State had upset two-seed Notre Dame and number-eleven Virginia Commonwealth University had taken out three-seed Purdue. And furthermore, number-twelve Richmond, who upset five-seed Vanderbilt in the first round, had defeated number-thirteen Morehead State, who upset Louisville, in a battle of underdogs. It didn't actually happen all at once, but I seemed to process it that way. Tournament craziness is a given, but I had never seen anything quite like it. The reality began to set in for each one of us in Johnny's that night: number-one Kansas was heading to the Sweet Sixteen in a region where the remaining teams were seeded twelve, eleven, and ten. The bracket for our region had completely fallen apart, and as we would continue to hear over the next three days, KU had one of the easiest paths to the Final Four in the history of the tournament.

Second Weekend, Part 1

On the Friday of Kansas's Sweet Sixteen game with Richmond I visited the Nelson-Atkins Museum of Art in Kansas City. When I lived in the city in the mid-2000s, I used to pass entire afternoons roaming through its corridors or sitting quietly on the great lawn with its uncanny and enchanting oversized shuttlecock sculptures. I came on that day because James Naismith's original rules of basketball were on display. The rules were touring the country before being installed permanently in the Booth Family Hall of Athletics in Allen Fieldhouse. It felt like the right excursion to make on this important day in Kansas basketball, and I was not alone. The usual dour, professorial raiment of most museumgoers had been replaced by the crimson-and-blue apparel of Jayhawk fans wanting, like me, to be close to history.

There were so many people that it felt odd, somewhere between a pep rally and religious pilgrimage. I suppose, in our own way, we were all there to view a sacred relic. It took a while to make my way up to the elevated glass display where the rules were suspended in space at eye level. Set against red matte were two sheets of yellowed, heavily creased paper. Above the thirteen original typed rules were the handwritten words: *Basket Ball*. In his book of the same name Naismith recounts how he had pinned the rules to the bulletin board in the gymnasium so that the young men of the YMCA would be able to consult them as needed, but one day they disappeared. Frank Mahan, a participant in the first basketball game ever played, later told Naismith he had taken the rules because he knew the game would be a success and "wanted a souvenir." Naismith was not disconcerted at the time, but in retrospect, having the vantage of knowing what his game became, he expressed relief that the young man had eventually returned them to him. From then on Naismith kept the original rules with him, and in the final decade of his life he added an interpolation, signed and dated 6-28-31, at the bottom of the rules in fine dark ink: "First draft of Basket Ball rules. Hung in the gym that the boys might learn the rules—Dec 1891." I leaned close to see the rules, my nose an inch away from the glass protecting them, and just stared for a long time. Like much of the artwork in the museum, it was both discomfiting and entrancing to be so close to something so old and important, to feel the breath of history on your neck. Some time passed before I realized there were others waiting behind me. I smiled at them as I moved away, unable to say anything.

By the time I had paid my respects to Naismith and the game he created, Todd was getting off work and I made my way to his house in Overland Park. We opened beers at the island in his kitchen and talked about that night's game. It was being played in San Antonio, where we won the 2008 championship, and though it comforted us to have the good juju we were both still anxious. We're always nervous before a game, especially at that stage and magnitude, but there was also an unspoken excitement that the draw had broken as auspiciously in our favor as it had. All week we had been hearing about Kansas's easy path to the Final Four, unlike the other favorite, Ohio State, who would have to go through a good four seed in Kentucky as well as a likely matchup against number-two North Carolina in the Elite Eight. The previous night, Thursday, we had celebrated as Arizona demolished number-one Duke in the West region, setting up a matchup against UConn on Saturday for a trip to the final weekend, while in the Southeast region number-two Florida would take on a surprise Butler team, seeded eighth. The upset virus had spread to other regions as well.

We recognized the opportunity Kansas had, and yet we also knew all too well our infuriating propensity to play down to our opponents. We didn't want to utter the sentiments everyone else was—that KU was a shoe-in— though we couldn't stop thinking about it. Instead we talked about how Richmond seemed like just the kind of team we would lose to, a team like Northern Iowa or Bucknell or Bradley, that would come out on fire and catch us on an off night. They were known for their outside shooting and we expected them to go eighteen for twenty from three. We began imitating the CBS announcers calling the game: "The Richmond Spiders have shocked the mighty Kansas Jayhawks—can you believe it!" We did our Kevin Harlan and Greg Gumbel voices and continued talking this way until the game started. Then we became stoics, stolid, impassive, trying to suppress the insanity going on inside our bodies and minds.

KU opened the game strong. While it remained close for the first six minutes, we gradually extended the lead, thanks to our outside shooting. Our fears of Richmond killing us from deep were quelled by multiple threes from Brady Morningstar, Josh Selby, and Tyrel Reed, igniting a 27–4 run that put us up 35–11. Meanwhile our defense was stifling, and we headed into the half leading 41–22. We clapped as we watched the team leave the floor and then realized we were making a racket while Rebekah was trying to put the baby to bed, so we decided to watch the second half in the basement. We packed a little Igloo cooler of drinks and snacks and made our way to the comfortable netherworld where I stayed when visiting. We cautioned ourselves against getting too excited or thinking the game was over.

"Good start," I said, "but we gotta finish the game."

"Need to keep up the pressure," added Todd.

"Totally."

"You know they're gonna make a run."

"No doubt."

"They're gonna start making shots."

"Of course."

"And we're gonna start missing shots."

"Yup."

"That's how it goes."

"Always."

"Long way to go."

"Twenty minutes of game time is an eternity."

"Let's go 'hawks."

"Come on, guys. Let's do this."

"Rock chalk."

"Rock chalk."

But much to our relief we continued our excellent play in the second half, and Richmond never got closer than fifteen. To every noninvested viewer it was a terribly boring basketball game—the antithesis of March Madness—because it went exactly according to script: the heavily favored Jayhawks won easily. To us, it was a savored gift this time of year. At times that season we had relied too much on the twins to carry us, but that night T-Rob put in a monster twelve-point/fourteen-rebound night and Selby knocked in three threes. But the real star of the game was Morningstar, who in addition to playing great defense led us in scoring with eighteen on seven-for-eleven shooting.

The privilege of playing first and winning was that then we got to sit back and enjoy the second game of the evening, the winner of which would be our next opponent. Florida State, seeded tenth, was the favorite over Virginia Commonwealth University, seeded eleventh, because they were from a major conference and because VCU's inclusion in the tournament was the most controversial decision the selection committee made. That year the tournament had expanded from sixty-five to sixty-eight teams and the NCAA developed a first round of games called the First Four to take place among the last four at-large teams and the four lowest-ranked automatic bid teams (sixteen seeds). For reasons that remain unclear to this day, the committee decided to include VCU over seemingly much more deserving major conference schools like Colorado or Virginia Tech. Many fans had advocated for the inclusion of more mid-major teams as at-large bids, but VCU's inclusion was pretty much a universally derided decision and one that was hard to defend. They finished third in the Colonial Conference and won only three of their final eight games. The VCU players had been so certain that they were going to the National Invitation Tournament—college basketball's freshman prom for teams that miss out on the Big Dance—that they didn't even get together to watch the selection show, as teams on the bubble normally do. To VCU's credit, however, given the opportunity, they made the most of it, taking out a string of higher-seeded teams: USC, Georgetown, and Purdue.

As we watched the ugly, offensively challenged VCU-FSU game, however, Todd and I noticed that there were much more interesting developments going on in the East regional, where Ohio State was in a close game against Kentucky, and we switched the channel. Ohio State was the better team, but they were struggling to score against Kentucky's tough defense and it remained a one- or two-point game the entire way. With thirty-six seconds left, Kentucky guard DeAndre Liggins hit a jumper that put UK up three. Todd and I let out screams that we immediately stifled, for fear of waking the baby. Then after an Ohio State timeout Jon Diebler, a deadeye marksman for the Buckeyes, nailed a three. While it was still a tie game and Kentucky had possession, there was the sense that the upset had been avoided, that if OSU could just get it to overtime they would take control and move on to play UNC Sunday. But with five seconds left, UK point guard Brandon Knight, who had otherwise had a dreadful night, knocked down a fifteen-footer. Again we screamed, rising from our seats as OSU missed a desperation three at the buzzer. We were running around the couch whisper-shouting, "Holy shit! Holy shit! Holy shit!" While I cheer for Kentucky in any game they're not playing Kansas, my support of the

Wildcats that night was intensified by the fact that they had just eliminated KU's biggest competition for the title. It took a few minutes for us to calm down before finally sitting down on the couch, where we switched back to the other game to find Florida State and VCU in overtime.

"Who do we want to win this?" I said.

"I don't know," said Todd.

We were still in the euphoria of the Ohio State upset, realizing that regardless of what had happened in our region our biggest impediment to winning a second national championship in four years had been eliminated. We were a little afraid to voice this, but we were both thinking about it, just as we were both afraid to say that we hoped VCU, a team that should never have been included in the field, would take out Florida State. We wanted the easiest possible road to the championship. And when that happened, VCU triumphing 72–71 in the extra session, we reacted calmly, as if to be excited might awaken us from this most excellent of dreams. We said things like, "They look tough" and "Gotta bring our A game," while inside my soul had already joined a metaphysical conga line that stretched from Todd's basement to Mass Street, where the championship parade would take place in a little over a week.

Yankee Town III

After the two-and-a-half-hour drive from Morganville, a small town in north-central Kansas, an area of the Great Plains known as the Smoky Hills, the Stonebacks, Harvey and Gertrude, along with their three boys, Irvin, Ray, and Dean, arrived in Lawrence. It was the Depression, and in Morganville there had been a semiregular flow of transients who were never turned away from a bite of supper or a night's stay in the barn's hay-covered loft, including the one whom young Ray would remember his entire life, a man who fished him out of the nearby river as he thrashed in the water, nearly drowned.

Like Reverend Fisher, the Stonebacks came from "a long line of Teutonic extraction," and had arrived in the United States sometime before 1890 and made their way to Kansas. Despite the hard times, Harvey had been able to purchase property in Lawrence in 1933 thanks to his shrewd and fortuitous crop speculation. There he built a farmhouse for the family to live, as well as a second, smaller house where his father, William Stoneback, would reside for several years in his old age. The farmland was in the undeveloped, far western part of Lawrence, which then must have been little different from the agrestic familiarities of Morganville, but by the time I was a boy fifty years later it was the location of my youth league soccer games and, twenty years after that, the site of an apartment complex where I lived after graduating from college.

And so they farmed. I use the plural because it was a family operation, as was usually the case up until later in the century when the consolidation of land and governmental largess by large corporate agribusiness made the notion quaint and nostalgic, even in a state like Kansas, where the identity of the place is so linked to the homesteaders and agrarian familialism of its past.

Though they lived on the outskirts of town, the Stonebacks certainly had more outlet and opportunity in Lawrence, especially the boys, who would work the plow to prepare for soybean and wheat planting or milk the cows for a few hours before and after school. Ray joked that he had been valedictorian of his country school in Morganville, the top student in a competitive class of eight. It's hard to imagine what walking the halls of massive Liberty Memorial High School must have been like by comparison.

The boys would graduate and all three traveled just a few blocks away to matriculate at the University of Kansas, where they shared a Studebaker convertible for a time, a wonderful asset to have in drawing the attention of attractive coeds. Irvin and Dean would go on to farm and ranch themselves, but the hard toil, the waking before dawn only to be smacked across the face by the tail of a cow he was trying to milk, grew tiresome for Ray, and in college he majored in finance and edited the School of Business newspaper. He was quite busy but found time to join the Sigma Phi Epsilon fraternity and enjoyed a nice social life when his school obligations allowed.

On the day he was to walk down the hill to receive his diploma in May of 1941, he spied a young woman standing by a piano in the fraternity house to which he belonged. She was a petite and pretty brunette with large brown eyes, a bewitching beauty that rousted in him the necessary courage and dash to interrupt the conversation she was having with the group around her and ask if she might consider having dinner with him that night. Her name was Martha Jane Miller, Martie to her friends, and she was dating a poetry student at the time, but Ray was persistent and handsome—tall and slim with striking strawberry blonde curls—and had a kind disposition and wonderful sense of humor, and soon his efforts would send his poor rival off to seek solace in the words of his fellow brokenhearted bards.

Upon graduation, the couple followed the right and only course their situation seemed to offer: to fall in love and begin a life together. It would be difficult, though. The attack at Pearl Harbor had just been carried out and after years of isolationism US entrance into the war was now inevitable. For a time, Ray worked for BF Goodrich, driving a sign truck, but soon he enlisted in the Army's Air Force division (the United States Air Force did not become its own branch of the armed services until 1947) and was stationed in bases in El Paso, Albuquerque, and Lompoc, California. But theirs was a courtship that even war could not derail. While back home on leave over Christmas in 1942, he proposed to Martha on the banks of Wyandotte

Lake in Kansas City, and they married at Saint Peter's Episcopal Church in Santa Maria on March 5, 1943. Nine months later he was assigned to the 12th Air Service Group and found himself aboard an ocean liner headed for Bombay, where he transferred to rail and ventured to Calcutta, and from there flew over the Himalayas—the site of which made such an impression that he could describe the scene vividly over fifty years later—to Kunming, China. For twenty-six months he served as a member of General Claire Lee Chennault's Flying Tigers. His long-distance vision prevented him from being a pilot, much to his disappointment, so he served as base commander in Guilin, where his efforts to save lives, making sure everyone made it to the trenches during Japanese bombing raids before taking cover himself, earned him the Bronze Star. By the end of his time he had grown gravely ill with hepatitis and was transferred to India to recover, though the disease left him weak; he was unable even to write letters to his beloved for six months. His already slim figure shrank to a mere 130 pounds. Martha barely recognized him when he finally returned home in 1946.

After the war, Ray went back to work for BF Goodrich, first serving as an assistant store manager in Sedalia, Missouri, before coming home to Lawrence to manage their store there. During this time, he and Martha had their only child, Lynn, and settled into the routines of a life they would lead together in Lawrence for the next forty years. By 1958 he had accrued enough experience, business savvy, and capital to open his own business. Ray Stoneback's Store was located at 929 Massachusetts Street, right along the main thoroughfare that Quantrill's men had left in ruins nearly a hundred years earlier. Initially he carried BF Goodrich tires, Schwinn bikes, and Kelvinator appliances. Later, in the mid-sixties, Ray expanded into the building next door, which allowed him to carry TVs, stereos, and appliances, as well as a state-of-the-art "listening room" he was quite proud of.

Like the rest of the country, Lawrence's economy and population boomed in the postwar years, and like the rest of the country the benefits were unequally distributed, overwhelmingly going to the 90 percent of the population of Lawrence that was white, to the exclusion of the remaining 10 percent, split roughly between African Americans and Native Americans. Despite its free state history, Lawrence was highly segregated, something that Wilt Chamberlain wrote about in his memoir.★ Having grown up in Philadelphia, he was no stranger to racism, but he found something more virulent in Kansas when he arrived to play ball at KU in 1955:

★Which carries my favorite title of all time: *Wilt: Just Like Any Other 7-Foot Black Millionaire Who Lives Next Door.*

Well, it took me about a week to realize the whole area around Lawrence, except for one black section in Kansas City, was infested with segregation. I called on a few of the alums who had recruited me, and I told them in no uncertain terms what they could do with Kansas if things didn't get straightened out in a hurry. A couple of them told me, "Look, Wilt, you just go wherever you want. You sit down in those restaurants and don't leave until they serve you." That's exactly what I did. It took me about two months, but I went into every damn place within 40 miles of Lawrence, even places I didn't want to go into. I'd just sit there and glower and wait. Finally, they'd serve me. I never got turned down or bad-mouthed or anything, and when I got through other blacks would follow me. I singlehandedly integrated that whole area.

This experience left a bitter taste in Wilt's mouth. He didn't return to Lawrence for over forty years. Of course, most people are not Wilt Chamberlain, not "just like any other 7-foot black millionaire who lives next door," not the star of the team that meant more to the town of Lawrence than just about anything, so it seems safe to say that few others, if any, held the same agency and were afforded the same passable treatment.

Housing, healthcare, education, and employment were rigged decks to draw a hand from if you were a person of color in Lawrence,★ leading to tensions that, again, like much of the country, would make conflict inevitable and necessitate the explosion of political and cultural activism of the sixties. As Rusty L. Monhollon writes in his excellent history of the period:

> Throughout the twentieth century KU was a magnet for alternate cultural, ideological, and social thought and activism, frequently to the disquiet of the townspeople, who often lamented "those people on the Hill." The contentious relationship between "the town and the gown," between a generally conservative (sometimes reactionary) and sedentary townspeople and a generally liberal (sometimes radical) and transitory university community helps define Lawrence's character. It was also a major source of conflict during the 1960s. The anti-intellectualism of many townsfolk,

---

★A family friend of Ray and Martha's, Jesse Milan, who was the first, and for some time the only, black teacher in post–*Brown v. Board of Education* Lawrence schools, recalled—in addition to sitting up at night with a shotgun to protect his family should the threats he was forced to endure actualize—looking for adequate housing for two years because white landlords would tell him the house had already been rented when he arrived for a viewing, and white realtors would routinely take him to houses with dirt floors and no indoor plumbing.

who saw the university community as "eastern snobs," was counterpoised
by an antiprovincialism from many in the university community.

And when the conflicts of that fractious decade did come, it would touch
everyone, Ray and his family included.

Ray was sympathetic to the plight and concerns of Lawrence's black
community, many of whom he broke bread with and passed the peace to
during church services, but like many conservatives and liberals alike he was
dismayed by the growing radicalism of the cultural and political movements
of the late sixties. As the gradualism of the civil rights movement and early
Students for a Democratic Society morphed into the increasingly militant
Black Power and Weather Underground antiwar movements, tensions rose
and the town seemed only a match-strike away from conflagration.

The Stonebacks were en route to Colorado for a brief vacation in June
of 1970 when Ray was notified that Doore's Stationery, the business next
door to his on Massachusetts Street, had been badly burned. There was said
to be smoke and water damage to his store as well. The vacation was over
before it had begun, and the family turned around so Ray could survey and
repair the harm. It was suspected that the fire had been a failed attempt to
burn the draft office, which was actually across the street above another
store called Gamble's, and which in time would be torched as well.

There was much protesting and activism throughout the latter half of the
decade, but things intensified in the spring of 1970, when arson, including
the burning of KU's Memorial Union, and bombings forced the suspen-
sion of classes at the university and put the town under curfew for a tense
period. By June most figured the town had weathered the worst of the
storm and that things would calm with the coming summer vacation, but
the situation hit a breaking point that July when Rick Dowdell, a young
African American KU student and activist, was shot in the back of the head
as he ran from a Lawrence police officer. Four days later, at a protest over
Dowdell's death, the police shot Nick Rice, a white KU student. The tensions and anger that had been kept just barely in check the previous spring
fully surfaced in July, making Lawrence as dangerous a place as it had been
since the days of Quantrill's Raid. Again, Monhollon:

> Lawrence in late July resembled a combat zone. Between Dowdell's death
> on the sixteenth and the end of the month, firebombs, arson, and van-
> dalism rocked the community nightly. Snipers blasted out streetlights and
> shot at police officers, firefighters, and ordinary citizens, including the
> local newspaper editor and radio station owner. The governor proclaimed

a state of emergency, sent the Kansas Highway Patrol to relieve the belea-
guered Lawrence Police Department, and mobilized the Kansas National
Guard to protect property and keep the peace. These efforts were not
enough for some residents. White vigilantes threatened to restore order by
killing "nigger and hippie militants." Business owners guarded their property with shotguns and rifles; several exchanged gunfire with unidentified
persons. Right- and left-wing radicals resented what each considered an
invasion of their space, and both vowed an armed defense of that turf.

It was in this environment, with much of the town still smoldering, that
Ray's daughter, Lynn, would start high school the following month.

Lawrence High School, which replaced Liberty Memorial, had already
been the setting of much activity in the years before the start of the 1970
school year. In the spring of 1968 black students and their families met with
school administrators to address concerns about black representation on
sports teams, in the curriculum, and on the faculty, and they had left the
meetings with assurances that steps would be taken. When little had been
done by the start of the following school year, however, students began
holding walkouts and occupying administrative offices, even starting a symbolic Afro-centric school right across the street from LHS in Veteran's Park
for a brief time. Dowdell had attended the high school and played a major
role in organizing the actions before graduating in 1969 and going down
the street to KU, where he joined the Black Student Union, in which he
would remain active up until his death. His presence was remembered and
his loss still painfully felt by the black students of Lawrence High School.

I spoke with Lynn about this time in her life and she recalled that shortly
before the start of school she was standing in the doorway of her father's
store, where she worked every summer, and watched as a group of black
men, most clad in black denim and berets, suddenly appeared, walking quietly as they carried Dowdell's casket down Massachusetts Street, blocking
all traffic. While whites took in the procession from sidewalks and behind
windows, the funeral march made its way from Saint Luke's AME church,
where services were held, to Oak Hill Cemetery, where his body was in-
terred. A sight to behold for certain. "I remember the silence as they passed
by," said Lynn.

It is easy to understand why, as Lynn told me, "I never really relaxed
at Lawrence High that year, or the next, honestly." A few weeks into her
freshman year—on her birthday, no less—a fight broke out in the cafete-
ria between white and black girls. They were screaming, punching, drag-
ging each other under tables by the hair. The police arrived, macing those

involved, and sent the entire school home for the day. Understandably, Lynn felt "shocked, numb, just in disbelief." The school was virtually divided into zones where, depending upon the color of your skin, you were either welcome or barred entry. Periodically several black students would link arms and walk down the hallway between classes, making it impossible for anyone to pass. Lynn was friends with several black girls, but they never spoke about the situation—even friendship failing to create the space where one might communicate and thus begin to bridge the divide that was tearing apart the school and the town. With time, things settled down and life in Lawrence regained a sense of normalcy.

Lynn graduated, first from LHS and then from KU, where she had fallen in love with a medical student named Steve. All the while, Ray continued to run his store, which, as any small business owner will tell you, was stressful but also a source of immense pleasure, allowing him to interact and chat with customers. Furthermore, it had by any measure been a successful venture, and by 1978, twenty years after first opening its doors, Ray Stoneback's Store was something of an institution in Lawrence, with a host of loyal customers. In 1980, as Lynn and Steve were preparing their wedding, Ray began the process of selling the store to one of his longtime employees. He would remain a partner for the next ten years, until the buyout was complete.* He enjoyed keeping a hand in things while also getting to focus on what he loved most: being husband, father, and soon grandfather to his family. But while that decade before retirement would bring the joy of those grandsons, it would also bring immense sadness when Martha passed away in April of 1985. Always important, his faith and involvement at church increased after her death, and in doing so he worked through his grief. He taught Sunday school, served on the vestry, and worked as an usher, among the many other roles he filled. A warm and gregarious man, his favorite job was to be a greeter, meeting congregants on their way inside, shaking hands, helping to hang coats. At some point during this period in the mid-to-late eighties, my mother, brother, and I walked through the red wooden doors of Trinity Episcopal Church and were greeted warmly by Ray.

My first memory of the man who would become my stepfather was the time Ray sneaked Brint and me back to the apex of the church to help

---

*In the fall of 2018, current owner Andy Vigna, who knew Ray well and worked at the store after graduating from high school, celebrated the store's sixtieth anniversary with longtime customers who still fondly recall Ray. While it is no longer located on Mass Street, it retains his name and there are a number of pictures of Ray on the walls. It is now known as Stoneback Appliance.

him tug the long, hawser-like rope that set the bell in motion, the clapper striking the flared rim of the cast–iron metal and sending out that gloriously soft boom all over Lawrence, filling me with awe. As my mother became more involved at the church, she and Ray, divorcee and widower, were often paired together as ushers. My mother, newly forty, still carried the beauty she had had twenty years earlier and drew the attention of many men, but she had dated sparingly since we arrived in Lawrence a few years prior, mostly, I suspect, because there was little time left for herself between caring for us boys and attending to the demands of her doctoral program.

For some time my mother and Ray were just friends who saw each other mostly at church. But he had a way of popping up in her life, always offering to lend a hand, whether it was watching Brint and me while she taught, or to help out with something around the house, or bringing her fish he had caught on one of his fishing trips in Colorado, or just happening to show up at the gym where she exercised. This was in part because it was in his nature to be a generous and social person, but undoubtedly there was some artful yet harmless guile at play as well; he was beginning his courtship that was obscured, at least on my mother's end, by their significant age difference: he was twenty-five years older than her.★ Those platonic years, it seems, was the incubation period necessary for a complex love to grow from the seeds of friendship.

It wasn't until 1990 that they started to date. My mother was nearing the end of her program, preparing to defend her dissertation while teaching at Rockhurst University in Kansas City. Ray would watch Brint and me on the nights Mom taught, taking us out for burgers or tacos and politely watching the horrible television we made him endure. Years later I felt utter shame for the fact that I'd sometimes catch him watching reruns of *Beverly Hills, 90210* when he thought he was alone. I loved the nights Ray would look after us. He was funny and had a wonderful energy, was always up for anything, always easy to laugh. My god, to see the man walk down Mass Street was an experience itself, almost mayoral. He knew everyone, it seemed, and always took a few minutes to stop and chat with folks.

One night when I was ten, my mother asked us what we thought of the possibility of her marrying Ray. Without hesitation, I said it would be great, thinking of my pal who bought me tacos and kept me company over

★Their difference in age did lead to some wonderful misunderstandings that have since entered the family mythology, as when on an early date, knowing my mother had served in Liberia in the Peace Corps, he thought she might relate to, and enjoy seeing, *Jungle Fever*, not realizing that the Spike Lee joint was a film about interracial dating in New York City.

bad television. Brint, however, told her not to do it. I remember being stunned. How amazing that moment was when I think back on it now. It wasn't that he didn't like Ray—he did so very much. It was that with my dad many years gone, Brint was the oldest male in the house, and even if that only meant being two and a half years older than me, he carried, had in fact been carrying for some time, a responsibility for our mother's welfare that I'd never realized, in part because he'd been looking out for me as well.

Despite my brother's reservations, however, my mother and Ray married, but not before something equally important happened. By 1992 my mother had earned her PhD and went on the job market. I remember the night she came into my room and explained to me that universities generally do not like to hire their own graduates. I'd assumed she would just become a professor at KU. While we had moved three times over the course of our near-decade in Lawrence, I'd never for a second considered the fact that we might leave the town, let alone the state. I pleaded for her to get a teaching job in Wichita or Kansas City, but there were none available, so as the market dictated, we left Kansas. I was devastated. My mother ended up accepting an offer from Central Connecticut State University in New Britain, Connecticut, and the reality of leaving brought her and Ray to an all-or-nothing moment in their relationship. They had known each other for several years but had only been dating a little over one. She was a professor, he was retired. She had a job in Connecticut, he had his family and friends and history in Lawrence. I still find it hard to fathom all that must have been weighing on him during this period of uncertainty, let alone the amazing leap of faith he took in coming with us. He had been living in Lawrence fifty-nine years and at the age of seventy-two was willing to uproot his life and follow a woman he loved to a state he'd never been to. Newly settled in a small town in the Farmington River Valley called Avon, they married that December of 1992. Almost a decade to the day afterward, in late November of 2002, Ray and I would find ourselves back in Lawrence.

At that point in my life I had graduated from the University of Arizona the previous spring and moved back to what had always felt like home, Lawrence. Though I had visited often over the years, it was my first time living there since we moved away. I rented an apartment with Todd, who had another year of school to finish up, and was working for Lynn's husband, Steve, as a surgery scheduler at his otolaryngology practice. I planned to go to graduate school the following year and came home at night to study for the GRE or to think about the fiction I should have been writing while I was fetal before the television, exhausted by my immersion in the real world. In the years after moving to Connecticut, Ray made a habit of visiting his family in Lawrence every two months, and so it was that he and my mother came to visit over Thanksgiving in 2002. She had to leave right after the holiday to make it back in time for the frantic rush of the end of the semester, but Ray planned to stay in Lawrence for an extra week to spend time with friends and family.

The afternoon my mom flew back to Connecticut, Ray told Lynn he was going to take a nap. When he appeared an hour later, he sat in the kitchen snacking on carrots as Lynn prepared dinner. "Where's Jane?" he asked, meaning my mom. Lynn reminded him that she had gone back to Connecticut for the end of classes. "Oh, okay," he said, nibbling on a carrot. He took a couple more bites and again asked where my mother was. He would continue to ask this question for days afterward, long after Lynn took him to Lawrence Memorial Hospital, and long after I visited him his first morning there and listened as Steve deciphered physician's argot to tell me that my stepfather had had a stroke.

For reasons I will soon elucidate, it needs to be said that my relationship with Ray had deteriorated over the years, which made the fact that I was the only one from our Connecticut unit there with him a little unusual. The experience over the next two weeks comes back to me now, almost seventeen years later, so clearly in part because it had an impact on me and my understanding of my relationship with Ray, and in part because I found myself taking a lot of notes, as I always do, scribbling in the notebook I carry with me, trying to observe and understand what is happening around me.

I walked into his hospital room the first day he was admitted, expecting to see him paralyzed, comatose, nonverbal, like stroke victims I had seen on film, but he looked exactly like his usual self, sitting up in bed, smiling at me as I entered the room. Lynn was there, her eyes puffed up like portabellas from a combination of crying and sleeplessness. I asked how things were going. "Pretty good, right, Daddy?" said Lynn, forcing a pained smile. He didn't answer her, just turned to me and asked if my mom was down at the beach. I soon realized that he thought he was in a resort. My mother, he believed, was always at the beach swimming.

"Daddy, you're in Lawrence Memorial Hospital," Lynn said, adding, "in Lawrence, Kansas," when he looked at her confused. The stroke left him with almost no short-term memory, so this was something we would repeat countless times over the next several days. I tried to explain the situation to my mother over the phone. I told her that physically he seemed fine, that most of the damage seemed cognitive. "It's like he's in a different, shadow world from ours," I said, but it came to feel like something I could never truly convey to someone who had not been in the room with him.

On his second morning at the hospital, he put on his clothes, took off his patches, wires, and IV, and walked out of his room, past the nurses' station, down the elevator, and out the sliding doors of the entrance. In a panic, orderlies and nurses pulled on their winter coats and descended onto the surrounding neighborhoods to search for him. When they finally found him a few blocks away, he was blowing into his hands, wondering where he could get a hot cup of coffee. I heard the story from Lynn when I arrived a little later, before work. The nurses were busy installing a door alarm that would beep anytime someone entered or left the room, an annoyance that would bring us all close to madness. "Daddy went for a little walk this morning," Lynn said, looking at him. She was shaking—with anger or fear, I wasn't sure, so I tried to hug her. As I wrapped my arms around her, I looked over her shoulder at my stepdad in bed, hands laced on his chest, blanket pulled up to his chin, and could see he had already forgotten about his exodus.

The doctor told us that Ray would need a pacemaker, that he would have to start taking Coumadin. He explained this as we sat beside my stepfather, who lay in his bed, taking it all in with a slight grin, like they were talking about someone else, possibly a friend of his. But it was his mind I worried about, his memory and his normal cognitive functions. Would they return? Maybe, the doctor told us. He didn't know. We would have to wait and see. I don't know whether it's ironic or simply fitting that it was his loss of memory that so preoccupied my concern, because that's all I have of that strange, sad, and occasionally beautiful time. Memories, lots of them.

I remember how even in this troubled state we kept up with basketball. One night we watched KU play. I was there with Lynn, Steve, and their sons. We cheered after each Jayhawk basket, Ray included, and at one point in the second half he pointed at the game clock on the screen and said, "Twelve dollars and forty-one cents. How about that!"

I remember how order became increasingly important to him. He would rearrange his bedside table, moving around his remote, ice water, orange, and blue-foiled yogurt a few inches every hour. He frequently read the time and date off the wall facing him and announced it to me, or counted the stacked boxes of Kleenex in the room over and over: One, two, three. One, two, three.

I remember stopping in one night after work to watch the evening news with him and Lynn. He couldn't follow narrative longer than a few minutes, and for this reason he enjoyed commercials, but he watched with us anyway. The main story was about the possibility of Iraq having nuclear weapons and whether the United States should invade. We watched in silence and when it cut to commercial Lynn looked at him and asked, "Well, what do you think, Daddy? Does Saddam have the nukes?" He was picking at the fingertips of his right hand with those of his left, as though removing lint from a sweater, and without missing a beat confirmed, "He's got twelve, but he's only going to use four."

I remember how the drugs they gave him after the surgery to put in his pacemaker made him slip in and out of sleep. He seemed to dream the second he closed his eyes. In sleep, his right hand would reach out before him. Initially it struck me as the pose of a conjurer, ready to bring something fantastic to fruition, but it came to look more and more like a hand reaching for something always a little beyond its grasp.

I remember taking a long walk one evening when I needed to escape the hospital and making my way to Mass Street, where I strolled past the closed and lighted shop windows of stores until I ended up at the building that used to house my stepfather's appliance store. Today it's a foo-foo European *marché*, something that tickled him because it seemed so silly and pretentious to a man who never put on airs. I stared into the window a long time, trying to imagine how it used to look, trying to picture him inside, joking with customers.

I remember the frustration finally beginning to show. Periodically he would take off the wires and get up from his bed, saying, "Well, I think I'm going to go home now. When Jane gets back from the beach, tell her I'm in the car." And when I or Lynn told him no, that he had to stay, he would say, "I do?" and then lean back down, gloomily conceding, "Okay." His arms were all iodine and bruises from IV insertions and injections. Once he lifted up his arms, turning them underneath the overhead light, and said, "What the hell happened to me?"

In all, he was in the hospital for a week, and he would rest at Lynn's for another ten days before being able to return to Connecticut with my mother. I offered to stay with him his last night in the hospital so Lynn could have her first and only evening at home. She had pretty much been living at Lawrence Memorial since he was admitted. I didn't mind because in a strange way I had come to actually like the whole roiling cosmos of the hospital—its regularity, the cycles of pills, meals, and tests, the abject grace seen daily in the broken bodies of the sick and dying. I'd been a little nervous about being alone with him in the room, the disquieting feeling of being implicated so fully in the experience of another person's delusions and fantasy. But I went, of course. It wasn't easy to sustain conversation with him, so that night, like usual, we turned on the TV. It was a Saturday night and NBC was showing *It's a Wonderful Life.* The two of us watched in the dark and periodically he laughed whenever someone said, "I wish I had a million dollars—hot dog!" And later, as Jimmy Stewart ran through the streets of Bedford Falls like an insane person, screaming joyful noise and yelling "Merry Christmas," trying to make it home to his wife and family, I began to cry. Though I am often moved, I'm rarely moved to tears, but not because of some idiotic notion that men don't or shouldn't cry. In fact, I often think there's something wrong with me that I don't more often, desiring some concrete manifestation of the immense depth of feeling I know to be going on inside me. This, however, was one of the times tears came: a big, sloppy crying jag. I was so emotionally scattershot I couldn't contain it anymore. Ray didn't seem to notice. I thought he had fallen asleep, but a few minutes later, as the credits rolled, he said, "That's a great show." Then he looked over at me in the dark corner beside his bed and saw what a wet-cheeked mess I was. He leaned forward a little, concerned. "Do you need some fire, Andy?" he said, pointing to the lamp beside him. "I've got some over here. Would you like some?"

I often find myself trying to understand what happened to us, how we fell out with one another. The poor man joined our family right as I entered my depressive teenage years, and in the navel-gazing that characterized that period I was only able to see, and at times even relish, my own anguish, blind to the emotional IEDs with which I maimed those around me. No one should have had to be around me, especially someone new to the family; I should have been quarantined until I turned eighteen and then let back into the world. In the years before I left for college, we each retreated to the comforts of the very things that only ensured our isolation from the other: me to my bedroom universe, where I stomped on my distortion pedal and banged loudly on guitars, performing my sulky melancholy for the entire neighborhood to hear, and he to the jeremiads of conservative talk radio and the watchful eye of the scrolling market ticker.

Other than our shared love and concern for my mother, the times we most came together were during basketball season. He attended every one of my games, chatting and cheering along with the other parents. Every once in a while I'll get out the old game tapes I forced my mom to film under the pretense of needing to study and learn from mistakes, but which was really a project of bottomless vanity—I wanted to bear witness to my own greatness on the court, to see myself as people saw me in the crowd. And as I watch the unsteady Zapruder-like panning of the camera, there is always the voice of my stepfather, cheering for me and my teammates, but also his wonderfully quotidian asides to those around him. During my senior year I was honored before a home game for having scored my thousandth point. My coach pulled me aside and told me that I was going to be given the game ball and that I should acknowledge the crowd and take it over to my family, then get my head back into the game as quickly as possible. My mother was teaching a night class at the university, so I walked over to the bleachers where Ray stood clapping, and I handed him the ball, which he proudly accepted and held up, displaying it to the cheering crowd.

And, of course, there was Kansas basketball. We followed religiously, watching every nationally televised game together, or at least up until the point at which his defeatism would force me into another room.* That was the thing—it wasn't just Kansas basketball we shared; it was Kansas. Ray was the only one in the family who could match—trump, even—the zeal with which I claimed my roots, for he was actually a native Kansan, whereas my allegiance was adopted by simply growing up there. Perhaps unconsciously we bore some enmity toward one another for the way our individual destinies, once concatenated, depended upon leaving the place we so loved.

The five and a half years he was alive after the stroke are marked in my memory as equal parts sad and happy. There were untold indignities to be suffered by Ray, as well as my mother, who bore most of the brunt of the hard duties required so that he could remain at home and not have to enter a care facility, but there was something amazing about it all, too. This was during my two stints in graduate school, and I would return to Connecticut

---

*He had the habit of announcing at moments ridiculously rash that Kansas was going to lose. KU could be down 15–14 with twelve minutes left in the first half and he'd say, "Well, looks like this one's over." It used to drive me crazy, but I realize now it was both a ward against caving to the intense feelings inside us that were overinvesting the game with import, as well as a shrewd, covert cheering strategy. If you always assumed Kansas was going to lose, you were pleasantly surprised when they didn't, which in those years was roughly 83 percent of the time. Interestingly, as I've grown older I've moved closer to Ray's cheering stance more than the hair-pulling, histrionic, this-is-how-much-this-game-means-to-me performance of team loyalty that characterized my teens. While they represent two opposing poles of temperament, they both roost in the same irrationality endemic to fandom: yelling at men on a television screen and expecting them to react is commensurate to the subtler games of erotic reverse psychology that are at play when I assume KU's defeat while leaving unuttered, yet implied, my needy but-if-you-really-loved-me-you'd-win guile.

on breaks and vacations to visit. What most struck me about Ray was that he seemed like another person. I don't mean this in a shell-of-his-former-self kind of way; I mean it felt like he had a fundamentally different personal genome than the man I had struggled to be around when I was in high school and college. And yet this new version of Ray wasn't new at all, I realized. It was a return to the version of himself I remember when I first met him: affable, quick to laugh, quick to compliment, kind, generous, affectionate. Sure, he had a spotty memory and occasional fainting spells, but most of the time his was the merriment of a grandfather who has had an extra finger of gin at the family get-together.

It was important for me to see him like that, to remember his innate kindness and joy, and to realize that whatever real or perceived sadness and negativity he was carrying during my teenage years was, for both of us, the product of particular circumstances, an aberration of one's self as opposed to its true nature, assuming there is such a thing. How amazing that at his most vulnerable, particularly in the final year or two when his condition worsened, a time when so many people in similar situations become understandably scared or angry, acting out against the ones trying to care for them, he was perfectly relaxed, never doubting for a moment that he was loved and cared for. What grace he possessed, even when most compromised. It was in this state that I really grew to love my stepfather as an adult, with a mature kind of love and in a way that I couldn't or wouldn't earlier in our relationship, when we had been unable to stay close because we couldn't find the will and words to express what we were feeling in the aftermath of leaving Kansas and becoming a new family in a new place.

In his last months, walking up the tall staircase became too taxing, so my mother moved a twin bed downstairs into the den, where her desk was, and where for so many years Ray would sit with her on the small sofa and rub her feet to help her relax after a long day at work. One morning in early July, two days after my mother's birthday and one before our Independence Day holiday, my mother came downstairs to check on Ray. He was sleeping soundly and she climbed into the bed with him as she often did in the mornings. Snuggling with her husband, head on his chest, she listened to him take what turned out to be his final breaths.

I remember being slightly annoyed when she called me soon thereafter. It was early and I was still asleep, in bed with H. My greeting carried a slight edge that dissipated when I heard the numb surprise in my mom's voice telling me he was gone. We had funeral services for him in Kansas and in Connecticut, and I can't help but think that their differences in style and tone capture some of the difference between his experiences in the two places. The funeral in Lawrence was packed, full of pomp and hymn, and he was buried with military honors in a pretty plot next to Martha in Oak Hill Cemetery, the same burial ground where Rick Dowdell, George Nash Walker, James Naismith, and most of the victims of Quantrill's Raid rest. The service in Connecticut was smaller, more personal. In place of the formal eulogy I had delivered in Lawrence, I played guitar as Brint sang Dylan's "You're Gonna Make Me Lonesome When You Go."

For a long time after he died, I regretted that we had not been able to repair our relationship prior to the stroke, when he was in his right mind. Only in the last few years was I able to see the sad miracle in his body betraying itself, the gift it had given us of being able to reconnect, in however diminished a capacity, and find our way back to one another. I wish I could have apologized to him for the past, but I'm so grateful I got to know what it felt like to love and be loved by him.

An unexpected thing happened the spring after Ray had the stroke. He had long since returned with my mother to Connecticut, and one afternoon late in the workday Lynn called to ask if I would join her family for dinner. That night as Lynn and Steve and their boys and I finished eating, tornado sirens began sounding all over town. We huddled in the basement, as Steve, despite Lynn's protestations, periodically sneaked out to try and get a peek at the funnel. When the tornado was gone, we emerged to survey things. There was that eerie, dead, green fog in the air that comes with twisters. Stuck up in the limbs of a tree beside their basketball goal was part of someone's roof. Watching the news reports, we realized that my apartment complex, just about a mile away, had been in the path of the tornado.

I called Todd and learned he was safe at his girlfriend's house. Then Steve and I drove over to find my apartment complex blocked off by police and firemen. The National Guard would come the following day. They weren't letting anyone in. The complex was made up of a dozen or so standalone clusters containing four units each. I could see, even at the distance we were kept, that ours had been hit. The roof of our apartment had been damaged. Later we would recognize one of the firefighters as the son of an employee at Steve's office and, despite concerns of structural soundness, he'd sneak me into my apartment to see what I could salvage. The apartment had been built with a bedroom on each side of the unit on opposite sides of the kitchen. When I got inside and ascended the staircase, I found that the entirety of roof over the kitchen had been sucked out, along with much of our kitchenware and appliances, but the roofing structure covering both my bedroom and Todd's had remained intact, if barely so. I stood in the annihilated kitchen staring out at the starlit sky for some time, and it didn't occur to me until later how strange it was that I could. I grabbed my Martin guitar, laptop, and a box of files containing my writing, and Steve helped me lug them out into the night to safety. I would live in Lynn and Steve's basement for months afterward before going off to graduate school.

Perhaps a month after the tornado, I took a friend to survey the state of the apartment complex. We found that every cluster, whether it had been hit or not, had been demolished. All that remained were the concrete slabs of their foundations. We parked and got out. It was a perfect summer evening, the light as flaxen as the wheat and tall grass that had once grown there. I walked onto the foundation of our apartment. "Here's where the door was," I said to her. I moved ten feet to my right. "And once upstairs, this is where our couch in the living room was." My friend stood still on the sidewalk, watching me as I moved around the foundation, giving her a tour of the ghost of what had once been my home.

It was 2003, the last time I would live in Lawrence and exactly seventy years after my stepfather's parents had moved the family to this land where we now stood. An odd symmetry to it all, in retrospect. In that time, Lawrence had steadily expanded west from downtown and the university, and now the tracts of Stoneback wheat and soybean were gone in total, replaced by my apartment complex, the Miller Mart where I filled up my car with gas, and the soccer fields I played on as a boy, as well as other newly built homes and subdivisions. For a brief moment, standing on the foundation, I was filled with the thought that in the tornado's wake it all might return to what it once had been. But of course the owners simply rebuilt new apartments that looked exactly like the ones in which I had lived. As my friend and I drove away, we passed the tall green sign bearing the name of a nearby street. I pointed that out to her, too. The street was named Stoneback Drive.

Second Weekend, Part 2

We lose.

Loss Redux

In hindsight, everything was wrong, even though, as is often the case, I had no ability to see it at the time. No matter how much I tried to tell myself that all we had was an opportunity to get to the Final Four and that that opportunity promised nothing if it were not taken advantage of, all my attempts at forbearance were masking an unconscionable hubris, that classic and most deserving flaw of the privileged and entitled. It seemed too good, impossible that given the unbelievably fortuitous way the bracket had broken we wouldn't win the region and, with Ohio State's loss, the entire tournament.

On Saturday, the day before our game against Virginia Commonwealth, this belief was bolstered by the results of two other Elite Eight matchups. Connecticut defeated Arizona, and while UConn was a three seed and considered a hot team, they also finished in a three-way tie for ninth place in the Big East. More significantly for KU, our opponent in the Final Four was going to be number-eight Butler, which upset number-two Florida in the Southeast regional final. KU now had a path to the championship game that required beating no team higher than an eight seed. I'd never seen anything like it. The lucky breaks were getting downright absurd. I remember watching the Florida game with Todd, standing before the television in his living room as Butler took control of overtime, and feeling a euphoric sense of disbelief. He shook his head. "I want Florida to win," he said. "I just feel like we should at least have to beat *some*body good."

For all the coach-speak and one-game-at-a-time platitudes being bandied about by the KU team and fans, if two adult men who know the history of upsets all too well—to say nothing of the general anything-can-happen unpredictability of individual one-and-done tournament games—as Todd and I did, were lapsing into this thinking, then how could we expect a group of nineteen- and twenty-year-olds to block out the reality of the situation, the air of inevitability, let alone silence the voice of commentators who were anointing them presumptive national champions?

I can see now that we had lost to VCU before we ever set foot on the court.

For reasons unclear to me now, I didn't watch the game with Todd, as I had most of the tournament. I was staying in Lawrence at Lynn's house and while I recall thinking I should go watch the game at Johnny's, that it would be fun to experience the rush of going to the Final Four with the Jayhawk masses, I came downstairs to find Lynn and her family all gathered around a small TV in the kitchen. They were watching the pregame, and while it wasn't the ideal viewing situation, I felt it might be impolite to take off on my own after they had been so kind and generous in putting me up whenever needed, often on short notice, during my months of intermittent wandering and transience. So I pulled up a seat and settled in for the game, which started as expected. We scored six straight points just like the dominant team we were, while VCU appeared overwhelmed, nervous on the big stage. It looked like it might be a wonderful snoozer of a game, a nerve-free blowout, as the Richmond game had been, but then VCU showed the intrepid toughness that had come to characterize that team. They didn't cower, didn't back down. They took it right at us and six minutes into the game had taken the lead. After ten minutes they extended it to double digits and with less than five minutes remaining it had ballooned to eighteen. We went into the halftime down fourteen, a what-the-hell-just-happened daze hovering over player and fan alike.

What was so impressive about VCU was that after the first couple of minutes they didn't play like the underdog. They didn't concede KU's athletic superiority. They didn't try to slow the game down and sit on the ball to limit our possessions. They beat us at our own game, getting out in transition, flying up and down the court. They got in our faces, taunted the overwhelmingly pro-Kansas crowd as if they were the favored team. They played an up-tempo anarchic defense their brash young coach Shaka Smart called "Havoc" that forced us into turnovers, but what really built their lead was outside shooting. While they were known for shooting a lot of threes, they were not necessarily known as a great shooting team; however, that afternoon they went nine for seventeen from the three-point line in the first half, which for even a good shooting team would be an excellent mark for an entire game, let alone the first twenty minutes.

As so often happens in games, when one VCU player got on a roll the energy and confidence became as contagious as the diffident defeatism that set in for KU. Simply put, as the clichés go, we couldn't throw it in the ocean, couldn't hit the broadside of the barn, our jumpers were broken. Which was frustrating because two days earlier, on the very same court against Richmond, we had been the ones to hit nine three-pointers. We were the best field-goal percentage team in the country that year, the only team to shoot over 50 percent on average, but on that day we didn't come close to that. A good deal of that was certainly due to VCU's excellent defense, but that by itself couldn't account for an almost historically poor shooting night, our worst in two years, in which we shot under 35 percent from the field, 53 percent from the free throw line, and 9 percent from three. Nerves. Once VCU showed they weren't scared, our puffed chests deflated and we revealed ourselves to be the mentally fragile team we are, one that while amazingly successful has also suffered some of the biggest upsets of the last twenty years. We got tight.

Still, we had our chances. When the second half began, their virtuoso shooting wavered, which allowed us to make a run and with thirteen minutes left in the game we had cut the lead to two. Finally it seemed we had righted the ship. It started to have the feel of a game where the upstart team plays great for a half but can't sustain it over the course of the full forty minutes, and the favorite, while receiving a good scare, proves itself to be the better team and restores the natural order of things. This time, however, we could never regain the lead. We didn't take advantage of their poor play, simply matching it with our own turnovers and missed shots, until they started to play better and again extend the lead. Impressively, VCU didn't cave when we put the pressure on. Any team can go unconscious for a half, but what happens when the shots stop dropping and the game gets close? They responded, as good teams should. We made a late last-ditch effort to steal the game, but it never really got close and they won by ten points, 71–61, our lowest point total of the season.

We were certainly the better team—the respective records, quality of play, and strength of competition throughout the season make that undeniable—and had this been an NBA-style best-of-seven series I would have bet a future firstborn child on us winning, likely in five or six games. However, it wasn't the NBA, and VCU was the better and deserving team on that particular day. They didn't luck into anything. They took it to us and, after the first few minutes, controlled the rest of the game. Of course, I can see and appreciate that only now. In the moment, there in Lynn's kitchen watching the game, I was—we all were—in the throes of anguish. I wouldn't call our behavior a high point of post-Enlightenment rationality. We regressed to our basest selves, Hobbesian monsters in human clothing. We yelled at the TV, chastising the players we had loved and supported all season. We became nativist paranoids, airing conspiracy theories that the refs were biased against Kansas—not the team; the state, the geographical unit. We even turned on each other for short spells, arguing about the solution to our shooting woes, debating strategy and whether Coach Self knew what the hell he was doing. We were red-eyed and hoarse from yelling, and by the end I felt not just resigned but exhausted, for my muscles, I realized, had been clenched for two hours.

When it was over, we sat quietly staring at the television, which showed VCU players celebrating their school's first trip to the Final Four while our team walked off the court, towels over their heads, arms over each other's shoulders. My mother, a neophyte texter, sent me a message: *Wha hapend?* Soon we all dispersed to different areas of the house to sulk. I called Todd, but there was little to say. We were too stunned, too disappointed. How had we blown a sure thing? I decided to go to Johnny's, where only a few hours earlier I had imagined the bacchanalia that would follow KU's victory, but now the mood was dismal and cheerless. The bar was half empty and the silence carried an edge that made me a little nervous, like the sorrow and frustration was so palpably intense that it wouldn't take much for a fight to break out. I did watch Kentucky beat North Carolina in the second and final game of the afternoon and was glad to see them lock up the last spot in the Final Four, happy for my Lexington family, but it did little to salve the wound of KU's defeat. I remember going to bed very early.

The next morning the fog of the loss still hung thick over Lawrence, and I figured the only way to escape it was to leave. As I'm sometimes given to do, I decided to get in the car and just drive, no destination in mind. During my time in Kansas over the previous months, I had spent most days at the State Historical Society in Topeka, researching and writing. As I drove west on I-70 and passed through Topeka, I thought I might stop at the archives and work, but I kept on, not wanting to get out of the car. I drove for one hour and then two, watching the rolling plains pass. It wasn't until I arrived at a gas station in Salina that I knew where I was going.

One of the places I wanted to write about in my book was a town called Nicodemus, Kansas. Located in the north-central part of the state, it is the oldest still-surviving black settlement west of the Mississippi. I had wanted to visit since returning to Kansas in January, but it was almost a five-hour drive from Lawrence, and I had yet to make the journey. Now seemed as good a time as any. Near Wilson I veered right, heading north on US-281 for twenty miles before catching US-24 just past Osborne, and fifty-four miles westward I found myself realizing I had driven right past Nicodemus and had to turn around. It is that small of a small town.

When I had righted my course, I pulled off the highway onto a dirt road that led to a street lined by tumbledown houses and parked near a pavilion beside a park that seemed to be, as far as I could tell, the center of town. I sat in the car for a minute before getting out. The town felt abandoned, giving the impression of having been evacuated some years before my arrival. I would see one person the entire time I was there, a woman who worked for the National Park Service (Nicodemus was declared a National Historic Site in 1996). I knew from my research that former slaves from Lexington and Georgetown, Kentucky, who came to Kansas to homestead and start a community of their own, founded it in 1877. They had struggled mightily, surviving just barely the first year, living in the ground in dugouts before more emigrants from Lexington arrived with supplies, horses, and farming implements, which enabled them to survive and endure. And they did so quite impressively, and with significant successes despite the considerable frontier tribulations. The town grew to as many as 450 people, but would suffer setbacks, including losing the bid to become the county seat when neighboring white towns colluded to have the railway avoid Nicodemus, and over the last hundred years the population has steadily declined. The woman from the park service told me there were only twenty-six people, most advanced in age, living in town at present. Someday soon, she speculated, there would be none, and, if so, she feared, the town would cease to exist as anything more than a museum, a ghost town like so many others across the Great Plains.

The town's history and continued existence were worthy of attention and celebration, but part of my fascination with Nicodemus had to do with a certain kind of improbable connection I felt to it. I didn't have roots or ancestors in the town, but my own family had mirrored the Nicodemus settlers' westward migration from Kentucky to Kansas. The connection I felt wasn't personal or historical so much as it was metaphorical. I'm aware, of course, that when factoring in matters of race, privilege, and circumstance, the town's inhabitants and their experience couldn't have been more different from my family and our experience. But, in a most basic sense, we had all come to Kansas from the same place, looking to start a new and hopefully better life than we'd had in Kentucky. I spent the afternoon walking around Nicodemus, thinking about the history of the town and trying to figure out how to tell a story that I wanted to tell. I recall now the lines from Kansan poet William Stafford that capture what it felt like to be there: "my father sifting his / fingers in that loose ground of the Indian / campsite said, 'Oh, Bill, to know / everything! Look—the whole world is alive, / waving together toward history.'"

But that day, more often than I'd care to admit, I found myself replaying bits of the previous afternoon's game over and over. The loss still ate at me, and I hated that it did, which is a significant difference between my experience of sporting defeats as a boy and as an adult. When I was young, a KU loss upset me primarily because I loved the players and because I felt protective of Kansas as a state, particularly after we had moved to Connecticut. Somehow in the logic of my callow brain, the loss of the team, as representatives of the state, seemed to deride further a place, I had come to understand only once I'd left it, that was commonly looked down upon as unremarkable or backward by much of the country. While I'm still protective of Kansas and quick to point out its more honorable history when the setbacks of the last decade have dominated headlines, as I aged into adulthood a loss by the KU basketball team began to upset me more because of the feeling of shame induced by the belief that a sporting contest should not upset me the way, say, Governor Brownback's tax experiments at the expense of Kansas schoolchildren should. Which is true; it shouldn't, I firmly believe, but that doesn't mean I shouldn't care about it at all. I realize now that the question that compelled me to write this book—Why do I care about basketball as much as I do?—was the wrong question to ask because it masked the assumption that there was something wrong with me for loving basketball. The real question was not how can I stop loving basketball, but how can I love it in a healthy way? And perhaps it has taken me this many years to write about an increasingly distant season in Kansas basketball to arrive at a simple acquiescence: it's okay that I love basketball.

There are astute critics who would disagree, most notably perhaps the renowned linguist and political thinker Noam Chomsky, who believes that, among other things, sports condition people for obedience to illegitimate authority, foment chauvinistic attitudes, and distract the population from engaging in more important—that is, political—affairs. Here are a couple of excerpts from interviews in his book *Understanding Power*:

> Well, in our society, we have things that you might use your intelligence on, like politics, but people can't really get involved in them in a very serious way—so what they do is they put their minds into other things, such as sports. You're trained to be obedient; you don't have an interesting job; there's no work around for you that's creative; in the cultural environment you're a passive observer of usually pretty tawdry stuff; political and social

life are out of your range, they're in the hands of the rich folk. So what's
left? Well, one thing that's left is sports—so you put a lot of the intelligence and the thought and the self-confidence into that. And I suppose
that's also one of the basic functions it serves in the society in general:
it occupies the population, and keeps them from trying to get involved
with things that really matter. In fact, I presume that's part of the reason
why spectator sports are supported to the degree they are by the dominant
institutions. . . .

But the point is, this sense of irrational loyalty to some sort of meaningless community is training for subordination to power, and for chauvinism.
And of course, you're looking at gladiators, you're looking at guys who
can do things you couldn't possibly do—like, you couldn't pole-vault seventeen feet, or do all these crazy things these people do. But it's a model
that you're supposed to try to emulate. And they're gladiators fighting for
your cause, so you've got to cheer them on, and you've got to be happy
when the opposing quarterback gets carted off the field a total wreck and
so on. All of this stuff builds up extremely anti-social aspects of human
psychology. I mean, they're there; there's no doubt that they're there. But
they're emphasized, and exaggerated, and brought out by spectator sports:
irrational competition, irrational loyalty to power systems, passive acquiescence to quite awful values, really. In fact, it's hard to imagine anything
that contributes more fundamentally to authoritarian attitudes than this
does, in addition to the fact that it just engages a lot of intelligence and
keeps people away from other things.

While there's much I respect and admire about Chomsky, I find his
riffing on sports unconvincing. It's the one area where his thought seems
rather lazy. It's not that there isn't some truth in what Chomsky argues, it's
that he almost fanatically refuses to acknowledge that anything good could
possibly come from sports. His critiques also carry the unpleasant whiff of
arrogance and elitist judgment: What brainless dupes we are to care about a
stupid game. Sports aren't inherently a soporific evil and a distraction from
more important things. Of course, they can be, but that's certainly not
unique to sports; we've invented myriad ways to avoid confronting aspects
of the human experience that while important are also difficult, scary, or
sad. What Chomsky misses, however, are all the aspects of the game that
are positive and beneficial. There are the aesthetic pleasures: the enjoyment
of watching something captivating and dramatic, at its best a true art form, I
would argue, as legitimate as so-called serious artistic practices like theater,
dance, music, film, visual art, and literature. It is also fun to play. When

uncorrupted, it does teach values I think most people hold dear: solidarity, teamwork, discipline, effort, self-sacrifice, sportsmanship, commitment to something bigger than yourself. While sports may have the ability to turn us into our less noble selves, the jingoistic automatons being conditioned for obedience that Chomsky claims, they also can help us to be our nobler selves by creating community, bridging divides, and helping to understand and respect others. As William C. Rhoden wrote in elucidating Frederick Douglass's complex relationship to sport: "Douglass recognized the power of athletics to either pacify or inspire." I believe, as Dave Zirin writes, that "if we challenge sports to be as good as they can be—a force to break down walls, a motor for inclusion—they can propel us toward a better world, a world worth playing in—and worth fighting for."

In the eight years since that day I wandered around Nicodemus taking pictures and scribbling in my notebook, I have come to believe that the key is not to accept my love and obsession for the game unconsciously, to apply critical thinking to sports as I try to do other areas of life. Love the game, but do so with perspective and self-awareness. Which may sound like no big insight, but nonetheless, for someone geographically predisposed to be obsessed by the game to the exclusion of most other things in life, it marked a big step forward for me, and this awareness began with the despair that overcame me after the Northern Iowa loss.

In the year that followed, I felt the beginnings of this recalibration of my relationship to the game. While it would have made for a better stand-up-and-cheer ending to this book if the season had ended with KU hoisting the championship trophy, in some sense it was the perfect test case to examine how I felt after an even more devastating loss than the one that prompted me to start asking questions. My spirits were low, certainly, and I was bummed that we had been unable to take advantage of a bracket the collective desire of Jayhawk fans worldwide seemed to have willed into existence: the all-but-certain Final Four and probable national championship. However, disappointment is not the same thing as despair. I wasn't that level of distraught. I was not paralytic under the weight of the loss as I had been the previous year. I was, in fact, doing something that felt meaningful in visiting a place that was important to my continued work on the book of short fiction.

I do think I have arrived at a healthier place with respect to my relationship to the game. Now when I watch Kansas, I still go nuts and cheer on the team. I still qualify as obsessed, but it's different. When KU beat Duke to go to the Final Four in 2018, I was doing snow angels on the carpet before the television, laugh-crying in joy and excitement as my girlfriend,

who is not a sports person, looked on as though she were engaged in some
kind of anthropological observation of a newly discovered civilization. And
yet when we got blown out by Villanova the very next game, ending our
season and a quest for another championship, I was disappointed, sure, but
it didn't leave me despondent. The same goes for seasons that don't end in
a run to the Final Four. For so long my obsession and love for the game
had actually prevented me from enjoying so much of the experience of
watching Kansas play. How strange it was to love something that gave me
so little pleasure. Now I try to enjoy it all, the wins and even a few of the
losses. We're often told to remember that it's just a game. Well, fine. So it
is. But what a beautiful and compelling game it is.

It grew late in the evening, the sun a pink flame falling on the horizon, and
as the temperature dropped, rather than returning to Lawrence, I decided
to stay overnight. There was nowhere to lodge in Nicodemus, so I drove
to nearby Hill City, where I passed the night in a roadside motel. In the
morning, I returned to Nicodemus and retraced my steps of the previous
day, took more pictures, made more notes. Beside the Nicodemus Town-
ship Hall, a large building constructed in 1939 as part of the WPA and
that now houses the museum that details the history of the town, was the
pavilion where I sat at a picnic table staring at the basketball court between
the hall and myself.

It's strange to think back on that uncertain and precarious time from the
stability of my present. I was rootless. I was alone. I was thirty-one years old
and didn't have a home, a job, or a plan for where to go next. My credit
card debt was growing, and my student loans loomed ominously ahead of
me like the peaks of an unscalable mountain in the distance. Beyond the
desire for a teaching job I was unqualified for until I published a book, I
had little sense of what I was doing with my life aside from trying to finish
the collection of short stories I had been working on for so many years.
There was so much that I didn't—that I couldn't—know. I didn't know
that within a week or two I would receive word that my first book was
to be published the next year, and that would allow me to secure my first
university teaching job. I didn't know that the following season, Thomas
Robinson, the tragic hero of this season that ended so disappointingly,
would lead what appeared to be the least talented Kansas team in a decade
on a run in the NCAA tournament all the way to the championship game,
where they would lose honorably to a historically great Kentucky team,

a game I would have the good fortune to attend in New Orleans with my uncles and cousins from Kentucky. And I certainly didn't know that I would be finishing this book, composing this very sentence, in fact, from my writing desk at my home in Lexington, Kentucky, that I would be a professor at the University of Kentucky just as my father had been when I was born. I could never foresee my life coming full circle, from Kentucky to Kansas and back again. My two homes, forever bound to me personally as they were symbolically that day in Nicodemus.

But that day I wasn't thinking about a future I couldn't possibly know. I was wondering how long I could stay in Nicodemus before hitting the road, not asking myself the more difficult question of where that road would end for me. As I made my way toward the Township Hall, I walked across the cracked cement of the basketball court. Near one of the goals, which were missing their nets, I spied a basketball. I stopped. I hadn't noticed it sooner because it was partially deflated and semiobscured by grass and weeds. For a moment I thought I might pick it up and shoot a few baskets, hoping that if there were any children still living in town they might hear the report of my dribble and come out and join me. But the ball was flat and I decided to let it be, nestled in that divot of weedy black earth beside the hoop, where, if unclaimed, it would continue to deflate until it looked like nothing more than a jack-o'-lantern weeks after Halloween. I walked past it and on toward the Township Hall, stopping to take a picture of the stone etching that marked its year of construction before heading inside. I stayed for a few hours, writing down in my notebook dates and facts that would inform the fictional story of Nicodemus I sought to tell, and then I got in my car and, once again, I started to drive.

Sources

Loss

Styron, William. *Darkness Visible: A Memoir of Madness*. New York: Vintage, 1990.

Portrait of the Ball Player as a Young Artist

Eliot, T. S. "Shakespeare and the Stoicism of Seneca." In *Selected Essays*. New York: Harcourt, Brace, 1950.

Zimmer, Carl. "This Is Your Brain on Writing." *New York Times*, June 20, 2014. https://www.nytimes.com/2014/06/19/science/researching-the-brain-of -writers.html.

Mama, You Been on My Mind

Bedore, Gary. "Dearly Missed: Jackson Opens Up about His Mother's Tragic Passing." *Lawrence Journal-World*, May 9, 2010. http://www2.kusports.com /news/2010/may/09/dearly-missed-jackson-opens-about-his-mothers-trag.

———. "Jackson Has Clear Mind, Big Ideas for Senior Season." *Lawrence Journal-World*, January 8, 2008. http://www2.kusports.com/news/2008/jan/08/jackson _has_clear_mind_big_ideas_senior_season.

———. "Straight from the Heart." *Lawrence Journal-World*, January 27, 2006. http://www2.kusports.com/news/2006/jan/27/straight_heart.

———. "Talk Helps Jackson." *Lawrence Journal-World*, February 15, 2007. http:// www2.kusports.com/news/2007/feb/15/talk_helps_jackson.

———. "Two Jayhawks Shaken by Relatives' Deaths." *Lawrence Journal-World*, February 23, 2008. http://www2.kusports.com/news/2008/feb/23/two_jayhawks _shaken_relatives_deaths.

Lybarger, Dan. "Jackson on Mend." *Lawrence Journal-World*, November 6, 2005. http://www2.kusports.com/news/2005/nov/06/jackson_on_mend.

McPhee, John. *A Sense of Where You Are: A Profile of William Warren Bradley*. New York: Farrar, Straus and Giroux, 1965.

Newell, Jesse. "Tough Enough." *Lawrence Journal-World*, January 28, 2006. http://www2.kusports.com/news/2006/jan/28/tough_enough.

Thompson, Hunter S. *Hey Rube: Blood Sport, the Bush Doctrine, and the Downward Spiral of Dumbness*. New York: Simon & Schuster, 2005.

Yankee Town I

Benjamin, Walter. "On Some Motifs on Baudelaire." In *Illuminations*, translated by Harry Zohn. New York: Schocken Books, 1968.

Faulkner, William. *Requiem for a Nun*. New York: Vintage, 2012.

Fisher, H. D. *The Gun and the Gospel*. Chicago: Kenwood, 1896.

Miner, Craig. *Kansas: The History of the Sunflower State, 1854–2000*. Lawrence: University Press of Kansas, 2002.

Schultz, Duane. *Quantrill's War: The Life and Times of William Clarke Quantrill 1837–1865*. New York: St. Martin's Griffin, 1996.

Sutton, Robert K. *Stark Mad Abolitionists: Lawrence, Kansas, and the Battle over Slavery in the Civil War Era*. New York: Skyhorse, 2017.

Basket Ball

Hyde, Lewis. *The Gift: Creativity and the Artist in the Modern World*. New York: Vintage, 2007.

Jamieson, Duncan R. "Muscular Christianity." In *Sports in America from Colonial Times to the Twenty-First Century*, edited by Steven A. Reiss, 634–636. New York: Routledge, 2011.

Keegan, Tom. "Booths Purchase Original Naismith Basketball Rules at Auction for More Than $4 Million." *Lawrence Journal-World*, December 10, 2010. http://www2.kusports.com/news/2010/dec/10/original-naismith-basketball-rules-set-go-auction-/.

Naismith, James. *Basketball: Its Origin and Development*. New York: Association Press, 1941. Reprinted with an introduction by William J. Baker. Lincoln: University of Nebraska Press, 1996.

The NIV Study Bible. New International Version. Edited by Kenneth Baker. Grand Rapids, MI: Zondervan, 1985.

Orwell, George. "Reflections on Gandhi." In *All Art Is Propaganda: Critical Essays*, compiled by George Packer, 352–362. Boston: Mariner Books, 2009.

Rains, Rob. *James Naismith: The Man Who Invented Basketball*. Philadelphia: Temple University Press, 2009.

Zirin, Dave. *A People's History of Sports in the United States: 250 Years of Politics, Protest, People, and Play*. New York: New Press, 2008.

'08

Baldwin, James. "Autobiographical Notes." In *Notes of a Native Son*. Boston: Beacon Press, 1955.

Orwell, George. "Why I Write." In *Facing Unpleasant Facts: Narrative Essays*, compiled by George Packer, 224–231. Boston: Mariner Books, 2009.

Yankee Town II

Caldwell, Dave. "The Long Decline of Haskell Indian Nations University's All-Conquering Football Team." *Guardian*, October 21, 2016. https://www.the guardian.com/sport/2016/oct/21/haskell-indian-nations-university-college -football.

Hughes, Langston. *The Big Sea*. New York: A. A. Knopf, 1940. New York: Hill and Wang, 1993.

———. *Not Without Laughter*. New York: Random House, 1930. Reprinted with an introduction by Maya Angelou and foreword by Arna Bontemps. New York: Simon & Schuster, 1995.

Johnson, Stephanie Anne. "George Walker (1873-1911)." *Black Past*, July 3, 2008. https://www.blackpast.org/african-american-history/walker-george-1873 -1911/.

Rampersad, Arnold. *The Life of Langston Hughes, Volume 1: 1902–1941*. London: Oxford University Press, 2002.

Schmidt, Raymond. "Lords of the Prairie: Haskell Indian School Football, 1919–1930." *Journal of Sport History* 28, no. 3 (Fall 2001): 403–426.

Sotiropoulos, Karen. *Staging Race: Black Performers in Turn of the Century America*. Cambridge, MA: Harvard University Press, 2008.

Statehood

Kansas Historical Society. "Home on the Range." *Kansapedia*. Last modified December 2014. https://www.kshs.org/kansapedia/home-on-the-range/17165.

———. "Kansas Day." *Kansapedia.* Last modified December 2014. https://www
.kshs.org/index.php?url=kansapedia/kansas-day/16773.

Lomax, John A. *Adventures of a Ballad Hunter.* New York: Macmillan, 1947. Reprint, Austin: University of Texas Press, 2017.

———. *Cowboy Songs and Other Frontier Ballads.* New York: Macmillan, 1922.

Orwell, George. "Bookshop Memories." In *Facing Unpleasant Facts: Narrative Essays,* compiled by George Packer, 38–43. Boston: Mariner Books, 2009.

Tanner, Beccy. "Home on the Range: Origins of Famous American Folk-Song
Grew from Historic Kansas Cabin." *Lawrence Journal-World,* January 24, 2011.
http://www2.ljworld.com/news/2011/jan/24/home-range-origins-famous
-american-folk-song-grew.

Yankee Town III

Bailey, Beth. *Sex in the Heartland.* Cambridge, MA: Harvard University Press, 1999.

Brainard, Joe. *I Remember.* New York: Granary Books, 2001.

Chamberlain, Wilt. *Wilt: Just Like Any Other 7-Foot Black Millionaire Who Lives Next
Door.* New York: Macmillan, 1973.

Monhollon, Rusty L. *"This Is America?" The Sixties in Lawrence, Kansas.* New York:
Palgrave Macmillan, 2004.

Loss Redux

Chomsky, Noam. *Understanding Power: The Indispensable Chomsky.* Edited by Peter
R. Mitchell and John Schoeffel. New York: New Press, 2002.

Chu, Daniel, and Bill Shaw. *Going Home to Nicodemus: The Story of an African American Frontier Town and the Pioneers Who Settled It.* Morristown, NJ: Silver Burdett,
1994.

Crocket, Norman L. *The Black Towns.* Lawrence: Regents Press of Kansas, 1979.

Painter, Nell Irvin. *Exodusters: Black Migration to Kansas after Reconstruction.* New
York: Knopf, 1976. Reprint, Lawrence: University Press of Kansas, 1986.

Rhoden, William C. *Forty Million Dollar Slaves: The Rise, Fall, and Redemption of the
Black Athlete.* New York: Three Rivers, 2006.

Stafford, William. *Kansas Poems of William Stafford.* Edited by Denise Low. Topeka,
KS: Woodley Memorial Press, 2010.

Zirin, Dave. *A People's History of Sports in the United States: 250 Years of Politics, Protest, People, and Play.* New York: New Press, 2008.

Acknowledgments

I'd like to thank Harriet Clark, Monika Gehlawat, Kevin Gonzalez, Charles Lesh, Hendree Milward, Stuart Nadler, Ted Thompson, and Renée Zuckerbrot for the helpful discussions and advice on this project over the last decade. I'm very grateful to the Lighthouse Works Fellowship Program, the Joshua Tree Highlands Artist Residency Program, and the National Endowment for the Arts for the generous time and support they provided me. I'd like to thank my family in Kansas, Kentucky, and elsewhere, in particular my mother and father, Jane Stoneback and Brint Milward. Thank you to Lynn Segebrecht for providing essential information and for her family's generosity in allowing me to use their home as base camp whenever I'm back in Lawrence doing my weird "Kansas things." Also, my basketball brothers and teammates: the Clinic, Chief, Nutso, Biff, and everyone I've ever been on a team with. Thank you to Dr. James Naismith for imagining this beautiful game into existence. Thank you to the Kansas Historical Society and the wonderful people who work there. Many thanks are owed to Kim Hogeland and everyone at the University Press of Kansas, who worked hard to make sure the best possible version of this book came into the world. And finally, my deepest love and gratitude goes to Stacy Kranitz, who has no idea what basketball is, but who does know that it is important and beautiful to me. Thank you for filling my heart with yours and for believing in this book.

Illustration Credits

Photo 1, page 129, Man standing on a pile of buffalo skulls, circa 1892. Photo courtesy of Wikimedia Commons.

Photo 2, page 133, The Tavernier Trio, 1964. Photographer unknown.

Photo 3, page 134, *The Tragic Prelude*, 1940, by John Steuart Curry. Courtesy of the Kansas State Historical Society.

Photo 4, page 136, Civil War reenactor, January 27, 2011. Photo by the author.

Photo 5, page 186, The author, 1999. Photographer unknown.